THE JOY
OF CRICKET

THE JOY
OF CRICKET

selected and edited by
John Bright-Holmes

'I doubt if there be any scene in
the world more animating or delightful
than a cricket match.'
Mary Russell Mitford

'If I knew I was going to die today,
I think I should still want to
hear the cricket scores.'
G. H. Hardy

SECKER & WARBURG

LONDON

First published in England 1984 by
Martin Secker & Warburg Limited
54 Poland Street, London W1V 3DF

Introduction and Selection copyright © 1984 by
John Bright-Holmes

British Library Cataloguing in Publication Data
The Joy of Cricket
    Cricket – History
    Bright-Holmes, John
    796.35:8:09, GV913
ISBN: 0-436-06857-5

Printed and bound in Italy by
Imago Publishing Ltd

Contents

Editor's Acknowledgements

An anthologist is only as good as his friends. Even though mine has been the responsibility for the selection, I have always found it helpful to be offered ideas and actual books to consider. In this case I have been lucky to have the help and advice of: David Ballheimer, Christopher Chadwick, Brian Cooper, Tony Harlow, the late Bernard Hollowood, Peter Johnson, David Negus, Bill Neill-Hall, James Wright.

David Ballheimer and James Wright both gave me valuable assistance with ideas, and also read through and commented upon the uncut manuscript. I am very grateful to them both.

I would also like to thank particularly J. W. Mackenzie, helpful and experienced bookseller of Ewell in Surrey, who specializes in cricket and who very kindly allowed me to pillage his shelves of books which I could then read at leisure. I would like to offer my thanks also for practical assistance to the staffs of The British Library, The Westminster City Libraries and of the Merton Library Service, at Wimbledon Library, and at Mitcham Library where Mr Mike Harkin is the fortunate curator of the largest collection of cricket books in the Library Service.

Introduction

When I was asked to put together a collection to be entitled *The Joy of Cricket* I was particularly delighted because the suggested approach demanded an emphasis on the positive elements of the game. But inevitably I was conscious of the dangers of offering yet another cricket anthology which, by its nature, would compete for material with several existing collections that have already given great pleasure. One has only to think of Eric Parker's *Between the Wickets*, Thomas Moult's *Bat and Ball*, Gerald Brodribb's *The English Game*, John Arlott's *Cricket*, Leslie Frewin's *The Boundary Book* and his collections of cricket fiction and verse, Kenneth Gregory's *In Praise of Cricket* and Benny Green's *The Cricket Addict's Archive* to realize the nature and quality of the competition. In addition, there is Alan Ross' *The Cricketer's Companion*, which I, as a publisher, commissioned in 1960 and which, in 1979, was republished in a second edition. Could I produce something which did not just repeat much of the same material? Happily, there is a continuing richness in cricket writing that helps to lessen even if it does not completely remove the problem.

In searching for a new approach the publishers have generously offered plenty of space for pictures, and I hope a lot of these will come new to readers since I have tried to avoid too many well-known studies of cricketers in action. When it came to working out how to arrange the text my thoughts kept returning to the shape of a day's cricket – not so much that of the three- or five-day first-class match as of the one-day or, indeed, afternoon game which is the cricket the majority of us enjoys the most. The shape seemed to offer the opportunity of combining, as the two principal sections or innings, a selection of mainly historical portraits and accounts of the events and players of the past and present. This plan I have stuck to; so that in what follows Section II, called 'Giants in Those Days', covers approximately from the 1770s to the 1930s, while Section IV, 'The Modern Game', concentrates on the post-1945 scene. Such divisions are admittedly somewhat arbitrary, especially as several of the players included span the pre-war and post-war periods; but the only one who is treated at length in both sections is arguably the greatest of all; and it so happened that in a book published only towards the end of 1981, Mr Alec Bedser wrote fascinatingly about himself and Sir Donald Bradman.

But everyone has his or her own approach to the game, not only to the great events, but to the ordinary, the day-to-day, the local. These themes I have deployed in the other sections, beginning with 'The Anticipation of Cricket' where, just as the player on the day contemplates the contest to come, different writers describe their early enthusiasms for the game, whether it be Geoffrey Moorhouse caught in 'The Spell of Cricket', A. A. Thomson playing Hirst and Rhodes on the hearth, or Michael Meyer recalling his greatest hero, Woolley.

The third section, 'Interval Talk', offers a change of pace into more imaginative and even imaginary flights. One can see John Cleese's dual 'dismissal' of Denis Compton and Bernard Hollowood's victims of gamesmanship being heatedly and hilariously discussed around tea table or bar; not to mention the strange behaviour described in the splendid doggerel of *The Cricket Club of Red Nose Flat*, or Norman Gale's hat-trick of curates. On the other hand 'Close of Play', after the second main innings, offers more of the nostalgia of cricket, old players, old heroes – including, via Alan Ross, my own – seen in that afterglow of enthusiasm which breeds romance. But romantic writing – even as good as John Masefield's – can be overdone; for it usually fails to give – as I hope this section and indeed the whole book does give – a sense that the joy of cricket is inseparable from the fact that a cricket ball is hard, that it can travel fast and that, when wrongly intercepted, it can hurt.

Strange as it now seems, cricket has in the past had bestowed upon it an aura which is different from other 'mere' games – the notion of the game as simultaneously a rule-book of morality, the acme of team spirit, and a handmaiden of the British Empire all rolled into one. Much of this is pretentious, often bogus. 'More than a Game?', the final section, tries to reflect some of these differing attitudes over the years through passages that mix an historical, sociological and even philosophical approach. C. L. R. James comments fascinatingly on the place of cricket in the development of West Indian culture and also demands a place for W.G. in works of social history since he was, after all, 'the best known Englishman of his time'; a place which Eric Midwinter, Grace's most recent biographer, attempts to define. But these themes underly the myriad joys of a complex and fascinating game which by its nature lasts long enough, as Bernard Hollowood puts it, 'for ritual and pageantry to be welcomed; long enough for individual character to unfold'.

What I have *not* tried to do in *The Joy of Cricket* is to present any formal selection, as such, of 'Cricket in Fiction' or 'Cricket Verse'. Nor have I sought to represent every major figure or event in the game's history, although I have aimed to pick out those players who tended generously to offer the writer and spectator the most pleasure. To do this comprehensively would of course require many more than the number of words placed at my disposal. Even so I hope the reader will not feel too many obvious omissions, and will understand, partly for this reason and partly because I was working out themes, that I have chosen to 'represent' such famous set-pieces as the *England, Their England* cricket match, or Siegfried Sassoon's *Flower Show Match* instead of quoting them at full length. On the other hand I have included certain other items – for example, Herbert Farjeon's classic joke about the Laws *Herecombe v. Therecombe*, Francis Thompson's *At Lord's* and Arthur Mailey bowling to his hero Victor Trumper – since no collection of *The Joy of Cricket* (which necessarily includes its obverse) would seem to me complete without them. I hope that readers will find both a satisfying overall pattern and enthusiasm for the game combined with pieces that he or she will not previously have known, or which now, because of a fresh, sympathetic context, seem new and surprising. For the gaps that may remain I can only apologize and hope that what is included will nonetheless justify the book.

One expects cricket, because it 'can be a cruel game', to be productive of lapidary phrases of the sort that might be suitable as epitaphs, like George McWilliam's 'to the end, a poor judge of a run'. There is also G. H. Hardy's memorable remark, quoted by C. P. Snow, 'If I knew I was going to die today, I think I should still want to hear the cricket scores', which justly stands with Mary Russell Mitford on the title page of this collection; for it encapsulates what so many cricket-lovers feel but might not so simply express – especially in these days when the county scores, particularly at the beginning of each season, seem much scrappier and less monumental and satisfying than in the years before so many different competitions were introduced. However, so far I have not seen used in any like manner that splendid cricket phrase 'Good enough to get a touch'. Maybe I have missed it? However, if anyone who reads this should ever feel indulgent to the point on putting on my own tombstone, or plaque, 'Good enough to get a touch', I shall be well content. It does, after all, say everything; and it also needs a modicum of explanation for the uninitiated. In short, the perfect epitaph.

I hope, too, that *The Joy of Cricket* will seem good enough to give you, the reader, a touch of that special glowing sense of joy which cricket, played at its best at any level, can kindle and rekindle.

John Bright-Holmes

I

The Anticipation of Cricket

'Well, there's one word that moved me when a boy
  That moves today,
It's when the umpire, to the general joy,
  Pronounces "PLAY!"'

Andrew Lang: 'Play!'

Morning of the Match

HUGH DE SELINCOURT

On Saturday morning, 4 August 1921, at a quarter-past five, Horace
Cairie woke up and heard the rustle of wind in the trees outside his
bedroom window. Or was it a gentle, steady rain pattering on the
leaves? Oh, no, it couldn't be! That would be too rotten. Red sky at
night shepherd's delight. And the sky last night had been red as a
great rose and redder, simple crimson. 'Now mind, if you over-excite
yourself and don't get proper sleep, you won't be able to enjoy the
match or anything!' his mother had said, and Horace knew that what
she said was true. Still, what was a fellow to do? Turn over and go to
sleep? If it rained, it rained, and there was an end of it: his getting up
to see whether the pattery, rustly sound was the wind or rain would
not alter the weather. For a chap of fifteen and a few months he feared
that he was an awful kid.

He got out of bed deliberately as any man and walked to the
window. He leaned out as far as he could lean and surveyed the
morning sky with the solemnity of an expert.

Not a cloud was to be seen anywhere; only a breath of wind
sufficient to rustle a few dried ivy leaves against the window-sill. A
delicate haze spread over the country to the hills.

What a day it would be to watch a cricket match, and suppose Joe
Furze couldn't turn out and he were asked to play! And suppose, when
he went in to bat five runs were wanted and he got a full toss to leg
and hit it plumb right for a four and then with a little luck . . . or
supposing Tillingfold had batted first and the others wanted six runs
and he had a great high catch and held it or a real fast one and jumped
out and it stuck in his fingers. Oh, goodness, what a clinking game
cricket was! Splendid even to watch. And old Francis always let him
mark off the tens and put the figures up on the scoring board.

Meanwhile it was still three good hours to breakfast, and if he
curled up in bed and went to sleep the time would pass more quickly,
and if he were wanted to play he would be in better form than if he
mooched about the garden on an empty stomach.

What a morning! What a morning! What luck!

'Now then, darling, you'll be late for breakfast.'

Horace leaped out of bed at his mother's voice.

'Is old Francis here yet?'

'Been here an hour or more.'

'Has he brought any message?'

'Not that I know of.'

'Oh, curse! Of course I shan't be wanted to play.'

'A very good thing, too, dear. I don't like your playing with men.'

The joy of watching cricket.
'Myself when young . . .'

'Oh, rot, mum! What complete piffle! I'm not a kid.'
He kissed her first on one cheek then on the other.
'You will never understand about cricket, will you?'

From *The Cricket Match* (1924)

Cricket in the drawing-room. Six
and out!

Cricket on the Hearth

A. A. THOMSON

Let me tell you about my first Australian tour. It was in the winter of
1903–4. P. F. Warner's MCC team played their Test matches at
Sydney, Melbourne and Adelaide. I played mine on the kitchen
hearth-rug. I was eight years old at the time.

What a team we had! Naturally the critics were against it, as critics
often are, for not ignoble reasons, against a side that contains so many
players that are young and untried. A team considered by many to
have been the best ever fielded by England had been beaten by the
Australian visiting team in 1902 and of the best English players
neither Fry, MacLaren, Jackson nor Jessop could make the trip. But I
knew nothing of the reservations of the critics; I only knew that
Warner's team were heroes, because they were the first side I ever
followed. The batting was not as strong as it might have been, but for
me it was princely. Macaulay once said that if every copy of *Paradise
Lost* were destroyed, he would be able to recite the whole poem from
memory. More diffidently I might say that I could remember the
scores in these matches if every *Wisden* were burned. This was its order
in the first Test: P. F. Warner, Hayward, Tyldesley, Arnold, R. E.
Foster, Braund, Hirst, B. J. T. Bosanquet, Dick Lilley (the wicket-
keeper), Albert Relf and a slim youngster from the Yorkshire village
of Kirkheaton, named Wilfred Rhodes. (What was Arnold, the modest
Worcestershire all-rounder, doing so high up in the batting order as
No. 4? He had been sent in as a night watchman and held up his end

[4]

with high credit.) It was not thought to be a wonderful eleven in October 1903, but I should not be churlish if I doubted whether any contemporary player except Hutton and Bedser would be worthy of it. Moreover, the whole side consisted of only fourteen men; there were but three reserves: Albert Knight, the Leicestershire batsman, Arthur Fielder, the Kent fast bowler, and Strudwick, who was to keep wicket for England over twenty years later. How did they manage on a bare fourteen bodies? Were they hardier then or is life harder now?

My pitch was the kitchen hearth-rug, with a steel fender running along the offside and the old stone sink at long-leg. While play was in progress I used to kneel down on the rug: my right hand was the batsman and my left hand was the bowler. The bat was a school ruler, the ball was a small rubber one, valued at a penny, and the wicket was a propped up copy of *Pilgrim's Progress*.

To the best of my small ability I tried to match my method to the individual style of each player. For Oxford's polished batsman, R. E. Foster, I would try to be wristy and elegant; for Johnnie Tyldesley I would execute the latest of late cuts; while, as for those fierce, daring pulls of George Hirst's, my poor dear Yorkshire step-mother went to heaven nearly thirty years later without knowing that it was a whole-hearted leg-hit by George Hirst that cracked the scullery window. I never told her. If I had, she would undoubtedly have said: 'You wait till I talk to George Hirst's mother . . .'

I varied my bowling, too, with a nice sense of contrast and character. This was necessary, because sometimes I was Hugh Trumble and sometimes B. J. T. Bosanquet, whom my step-Uncle Walter called Bozzikew. I had not the faintest idea of what a googly was, except that it was vastly peculiar, and I tried to stimulate it with a high bouncing delivery which the batsmen found difficult to time. I was, as I have always been, the slave of my own rules, and strove, within the limits of patriotism, to be scrupulously fair to both sides; that is, I would try to bat just as well for Trumper as for Hayward and Tyldesley and bowl as well for the Australian bowlers as for the English . . . well, all except Rhodes. It was impossible to keep Rhodes down to an ordinary level of excellence. The man who in the second Test at Melbourne took 15 wickets for 124 could not be judged by ordinary standards. I did not know then what a 'sticky' wicket might be, except that it was something terrible, and I pictured, not unjustly, a state of affairs in which the batsman's feet were glued to the ground and his freedom of movement horribly hampered. Morally, I was right, though it was difficult on an honest hearth-rug to reproduce the horrors of a Melbourne 'sticky dog'. It was on that same Melbourne wicket, later in the tour, that the tourists put Victoria out for the fantastic total of 15. On that occasion Arnold took 4 for 8 and Rhodes 5 for 6. Two chances were missed and Rhodes said afterwards: 'We ought to have got 'em out for under ten.'

No wonder I cheated just a little on Rhodes' behalf by not quite letting my right hand know what my left hand was doing.

From *Cricket My Pleasure* (1953)

Tinnin don't Lie

UNDINE GIUSEPPE

Brilliant sunshine flooded the morning air as he tucked his home-made bat under his arm, and walked whistling out of the house.

'Where are you off to now?' called his grandmother from the kitchen, busy with her regular daily chores.

His answer, if he gave one, was lost in the shouts of a group of boys outside his home. They had gathered in the street, eager for him to join them. Now they greeted him noisily as he approached.

'That boy!' muttered his grandmother with a shake of the head, but she smiled as she looked through the window and saw the group disappear down the street.

The boys scaled the wall of the Empire Cricket Club ground, dropped on to the green grass below, and soon they were lost in a world of their own – a world of fun and games.

'Tip-and-run,' called out Leroy Crichlow, one of the biggest boys in the group. 'You bat first, Frank. I'll bowl. And today I'll knock your wicket right down with the first ball.'

The others laughed. Leroy was always threatening to do this, but somehow he had never yet succeeded.

'Go ahead and try,' retorted Frank. He was slim, and smaller than Leroy, but that did not worry him. He was not afraid of Leroy's bowling.

Frank took up his position before the wicket which two of the other boys had set up.

The wicket that day was a piece of galvanized iron propped up with a stick and two stones. Whatever drawbacks it may have had in appearance, it nevertheless had its advantages. In such games, there was never any doubt when a batsman was bowled. The loud 'Tock' of the ball on the 'galvanize' always settled the matter without any fear of argument.

'Tinnin don't lie,' is a popular Barbadian expression.

Leroy came running up to the crease, and delivered the ball with all his might.

It went a bit wide, but Frank, more daring than wise on this occasion, reached out at it. It glanced off his bat, and fell a short distance away.

'Wow!' gasped Frank, as he started to run. That was one of the rules of the game. As long as the ball 'tipped' the bat, the batsman had to run. The object was to get down to the other end before the ball was thrown in, a job which was far from easy when the ball had not gone far. But the practice in running between the wickets was good.

Denzil Hunte, a short, thick-set fellow, grabbed the ball and threw it at the wicket as fast as he could.

'Tock!' went the ball, and down fell the wicket.

Tossing for innings, one of several versions of this basic idea (artist unknown; possibly Robert James)

Leroy jumped up in the air, laughing and clapping his hands in delight.

'Out, first ball!' he cried.

'Out, but not bowled!' replied Frank.

Years later Frank was to look back on days like this, days when he and his companions played 'Tip-and-run' and other such games for hours on end, and think that they had in some measure helped to make him the cricketer he had become. Now, however, there was no Future, there was no Past. The Present was all that mattered to him.

From *Sir Frank Worrell* (1969)

Glorious August

BRUCE HAMILTON

More dear to them than school matches were the long golden afternoons of those last two summer holidays. Somerset House played their games on a corner of the county ground, and this gave the pupils not only the right of free admission to all matches, but the privilege, modified by the frequently surly temper of Goddard, the head groundsman, of playing privately in the holidays, provided one got in no one's way.

Boys in Hyde Park

In retrospect, there always seemed to Teddy to have been something indescribably moving about that holiday – he was to go to the Grammar School next term. It was a glorious August, day after day of deep burnished indigo skies without a cloud. The county had three or four home matches, watched by the boys from the side of the screen, or sometimes from near the professionals' pavilion, where the demeanour of the heroes, emerging to bat, hopefully, or indifferently, or nervously, and returning with elation, nonchalance, or dejection, could be studied at close range. The two boys spoke very little, and resented the ignorant chatter of children and fools around them. At lunch-time they brought out their sandwiches, munching in a deep trance-like satisfaction, and presently their silence would break down into monosyllabic comment. Then the first bell; the clearing away of ropes, vacuous inspectors of the pitch, and flying boys with tennis balls; the slow umpires' procession; and, at last, the cricketers again, bringing another deep hush.

Tea was the climax of the day. They needed drinks, and had nothing left from lunch. They would thrust in competition with the men at the bar, opposing to the stentorian calls for bitter, weak appeals for ginger-beer and a pennyworth of Garibaldi biscuits, fussing in their fear that they would not get back to the game in time. Afterwards, the shadows of the pavilion, and of the elms behind it, advanced stealthily to the wicket, the white gold of the atmosphere became a yellow gold, and presently it was half-past six. Outside the ground there was a civil exchange of good-byes – 'Same time tomorrow.' Each had spent a perfect day, perfectly companioned.

But more often there was no match at the ground, or no match worth watching. Then French would be round at half-past ten with his private knock on Teddy's front door. Teddy was generally waiting, with bat and ball ready, and they were soon up at the ground. At the north end, behind the screen and in front of the tennis courts, they would improvise a wicket, with a blazer and a broken chair. Till one o'clock they batted and bowled, at intervals resting flat on their backs, their faces upturned to the sky. Then it was time to go home again to dinner, but before half-past two they were at it again. The bar was closed when there was no county match, but it was hardly worth while going home for tea. Towards five they would climb, bat and all, over the spikes of the closed gate at the north-east, and go to Carter's little shop a few yards away for doughnuts and Penny Monsters. Teddy, the affluent one of the pair, nearly always stood treat. The seriousness of the last hour of their day, after they had scrambled back, was somewhat relaxed. They might play French cricket, or even not play at all, but watch, in convulsions of ill-stifled merriment, the ridiculous antics of the lady archers, who were hated because they had certain rights on the north end of the ground, and sometimes made themselves a nuisance.

From *Pro* (1946)

Sunday was Our Field Day

LEARIE CONSTANTINE

It was about 1908 that we moved from Maraval to St Ann's, my father taking charge of an agricultural (mainly cocoa) estate there. Soon a wicket made of red earth was prepared, secondhand matting bought, and this was stretched tight over the solid, red earth wicket, watered and rolled to perfection. It was on this sort of wicket that all Trinidad and Tobago cricket was played. Rain or fine, it did not matter, and even if the water was up to the ankles, we could always practise catching. In the West Indies we have no winter, in fact there are two seasons, the wet and the dry. We played every day in the dry season and waited for the pitch to dry in the wet season. For players we were never short, whoever was straying around we gathered together for a game, and after a time we did not need to look, they were always there.

After a day's work my father used to join us and began giving instructions according to his own ideas. Batting was essentially the individual's choice and in his style. So long as he was comfortable in his stance and lifted the bat freely, he was left alone. Gross errors were corrected and whatever explanations we called for he would deal with, but on the whole he interfered very little.

For bowling, he told us of the cart-wheel action, hand as high as

possible, what an off-break was and how it differed from a leg-break, and stressed the value of length. But fielding, yes fielding, he took into his own hands, and what a martinet he was! You were not allowed to miss anything. If you were within range of his hand after making two mistakes, either catching of fielding, you had one of two alternatives thereafter, catch it, field it, or keep out of his range.

'Concentrate,' he would say. 'To mis-field or drop a catch is sheer carelessness.' This was an unforgivable sin. All kinds of tricks were devised to catch us out. We would be put to stand a few feet behind his back and with his strong wrists he would hit the ball in any or all directions – hitting it very hard at times, and we were expected to take the catches. His theory was simple – if you were paying attention you did not miss. So, 'Pay attention.' 'Pay attention.' and again, 'Pay Attention.' I developed an attitude to fielding, and wherever I was standing, whether in the slips, gulley, or cover, I watched the bowler run up, watched him deliver the ball, and as soon as it was in the air, I followed it to the pitch and then watched the batsman's movement, so that my anticipation took me to where the ball was directed or played by the batsman. The only exception to this general rule was when fielding at silly mid-off or silly mid-on. There I would watch the bowler start his run and immediately transferred my attention to the batsman, having a fair idea when the ball was going to be delivered, and see whether the batsman would be on his right foot or move into the pitch of the ball. All through my playing life I paid attention, and when for some reason or other I did not, my side suffered. It would not be immodest to say that after a time I remembered the catches I dropped, not those I had taken, except of course if there was some uncommon element about them.

The joy of cricket: on the sands in Barbados; in a Karachi street

Sunday was our field day; it was not merely a family affair, but a village encounter. Uncle Toy (Victor Pascall), now a full-fledged Trinidad representative, would come over sometimes; Morris, my father's nephew, would join, and we played after church, or after breakfast, which was the midday meal in Trinidad, until dark – 6·15 or 6·30.

My mother used to keep wicket and my sister Nora played as hard for her innings as any of the boys. The problem was how to get the batsman out and when the younger set failed to dislodge him or her and were losing hope, my father would take the ball himself, set his field and then came the battle. You gripped your bat, and, fortified by the earlier defiance of the younger brigade, you took your stance and played as if for your life. Slips, silly mid-off, short fine-leg, everyone plotting and waiting greedily for your downfall. You might last three or four overs, and my father would remark that you were improving, but this compliment, though giving pleasure, would at once warn you that the attack would be all the more concentrated. Still you held on. The off-break, which was his normal ball, the flighted one, the quicker one and all the guile that experience had taught him would be brought into play. Until, at last, a floated one looking like the off-break but going straight through crashed against the stump, amid the cry of triumph all round, indicating that the old man had got through at last. The joy, the tension and exhilaration, and the happiness those Sundays brought into our lives served as a cushion, I am sure, for the sterner life which was ahead for all of us.

From *The Changing Face of Cricket* (1966)

Mixed Emotions

NEVILLE CARDUS

A boy looks upon his heroes at cricket with emotions terribly mixed. He believes they are as gods, yet at the same time he has no real confidence in them. He thinks they are goint to get out nearly every ball. At least that is how I suffered on every day I sat in the sixpenny seats at Old Trafford and looked at MacLaren and Spooner and Tyldesley. An iron rail ran round the green circle of Old Trafford, and when I got a place on a front bench I would press my forehead against this iron rail and pray for heavenly aid for my heroes, as I saw them exposed to the barbarians from Yorkshire – George Hirst rolling up the sleeve on his great ham of a left arm, ready to swing it and hurl a new red ball at the wicket of Reggie Spooner, hurl it like a live coal; and Spooner seemed frail and his bat scarcely a solid, while all the other Yorkshiremen swarmed round him. Then would I pretend to be looking on the ground for something while I closed my eyes and prayed that God would make George Hirst drop down dead before bowling the next ball. I loved Spooner so much that I dare not watch him make stroke. It is a curious thought – I probably *never* saw him at the moment which he actually played a ball.

Strangely indeed does a boy think that his favourite cricketers are the best in the world but still the most fallible and in need of his every devoted thought. I used to walk the Manchester streets careful not to tread on cracks between the pavements; or I would touch each lamp-post as I passed, and like Dr Johnson I would go back if I feared I had missed one or not touched it with enough thought. But I was not propitiating the gods on my own behalf but on behalf of my darlings of cricket. The trials and suspense of my adoration of them! I cannot tell how the slender nervous and physical system that was mine ever survived the strain and wear and tear. No later crisis of life – and I have known a few – have so sorely tried me.

Sometimes I got myself into difficult positions with God. There was Victor Trumper, for example, next to MacLaren and Spooner my most adored. He was an Australian and I was a patriotic English lad. I wanted him always to score a century, but I also wanted England to get him out first ball and win the match. Obviously, I realized, it would be unreasonable to expect God to do for me these two things at one and the same time; for even He could not make Trumper score a century and be defeated first ball; there were, I knew, limits to Divine Power, and I was reasonable enough not to embarrass God, so I reflected carefully about it, and presented my petition in the most accommodating terms I could think of: 'Please, God, let Victor Trumper score a century today for Australia against England – out of a total of 137 all out.'

From *Autobiography* (1947)

The Spell of Cricket

GEOFFREY MOORHOUSE

I first fell under the spell of cricket, as every other small boy will have done, by batting and bowling on the nearest available space the moment I got home from school. With the other lads of the village, I used to spend hours in the field beside our house with a rubber ball and a home-made bat, whose handle was fashioned from an old carpet-beater, with a bicycle inner-tube rolled double down to the shoulder of the blade, which had once been a mahogany shelf. I first saw professional cricketers play in a charity match down in the town towards the end of the war. Eddie Paynter batted in that game, a legend in our part of the world and only just past his great days. So did E. R. Conradi, later to become a Cambridge Blue. And there were three great West Indians – Martindale, Achong and St Hill – who probably impressed me with their colour as much as by their skill, for almost certainly they were the first black men I'd ever seen. I cannot, alas, remember anything else of that match, though many times since I've tried to recall how it went. But I know that, after that, I went looking for cricket to watch. I found it mostly in the Lancashire leagues to start with but, when 1946 came, I entered Old Trafford for the first time. It was a lovely sunhazed day and the county ground seemed enormously grand, and Alf Gover was bowling with that curious cocktail-shaker action to Washbrook and Place. I sat there entranced, hoping it would never end: and, in a sense, it never has.

From *The Best Loved Game* (1979)

None has Matched Woolley

MICHAEL MEYER

A child needs heroes, and mine were cricketers. I collected their likenesses on cigarette cards. Though born north of the river, only a few hundred yards from Lord's in Hamilton Terrace (on the first day of the 1921 Lord's Test *v* Australia, when Woolley scored 95 out of an England total of 187), I supported Surrey, because my nurse came from Wonersh. She was the most important person in my life, my mother having died when I was very small, and although we still lived near Lord's in Portland Place I faithfully made the long Tube journey to the Oval and watched most of my early cricket there. Three years later I saw Hobbs, then over fifty, hit the West Indian bowlers for a double-century in a day.

My father loved furniture and Dutch paintings, boxing and rugger, but was bored by cricket; but when we were on holiday I sometimes persuaded him, or some other adult in the seaside hotel, to take me to a game, and later in that first cricket-watching summer of 1930 I saw Tate take six Australian wickets for 18 before lunch at Hove, including Ponsford clean bowled second ball of the match. That, too, was a day to remember, for Alan Kippax scored the most graceful century and the last pair, Hurwood and Hornibrook, added 100 – to my rage, for they left no time for me to see Duleepsinhji bat. I saw Lionel Tennyson, huge and ponderous, at Southampton, and heard the professionals address him as Milord; but mostly, we stayed at Hythe, and in the late thirties I watched many games at Canterbury, Dover and Folkestone. Woolley was then in the twilight of his career, but he was still in wonderful form – he had been recalled, albeit unsuccessfully, to the England side in 1934 at the age of 47 – and whenever I saw him bat he made runs, except once, and even that day was to be gloriously redeemed.

None of my many heroes, then or since, has matched Woolley for excitement and romance. To describe him in terms of modern batsmen, he combined the grace of Graveney with the power of Dexter – or, if you are too young to have seen them, the grace of Gower with the power of Botham. Once, as he waited to bat at Canterbury, I saw him dozing in a deckchair in the sun; a wicket fell, the applause aroused him, and out he strolled with that awkward, stiff-legged stride. There was an extraordinary negligence about his batting, as though his thoughts were elsewhere, but what terrible things he did to bowlers! In my memory he is continually lofting the ball, though lofting is a poor description of those blistering, low-trajectory drives, straight or over extra-cover, seeming to gather pace as they skimmed first-bounce into the crowd.

My late agent, David Higham, told me how one lunchtime in 1911 he hesitated whether to spend the afternoon on the beach or at the county ground, chose the latter and saw Alletson of Notts hit 142 out of 152 for the last wicket in forty minutes. I was almost as lucky, for in 1937 I witnessed every ball of the famous Kent v Gloucestershire match at Dover. Charles Barnett hit 70 in the first half-hour, G. W. Parker scored a double-century in four hours, and Gloucestershire ended with 434. Woolley, just past his fiftieth birthday, bowled 24 overs of left-arm spin and took 3 for 82, including Hammond caught at slip for 3. Next day Kent replied with 399, Woolley 100 in two hours. No hope of a result, we thought, but along we went on the final day – after all, Barnett and Hammond would be batting, and one might catch another glimpse of Woolley. Gloucestershire were all out for 182 (Hammond 52), leaving Kent to score 218 in under two hours. We sat resignedly to watch the match peter into a draw, but Kent got the runs in 71 minutes. Woolley hit 44 out of 68 in 25 minutes, Ames 70 out of 100 in 26 minutes, including a direct hit on a uniformed constable, and Watt 39 of the last 51 in 10 minutes. Ashdown, the anchor-man, was left 62 not out. Gloucestershire, to their credit, bowled 23·2 overs in that time; would any side have done the same today? Poor Tom Goddard, that great off-spinner, was clouted for 98 in 8·2 overs.

In 1938 Woolley played his last game at Canterbury. It was against Bradman's Australians, and Australia batted all the first day for 479. Next morning, before a huge crowd, Woolley pushed the first ball of the innings a yard down the pitch and went for a short run. We all laughed happily, for there was no close fielder in front, but Walker, the wicket-keeper, somehow moved quickly enough to throw down the bowler's wicket. Surely Woolley could not be out; everyone knew, for the papers had told us, that this was to be his last appearance on his favourite ground; but the umpire's finger was raised. Never, even in the darkest hour of a Test match, have I known such a silence settle on an English crowd. Woolley run out first ball of a lovely sunny day.

Kent crumbled quickly, and in mid-afternoon followed on. Woolley came out for his positively last innings. His second or third ball he lofted head-high dangerously close to the right of mid-on. It went for four but I remember wondering at the time whether the fieldsman tried as hard as he might have done to reach it. The next hour was as magical as any I have spent at a cricket match. The old man hit the Australian bowling all over the ground. One passage I especially remember. He drove Fleetwood-Smith (I think) over extra-cover for four. Bradman moved the fieldsman back thirty yards and the next ball went over his head first-bounce over the ropes. Back went the fieldsman to the edge, and the next ball, or was it the one after, soared high over him into the crowd. In under the hour he hit a six, a five and fifteen fours. At 81 he was brilliantly caught at deepish mid-on off a low, skimming drive by, appropriately, Bradman. *Wisden* tells me that Ames scored 139 and added with Brian Valentine 95 in 45 minutes, but I don't remember that.

From *Summer Days* (1981)

Omens

SIEGFRIED SASSOON

Leaving my pads to dry in the sun, I sauntered contentedly back to the house to have a squint at the morning paper, which never arrived until after breakfast. I had a private reason for wanting to look at the

Morning Post, I was a firm believer in predestination, and I used to improvise superstitions of my own in connection with the cricket matches I played in . . . I searched assiduously through the first-class scores, picking out the amateurs whose names, like my own, began with S, and whose initial was G. There were only two that day: the result was most unsatisfactory. *G. Shaw run out,* 1 : *G. Smith, c. Lilley, b. Field,* 0. According to that I should score half a run. So I called in professional assistance, and was rewarded with: *Shrewsbury, not out,* 127. This left me in a very awkward position. The average now worked out at 64. The highest score I had ever made was 51, and that was only in a practice game at Ballboro'. Besides, 51 from 64 left 13, an unlucky number. It was absurd even to dally with the idea of my making sixty-four in the Butley Flower Show Match. Anything between twenty and thirty would have been encouraging. But Aunt Evelyn's voice from the drawing-room window informed me that she would be starting in less than ten minutes, so I ran upstairs to change into my flannels. And, anyhow, the weather couldn't have been better . . . While we were walking across the fields Aunt Evelyn paused on the top of a stile to remark that she felt sure Mr Balfour would be a splendid Prime Minister. But I was meditating about Shrewsbury's innings. How I wished I could bat like him, if only for one day!

From *Memoirs of a Foxhunting Man* (1928)

The Free Seats

ROY HATTERSLEY

At half-past two on a summer's afternoon I can become a vagabond who need not return to middle-class respectability until stumps are drawn at close of play. I rest my caravan in the Free Seats at Lord's.

They are only free insomuch as spectators who have already paid entrance money are allowed to park their posteriors upon them without extra charge. But the view which they afford the enthusiast is beyond price. For high above the boundary at the Nursery End the bowler's line and length and the batsman's ability to get his foot to the pitch of the ball can be judged without interference from either umpire or wicketkeeper. Certainly balding fielders have the signs of age more cruelly exposed to the occupants of the Free Stand than to the MCC members in the pavilion or the weather-conscious troglodytes who huddle in the subterranean depths of the barrack block called the Lord's Grandstand. But the Free Stand is the perfect vantage point both for the expert witness and the casual caller who means to pass the afternoon with only one eye on the ball.

The Free Seats at Lord's

For it is flanked by horse-chestnut trees which, though still to blossom at the start of the season, are in full conker before the championship is decided. And the native fauna are just as interesting as the indigenous flora.

Ancient workmen set up benches on the tarmacadam paths around the ground and plane pieces of wood which become the bevelled backs of Long Room chairs and rasp away at steel rods that are destined to reinforce the railings which keep Middlesex members quarantined in the Q Stand. And all these sights and sounds of Old England are accompanied by the cries of MCC young professionals practising in the nets and a soft drone which is not the sound of the bumblebee, but a mysterious noise that drifts out of the Ladbroke betting tent.

The Free Seats are also the proper place for the *aficionados* who want no diversion from rigorous concentration on the game, the absolute antithesis of the private box hired by the limited liability company or public corporation. Official hospitality is an organised conspiracy to prevent the uninterrupted watching of cricket, based on a constant invitation to 'have a drink' or 'meet our sales manager from Slough'. Just as the true devotee turns his back on the pitch to have his glass replenished or to shake hands, a wicket always falls.

[17]

In front of what used to be a real Tavern at Lord's, the distractions are different but barely less disconcerting. It has become the home of hard drinkers, and the haunt of Australians with hairy chests and huge stomachs. These days my ambition, once I am established in the Free Seats with cushion and score card, is not to leave my seat at all.

During my impatient boyhood I used to hate the tea interval. It was simply twenty minutes with nothing to do except count the seconds to the pavilion bell and the reappearance of the umpires. Now I think of it as an essential opportunity for meditation. For cricket is a contemplative game and these days, unless there is a pause during which I can take stock, I miss part of the pleasure. Cricket's true beauty lies in the way it interleaves a moment's frenzied action with a minute for reflection. Now, after 30 years of concentrated watching, I need time to pull my memories together.

The Free Seats at tea at Lord's are the perfect place for controlled nostalgia with Father Time pointing in whichever way the wind blows. On a clear day Don Wilson – once Yorkshire left-handed pride and now the senior MCC coach – can be seen in the nets. And other spectators are always willing to jog the forgetful memory about how many runs Denis Compton scored in 1947. Indeed the regulars in the Free Seats are the ideal cricket companions.

Ask one of them if a catch carried or if byes were signalled and the reply will be brief and courteous. There is neither rambling about weather or traffic nor the beginning of a fleeting conversational friendship. The true cricket enthusiast needs to pass freely in and out of solitude with concentration only occasionally broken by comment and reverie, rarely disturbed by raconteur. That bliss he is allowed in the Free Stand. And sometimes there is quite a good cricket match going on down at ground level.

From the *Guardian* (7 May, 1983)

II

Giants in Those Days

'Here lives John Small,
    Makes Bat and Ball
Pitch a Wicket, Play at Cricket
With any man in England.'
    Painted sign in front of
    John Small's house in
    Petersfield

From Broad-Halfpenny to Lord's

NEVILLE CARDUS

It is because cricket does not always hurry along, a constant hurly
burly, every player propelled here and there by the pace of continuous
action, that there is time for character to reveal itself. We remember
not the scores and the results in after years; it is the men who remain
in our minds, in our imagination. Nobody asks what was the batting
average of Joseph Guy, a Nottinghamshire cricketer of whom it was
said by William Clarke, who got together and captained the first All-
England XI, that he was 'elegance, all elegance, fit to play before the
Queen in her parlour'. Ponsford made more runs than R. H. Spooner
– and there are more notes in a symphony by Shastakovitch than in
one by Mozart. The man is the style at cricket.

   We do not know, and we are not curious about the bowling averages
of 'Lumpy' Stevens, who rose early on summer mornings at Hambledon
to pick a wicket; for in those days the spin of a coin decided not only
first innings but also gave the winner the right to choose the pitch.
'Lumpy' loved to send fast 'shooters', and he invariably chose a wicket
with a downward slope – 'for honest "Lumpy" did allow, He ne'er
could pitch but o'er a brow.' Lineal descendents of 'Lumpy' were
Emmott Robinson and Rhodes, who once inspected the wicket at
Leeds after a wet morning. The sun was shining just before lunch, and
Rhodes and Emmott pressed expert fingers into the texture of the turf.
'It'll be "sticky" at four o'clock,' said Rhodes. Emmott pressed and
fondled the turf again, then answered: 'No, Wilfred; half-past.'

   The state of the turf is the clue to every cricket match; no other
game comes as much under the influence of material circumstances;
the elements are cricket's presiding geniuses. The wicket not only
makes a valuation of skill, but also of character. A score of 100 for 3
might be good or ruinous, according to the state of the wicket... Not
until we have considered the material conditions and environment of
cricket – which include the implements, especially the heavy roller –
can we measure exponent with exponent and period with period. Of
the early Hambledon epoch we must be content to savour the character
and the spirit; for technically the Hambledon game is scarcely linked
even to the cricket of only fifty years afterwards. Hambledon men, as
we know, bowled under-arm; it was later than Hambledon, May
1828, when the MCC legalized the round-arm action. The new rule
permitted the hand to be raised as high as the elbow, and the arm to
be extended outwards and horizontally. Seven years later, the law
compromised again; the hand in delivering the ball could now be
raised as high as the shoulder. As far back as 1788, Tom Walker of

Hambledon had experimented with a round-arm action; but it was left to John Willes, in the year 1822, to wave the red rag of revolution under the nose of Lord's itself. He opened the attack for Kent against the MCC and was promptly no-balled; and promptly he refused to play and got on his horse in dudgeon, and, as H. S. Altham says, rode out of Lord's and out of cricket history.

But the way was shown, and wide open now. The 'new' bowling became the rage at once; and a Sussex team, with Lillywhite in it, used round-arm so drastically that they thrashed All-England twice in three matches. For thirty years to come, this bowling set the general technical stamp and provided the most important bridge passage in cricket's symphonic progress; it was cultivated to the highest possible potency by Alfred Mynn, Lillywhite, and Caffyn. Here was the beginning of 'modern' cricket.

But the Hambledonians apparently discharged their bowling with characteristic vehemence. David Harris could cause an 'under-arm' to rise abruptly from the pitch. He could 'grind a batsman's fingers against his bat'. Brett's attack was described as so 'tremendous' that Tom Sueter, the wicket-keeper, was acclaimed a hero because he could stump a man off Brett; and he wore no pads or gloves, nor did the batsman. The inexplicable point of style about the classic masters' under-arm is their method of propelling the ball down the pitch, not with the lobbing action most of us moderns know, a variation of the quoit throw or the obeisance of the bowling green. Nyren describes how David Harris forced the ball away from the level of his armpit; and half a century later, Richard Daft tells of Clarke, 'at the last moment he bent back his elbow, bringing the ball almost under his right armpit...'

Brown of Brighton bowled under-arm at such velocity that history asserts he killed a dog on the boundary; and the ball had passed through a coat held protectively by long-stop. But this event is dated round about 1818, after the sun set upon Hambledon. Probably Brown of Brighton was one of the stealthy advance guards of the revolution; I doubt if he killed his dog truly under-arm, unless he bowled like Mr Luffey, who in *Pickwick* retired a few paces ('amid a breathless silence',) applied the ball to his right eye for several seconds, then cried 'Play!' whereat the ball flew straight and swift towards the centre stump of the wicket defended by Mr Dumkins.

Yet, is it absolutely certain that on a Hambledon turf, against the underarms of David Harris and equipped and armed in the period's garb and implements, a tricorn hat on his head, the average contemporary batsman would find an innings of fifty runs child's play? In the Golden Age of batsmanship, on flawless wickets and in conditions as 'modern' as yesterday, Simpson-Hayward bowled lobs to the acute discomfort of stroke-players as sophisticated and brilliant and quick-footed as Johnny Tyldesley, A. C. MacLaren, David Denton; and in three Test matches in South Africa he took 21 wickets for 15 runs each, and he was coping with the finest batsmen ever produced from South African cricket – Faulkner, Nourse, Gordon White, J. H. Sinclair, Tancred, and so on. There was also D. L. A. Jephson and Walter Humphries, each with only half of Simpson-Hayward's tricks; and they had their moments of mastery with under-arms on 'modern' wickets against batsmen, not inferior to say the least, to today's. So it is a fair inference that if they were suddenly whisked to Broad-Halfpenny Down, there to defend wicket and shinbones against 'Lumpy' at the base of the brow of a hill, one or two of our contemporary heroes would find themselves, like Bottom, terribly 'translated!' It is certain that on the rough turf of the heyday of the round-arm attack, they would appreciate the emotions of the poor cricketer named Ludd, who was struck on the foot by John Jackson, a giant in Nottinghamshire before Larwood, 1856–1862 to be precise. Poor Ludd hobbled in agony while Jackson appealed for 'leg-before'. And when the umpire announced 'Not hout!' Master Ludd said, 'Mebbe not, but I'm a -goin'.' John Jackson scaled fifteen stone and he measured six feet in his socks. He once lamented that he never achieved the distinction of taking all ten wickets in one innings but he brightened when he remembered that once, 'playin' for North against South, 'Ah bowled out nine of them and lamed Johnny Wisden so's he couldn't bat, which was just as good wasn't it?'

We might conjecture without too much fancifulness that the advent of the fast 'round-arm' attack hastened the passing of the tall hat which superseded the pretty three-cornered hat worn at Hambledon when the game was called 'elegant and manly'. The first All-England XI sported the topper; its stately balance no doubt suited the tall forward style of Fuller Pilch, who, though he was a right-handed batsman, born in Norfolk, I shall take leave to describe as the Woolley of Kent cricket of the years 1835–1855. He mastered the round-arm cannonade even on turf so rudely close to nature that at the beginning of one match he felt obliged to borrow a scythe and mow the grass a little smoother. Not until 1849 was it legal to sweep or roll the pitch between innings; and even then it was prepared in the simplest way, and the roller was probably no heavier than the one we use nowadays for the garden lawn. Bats were without 'humps'; the blade was of uniform thickness – or thinness – and there was no 'sprung' handle; in fact the whole bat, handle and blade, was cut out of one piece of wood. Much physical pain and nervous shock was presumably sustained by the batsman who 'came down' hard on a 'shooter', or drove a fast ball with the bottom of the bat. The first cane-handle was an innovation of 1853. Pads, unknown to Hambledon, were experimented with round about 1836; then the onslaught on shins by the new fast bowlers quickened Mother Invention sharply and in the 1860s pads and gloves became a necessary fashion, both of them almost apologetically frail, not at all a first line of offence, as the modern hardy warriors of Lancashire and Yorkshire wear *their* pads.

The danger of severe physical hurt has almost passed from first-class

‘Kind and manly Alfred Mynn’
by John C. Anderson

cricket. Even when Larwood bowled the body-line attack, so called, nobody was killed, or critically injured; and the danger was palpable with notice given open and unashamed. But the perils faced by batsmen on the crude turf of the older times against fast bowling – and it *was* fast – could not be anticipated; they came without warning; the best length ball might at any moment fly upward and knock a man out. As early in the history of fast round-arm as Alfred Mynn, he was once so severely damaged on the leg during a long innings that he could scarcely stand; at last he was obliged to retire when, narrates Richard Daft, ‘his leg was found to be dreadfully injured. He was confined to his bed for a long period, and it was thought his surgeon would be obliged to take the leg off; but happily this extreme measure was not resorted to, and Mr Mynn was afterwards quite sound again.’ Mynn was born in 1807, a yeoman of Kent who, from early manhood until a few years before his death in 1861, was the first universally acknowledged of cricket’s ‘champions’. In his heyday he stood six feet one inch high; and he weighed nearly twenty stone but, vows Daft, ‘there was nothing clumsy about his movements; they were, on the contrary, stately and dignified at all times'. He was the first really great fast round-arm bowler and there is strong evidence that he could pitch the ball on the leg stump and break to the off. When he died at the early age of fifty-four, he was immortalized – not by the statistics of his batting and bowling; no, he was remembered for his 'brave heart', 'ever warm'. Some verses appeared in *Bell's Life* signed W. J. Prowse, and the closing stanza made a cadence of true poetry:

> With his tall and stately presence, with his nobly moulded form,
> His broad hand was ever open, his brave heart was ever warm,
> All were proud of him, all loved him. As the changing seasons pass,
> As our champion lies a-sleeping underneath the Kentish grass,
> Proudly, sadly, we will name him – to forget him were a sin –
> Lightly lie the turf upon thee, kind and manly Alfred Mynn.

No other game could inspire such a requiem for one of its players. There is scope at cricket for men to reveal themselves. For hours they are gathered together; and the ball is not flying here and there, leaving no time for ayes and noes or any other revealing conversation or exchange of spirit. Between overs, at the fall of a wicket, in the slips while the fast bowler is walking back to his starting place – there is opportunity for human nature to 'come out strong'. And all the time the crowd sits around, and the players seem oblivious that they are being scrutinized, even though often the rhythm and procedure of cricket renders them as much exposed as actors on the stage. In truth when we look over the 'changing seasons' and remember them, we do not dwell on the records, the scores, the results; we see and savour again the men, the originals, the characters, all sorts and conditions, in a cavalcade of English character that travels slowly down the years from the meadows of Broad-Halfpenny to Lord's in June.

From *English Cricket* (1945)

W. G. Grace – The Making of a Champion

BERNARD DARWIN

1865 was to be a memorable summer in which the boy of sixteen was to play regularly in first-class cricket, and the tide, which had set so long and so fiercely against the Gentlemen, was to turn with his coming against the Players. W. G. was still quite a boy, but he was a very big boy, for he was more than six feet in height and weighed eleven stone, tall and lanky, with no premonition of the massive splendour that was to grow on him; indeed he had, according to Lord

Draw him like y on Stone by me, [G. F. Watts]

Cobham, 'some appearance of delicacy'. Already there was a black scrub upon his chin, and he seems never to have shaved till 1870 or 1871. Then he made the effort for a year or two, before finally letting his mighty beard blow where it listed. The leanness and lankiness are worth emphasizing, because W. G. was in those days a very good runner and won many prizes. We think of him now as fielding at point, a very fine point, but never to be compared, by those who knew, with the cat-like E. M. When he first burst on the world, he was magnificent in the outfield, alike through his pace and his great power of throwing. Indeed one famous cricketer who played with him in those days declared, in an illuminating paradox, that the really good part of W. G.'s cricket was his fielding . . . .

W. G. began this season as one who (as John Lillywhite had said) 'promises to be a good bat'; when it ended he had played twice for the Gentlemen against the Players, once for the Gentlemen of the South, and once for England against Surrey; in short, he had gained all the representative honours open to him. He had caught up, if he had not actually passed, E. M., who, by the way, nearly distinguished himself this summer by causing a free fight at the Oval. Something had to be

[25]

A cricket match at Wittersham,
Kent, c1840–50; attributed to
Charles Deane. Kent 23 for 2

done to get Jupp out, and E. M. conceived the luminous notion of
pitching a lob high in the air so that it descended on the top of the
stumps. The Graces were always resourceful, but the crowd did not
this time approve of E. M.'s ingenuity; the match was stopped, and
players tore up the wickets as weapons, but, in the end, Jupp had to
go, and his side, the United South, was duly beaten.

W. G. began by playing for the Gentlemen of the South against the
Players of the South at the Oval. He was stumped for a duck, but he
bowled unchanged through both innings, and took thirteen wickets
for 84 runs. This state of things seems almost contrary to the laws of
nature, but it was not thought so then, and it was probably his bowling
that gained him his place. Mr C. E. Green saw him for the first time in
that match, and thus describes his bowling: 'His arm was as high as
his shoulder – that is as high as it was then allowed by cricket law –
and while his delivery was a nice one, his action was quite different to
what it was in his later days; it was more slinging and his pace was
fast medium. He had not then acquired any of his subsequent craftiness
with the ball. He used to bowl straight on the wicket, trusting to the
ground to do the rest.' It was his bowling again that was the most
distinguished in his first Gentlemen and Players match at the Oval –
seven wickets for 125, as against 23 and 12 not out. At Lord's he went
in first with E. M., and made 34 in the second innings; he was run out
in the first innings, and if this was E. M.'s fault it was probably a good
thing that he was by seven years the elder brother. These two also
went in first together for England against Surrey, and made 80 for the
first wicket.

Of the two Gentlemen and Players matches, the Gentlemen lost at
the Oval but won at Lord's. There were fine batsmen on the
Gentlemen's side, for, besides the Graces, there were I. D. Walker,
R. A. H. Mitchell and C. F. Buller, and these are great names. The

W.G. Grace by 'Spy', 1877

fact that after long lean years the amateurs began to hold their own again was not all due to one man, but it is significant that the tide turned. The hour had come, and the man. The professionals had always depended a great deal on their bowling, and with the bad wickets to help them, this had been much more than enough: they had perhaps a little neglected their batting, as they could afford to do. Soon they were to face a scoring machine such as they had never dreamed of, and, in addition, a fine, hostile spirit that rose to its highest on the great occasion of the year. That 'promises to be a good bat' of John Lillywhite's was for the Players the writing on the wall.

In 1866 the Players won at Lord's, and the Gentlemen at the Oval, with W. G. more successful as a bowler than as a batsman. The Players had not yet felt the full scourge of his bat, but one county did; Surrey tried to play England; no county tried the experiment again for eleven years, and then the county was that of the Graces. England won the toss, and W. G. went in third wicket down. They were all out for 521, and the boy, now just eighteen, carried his bat out for 224. It was his first hundred in first-class cricket, and it was characteristic of him that he made a thorough job of it. Not for him the light heart when the first hundred was made, nor the touch of mercy towards the bowling; he was never tired of making runs, and went on piling them up with a cheerful ruthlessness. There used to be an old gentleman at St Andrews whose golfing maxim was, 'When I am five up, I strive to be six up: when I am six up, I strive to be seven up.' W. G. would highly have approved of that; with him the appetite for runs came in the making of them. His own memories of this innings were of feeling slightly nervous at the beginning of it, and then, after a blank, of the shouting at the end. The Surrey wickets fell fast before Willsher and Wootton, and England won by an innings and nearly 300 runs. On the last day, Mr V. E. Walker allowed the young hero to go away to the Crystal Palace to run in a hurdle race. It seems a little casual, and W. G., afterwards at any rate, thought so himself. 'I know what I should say,' he remarked, 'if I were the captain.'

Three weeks or so later there came a second innings of over a hundred – 173 not out for the Gentlemen of the South against the Players of the South at the Oval; his recollection of it was that there was 'more hitting in it than in the previous match', and that he 'played more confidently'. That 173 was out of a total of under 300, while the great innings against Surrey had represented nearly half his side's score. That is worth remarking, because W. G.'s scores in his youth constantly represented so very large a proportion of the whole side's. As Alfred Shaw, when an old man, said of him, he started so quickly, he hit the ball so hard, he travelled at such an even pace: other men might be not out 70 at lunch, W. G. was not out 130. Scoring as a whole was not large when he began to alter men's notions of what was possible; the great professional batsmen of the All-England Eleven had been content with averages of 20 or a little over. Gradually batting improved, and, still more markedly, the wickets improved, but W. G.'s long innings were colossal as compared with those of the rest of the side. This is a fact patent to anyone who looks at the scores, and it needs emphasizing when any attempt is made to compare him with modern batsmen. Incidentally this innings of 173, which he called 'one of my best', had been preceded by his taking seven of the Players' wickets, and bowling right through their innings.

Of the wickets on which W. G. was making these scores, something may here be said. Speaking of wickets in general in the early 1860s, he himself wrote this: 'Up to this time many of the principal grounds were so rough as to be positively dangerous to play upon, and batsmen were constantly damaged by the fast bowling. When the wickets were in this condition the batsman had to look out for shooters and leave the bumping balls to look after themselves. In the 'sixties it was no

1. Lyttleton Waiting for a Rise.—2. Called Back : The Bobby and the Pickpocket.—3. The "Demon" Bowler.—4. "Better Not Play Any More, Blackham."—5. Grace and Steel Practice Catches at the Fall of Spofforth's Wicket.—6. "How Shall I Manage Barlow?" "Put On the Pace."—7. Well-earned Repose.—8. Lord Harris's Carriage at Lord's.—9. Behind the Screen.—10. Bigger than the Giant Bonnor.

AUSTRALIA v. ENGLAND AT LORD'S, JULY 21, 22, AND 23, 1884

unusual thing to have two or three shooters in an over; nowadays you scarcely get one shooter in a season. At this time the Marylebone ground was in a very unsatisfactory condition – so unsatisfactory that in 1864 Sussex refused to play at Lord's owing to the roughness of the ground. When I first played there the creases were not chalked out, but were actually cut out of the turf one inch deep, and about one inch wide. As matches were frequently being played, and no pains were taken to fill up the holes, it is quite easy to imagine what a terrible condition the turf presented.' He added that he could remember the

time when he could go on to the pitch and pick up a handful of small pieces of gravel. In 1865 a large piece of the ground was levelled and returfed. Lord's gradually improved, but in 1870 it was still capable of an almost murderous condition. It was in that year that he made a historic 66 against Freeman and Emmett. 'Tom Emmett and I,' said Freeman, many years afterwards, 'have often said it was a marvel that the Doctor was not either maimed or unnerved for the rest of his days or killed outright. I often think of his pluck when I watch a modern batsman scared if a medium-paced ball hits him on the hand; he should have seen our expresses flying about his ribs, shoulders and head in 1870.'

With the end of 1866, W. G., now eighteen years old, was fairly established as what Pierce Egan would have called a 'nonpareil and an out-and-outer'. He was no longer climbing the ladder; he had got to the top, although he was still destined to add a few more rungs to it, dizzy rungs utterly beyond anyone else's reach. Henceforth he had great, greater, and greatest years, but they no longer belong to the making of a champion.

From *W. G. Grace* (1948)

The Maker of Modern Batting

K. S. RANJITSINHJI

There is one great landmark that separates the old batting from the new – the appearance of Dr W. G. Grace in the cricket world. In 1865 W. G. came fully before the public that has admired and loved him ever since. He revolutionized batting. He turned it from an accomplishment into a science. All I know of old-time batting is, of course, gathered from books and older players, but the impression left

on my mind is this: before W. G. batsmen were of two kinds – a batsman played a forward game or he played a back game. Each player, too, seems to have made a specialty of some particular stroke. The criterion of style was, as it were, a certain mixed method of play. It was bad cricket to hit a straight ball; as for pulling a slow long-hop, it was regarded as immoral. What W. G. did was to unite in his mighty self all the good points of all the good players, and to make utility the criterion of style. He founded the modern theory of batting by making forward- and back-play of equal importance, relying neither on the one nor on the other, but on both. Any cricketer who thinks for a moment can see the enormous change W. G. introduced into the game. I hold him to be, not only the finest player born or unborn, but the maker of modern batting. He turned the old one-stringed instrument into a many-chorded lyre.

From *The Jubilee Book of Cricket* (1897)

Jessop's Match

BEN TRAVERS

After almost eighty years, Jessop's Match still seems to retain a special sort of fabulous and glamorous reputation of its own ... [but] now that I come to write about it I find myself faced with the fact that the first two days' play contained some incidents which tickle the memory but few to haunt it.

I am glad now that I watched Trumper starting off the match with

Another great batsman who employed a high backlift and an equally high follow-through — Victor Trumper, by G.W. Beldam

a characteristic 42, for it was the only time I ever saw Trumper make double figures. But the latter-end of the first day's play produced in me a good deal of lingering resentment and muffled snorting as Trumble persisted in a long and stubborn tail-ender's innings of 64 not out ('pottering about' in my view) and, along with Hopkins and Kelly, put on about 150 for the eighth and ninth wickets. The second morning belonged to Trumble too, as bowler this time, unchanged throughout England's first knock and taking 8 for 65. As a result England were left 141 behind, which was all pretty depressing, but we had a great stroke of luck when Australia batted again. Trumper had only made two when he went for a quick run, stumbled, fell flat halfway down the pitch and was run out. Then Lockwood put in a great spell of bowling and Australia were all out soon after the start of the third morning for 121 (Lockwood 5 for 45). So the second day was a great deal more eventful than the tedious first and I am sure I watched every ball with those hopes and fears which only the cricket-lover can appreciate. But it is no good pretending that I can still give an eye-witness account of all that happened. Some of those for-no-particular-reason incidents survive. I remember one immaculate cover-drive of Palairet's better than I remember any individual cover-drive of Hammond's or Hutton's. Above all, two first-slip catches by MacLaren. They were not difficult catches; they came straight into his hands. It was the manner with which he accepted them. He took the ball and tossed it, not over his head to recatch it, but away into outer space with a flick of the wrist in the most disdainful fashion. 'Take it away: it stinks.' . . .

Trumble and Lockwood must in turn have demonstrated that, ever since the first day, the wicket had got worse and worse. After England's first innings total of 183 and Australia's second innings total of 121, how could we possibly be expected to make 263 to win? We couldn't, of course, but the impossibility needn't have been rubbed in to me so cruelly. That hateful Saunders [who had skittled the unfortunate Fred Tate in the previous Test] immediately came sailing in at the Vauxhall end, slinging destruction. MacLaren b. Saunders 2, Palairet b. Saunders 6, Tyldesley b. Saunders 0, Hayward c. Kelly b. Saunders 7. Jackson, at number five, was not out at lunchtime. Braund had joined him, but only for a very short time (c. Kelly b. Trumble 2).

During the lunch interval I noticed quite a number of disgruntled elderly members gathering up their belongings in the pavilion and departing home, unable to face the indignity of witnessing England's abasement. And I wonder what MacLaren had to say about what was served up to him for his mid-day meal.

So, then – Braund out but Jackson still there and appearing remarkably unruffled. And in came Jessop.

Jessop was a favourite subject for Craig's contemporary rivals as cricket poets. I recall two pleasing lines from an unidentified bard:

> At one end stocky Jessop crouched,
> The human catapult –

Crouched was an obvious description: 'the croucher' was a familiar nickname for Jessop owing to his stance at the wicket. 'Stocky' was descriptive of him too, though I think 'jaunty' would be nearer the mark. I knew, of course, all about his reputation as the biggest hitter in the game, but he had disappointed us in England's first innings (b. Trumble 13). Oh, well – perhaps he might treat us to a good slog or two before the inevitable and dismal defeat.

Again I must stick to my genuine and lasting recollections and impressions. It is obviously impossible to recall that Jessop innings in detail but there are certain features of it, and of its effect upon the crowd, that remain as clearly in my mind as though it all happened yesterday. To begin with, I was struck by Jessop's undaunted, almost it seemed heedless, approach – no 'desperate situation' about it. Jaunty. He was his own aggressive self from the start. Before long he took the triumphant Saunders in hand, to my especial delight, and hit him for two fours off successive balls to the long-on boundary. Darling immediately posted two fielders out there but Jessop ignored them and hit Saunders' next two deliveries between them or round them or through them as well. However despondent the crowd must have been during the morning, Jessop aroused them now to a state of wild exhilaration and Jackson must have been scoring steadily on his own. But I confess that the only thing I can remember about Jackson's invaluable innings is his getting caught and bowled by Trumble when he had made 49 and Jackson's exasperated thump with his bat on his pad as he turned to go.

Oh, damn and blast. Any faint gleam of hope of our getting those 263 runs vanished with Jackson into the pavilion. But the Australians

had still another Yorkshireman to deal with. Confidence was the last thing that Jessop seemed to require but, had he needed it, George Hirst was the man to supply it – sturdy, defiant and the best all-rounder in the country in his day. (No one else had ever taken 200 wickets and made 2,000 runs in one season and they never will.) Sure enough, Hirst settled down while Jessop continued as before. Trumble was still on at the pavilion end. Still on? He was never off throughout the whole of England's two innings. Jessop hit him for six on to a canvas awning above part of the members' enclosure. The ball came back only to land on almost exactly the same spot immediately afterwards.

On they went, Hirst unmoveable, Jessop irrepressible. Presently the roars of the crowd subsided and gave way to an awesome, aspiring hush. They had roared Jessop to the verge of his century.

How well all cricket-lovers know that tremulous moment and, goodness me, how often have I experienced it myself, but never, never in my whole life has it meant to me what it meant then.

Hush. Jessop crouched. The bowler started his run. It was just as well for me that my heart was only fifteen years old. The bowler bowled. Bang. Uproar.

The conventional Londoner wore a hat in those days and the conventional hat he wore was a straw boater. As Jessop made that stroke dozens of straw boaters were sent sailing from the crowd like boomerangs. Unlike boomerangs they failed to return to the owners, but who cared?

Like all cricket devotees I have many, many times shared with all around me that infectious, 'breathless hush' tension as a batsman, however well-set, however self-possessed, has to face up to the obligation of scoring that hundreth run. He brings it off and, amid the general enthusiasm, one feels a spasm of pleasurable secret relief and a glow of fraternal satisfaction in the case of a batsman one is particularly fond of. I know I was young and almost foolishly impressionable at the time but I have always treasured and still treasure that century of Jessop's above and apart from all the rest.

The frenzy gradually subsided; boaters were or were not recovered; the crowd settled down. England still had a long way to go; but so long as Jessop and Hirst were there . . . Then, oh, no, Jessop mistimed a hook-shot and was caught at fine leg. What a tragedy. But that seemed to settle it; that stupendous effort of 104 was sacrificed. We couldn't hope to win now, could we? Hirst was still battling away and scoring steadily but Lockwood didn't last long. Lilley did, though. Beyond all expectation Lilley stuck there with Hirst. The score crept up – 230, 240 – the whole Oval became almost as intent and intimidated as I was, hesitating to applaud too loudly for fear of inciting Hirst and Lilley to rashness.

Lilley got caught for 16 when the total had reached 248. Fifteen wanted and Rhodes came in to join his fellow-Yorkshireman for a last-wicket partnership which was to become a sort of historic addendum

Left: a crouch and a front footed hook. No wonder Jessop used to score so fast (G. W. Beldam)

'And what do you think is the best thing in cricket?' 'Why, being an all-rounder, of course,' replied George Hirst. 'When you're both a batter and a bowler, you enjoy yourself twice as much.' From *Cricket, My Pleasure* by A.A. Thomson (1953). Picture by G.W. Beldam

to Jessop's hundred, though the legend that Hirst greeted Rhodes with the pronouncement, 'We'll get 'em in singles,' was later refuted by Rhodes himself. They got 'em steadily, a single here a couple there, until they had levelled up the match at 262.

That is the moment – or rather the marathon minute – which remains clearest of all in my memory. Duff was fielding at deep long-on to Trumble, who was bowling, as ever, from the pavilion end. An Australian from his seat in the stand a few rows behind me shouted, 'Never mind, Duff; you've won the Ashes.' I saw Duff turn his head with a quick resigned grin and return at once to attention. He of all the Australians in the field was required to be at attention. Trumble, as crafty a bowler as ever existed, presented Rhodes with a slow half-volley on the leg stump. How could any human batsman resist such a heaven-sent gift? 'Hurrah, here it is and here it goes' – wallop. And the ball would sail high into the outfield and, well within the range of possibility, into the safe hands of Duff. Not Rhodes. Not Yorkshire. Rhodes tapped the ball gently past square leg, ran the safe single and the match was won.

When by some means long forgotten I managed to arrive back home that evening, there was my father waiting to welcome me in the open doorway, his arms outstretched in mutual rejoicing. I felt a bit of a hero at having actually been there on Jessop's Day. I still do.

From *94 Declared: Cricket Reminiscences* (1981)

Ranjitsinhji and Trumper

A. E. KNIGHT

Prince Ranjitsinhji is unlike all players, English or Australian, in his wonderful suppleness and freedom of wrist and limb, in quickness of eye, and has brought to perfection many strokes the attempt to emulate which must lead less gifted batsmen to direct and inevitable disaster. No number of short legs can cramp the delightful leg glances; no slips tame the felicities and facilities of his late cutting. His driving is fine, and he uses his feet very frequently in executing the stroke, indeed his 'walking out stroke' in order to play forward or hit seems quite an unnecessary tempting of providence, or rather it would be so to any one not so uniquely gifted. His innate natural quickness is such that when apparently caught in two minds, his subsequent stroke is still a perfect one, he can play the ball as it were 'the other way'. Something of the languidity of the Orient and a playfulness akin to jugglery tincture his batting, at times somewhat unpleasantly conveying the impression that he merely toys with, rather than attempts to master, the bowling.

On sticky wickets, occasionally, one has observed manifestations of this too easy watchfulness, and on that kind of wicket he never appeared to me to possess the perfect mastery of such a scientist as Arthur Shrewsbury, although I do not doubt that those who have seen him play a great innings upon such wickets will entirely disagree. On really fiery and bumpy wickets he is as incomparable as on those good ones, where getting out seems so entirely a matter for his personal choice. I remember the professional bowler Woodcock, a few years ago the fastest in England, telling me that he had been bowling at Ranjitsinhji, and had tried and failed to hit the back of the net, much less was the wicket possible for him to find. The same bowler told me how in a scratch game at Bexhill, on a positively dangerous wicket, Ranjitsinhji had repeatedly put to the leg boundary rearing balls which would have smashed his eye but for the intercepting bat. The very qualities which make for fickleness and indifference evoked in this superb player the possibilities of his genius.

I think, however, that the 'lyre' of willow has an even greater master. In Victor Trumper we have seen the very poetry and heard the deep and wonderful music of batsmanship. Not the structures of a great mentality, not the argument of logic, but a sweet and simple strain of beauty, the gift of the gods alone. Stylish in the highest sense, orthodox, yet breaking all canons of style, Trumper is just himself. On the occasion of a great Test Match at Sydney, the Englishmen had built up a colossal score after a relative Australian failure in the first innings, Mr R. E. Foster playing the record innings of his life and of these great contests. The Star of Australia seemed fast setting, but a couple of tail-end batsmen played out the last hour of the day with a quite heroic barndoor performance of exasperating correctness. The morrow dawned, and faint hopes glimmered in forty thousand minds, when, with the dismissal of one of these monuments of scientific patience, the young Australian champion emerged on to the green.

A slender figure, wan and drawn of face, cadaverous, but spiritualized with the delicacy of ill health, glides to the wicket. Not ornament nor colour marked his featureless attire, the personality was all-dominating. He took guard quickly, more quickly took a glance around the field, and received his first ball. 'Dreams of summer dawn in night of rain' presented no fresher vision than this boy's play to that black sea which hid the blistered grass of the Sydney hill. Not in his fascinating collection of strokes, nor in their frank and open execution merely, lay the charm; it was a man playing away a power which was himself rather than in him. With luxuriant masterfulness, yet with the unlaboured easy naturalness of a falling tear, or rather of showers from the sunny lips of summer, he diverted the ball in every conceivable direction which his genius willed. Not violently nor recklessly, like his comrade Duff the revolutionary slashing with his pike, not with the careworn, anxious deliberation of Noble, does he reach the heights, but, insensibly and unconsciously, lifts us with him to where winds blow cool and the outlook is infinite . . .

With bat whipping like a flail, he drove the fastest swervers of Hirst, and jumped in with fearless precision to the tempting slows of Rhodes, hooked the dropping 'googlies' of Bosanquet, and alternately late cut or pushed to square leg the pace-making deliveries of Arnold. One by one his colleagues fail and pass before an attack of magnificent precision and persistence. 'Our Vic' remains, and when a partner's lazy incompetence rendered his last effort to secure the bowling futile, with his colleague's loss, he left the field still undefeated. He had given to his country at least an outside chance of victory, and the glow of a hope once seemingly impossible. Nothing akin to jugglery or contemptuous languor mars the incomparable grace and simplicity of this perfect batsman. His greatness is of that high kind which appeals to the technical no less than to the more human critic. His simplicity has no faintest touch of *simplesse*, he convinces the onlooker and the bowler that the stroke he executes is precisely what should be done. There is no subtlety, no show miracle, but the perfect openness and the direct simplicity of a master.

Like Ranjitsinhji, if apparently in doubt, his celerity is such, mind and action following judgement so directly, that jumping out to drive on a fast pitch to a fast-medium bowler, he seems to have ample time to return to his crease and late cut the same ball. His wonderful eye, his great reach, so remarkable in one not over tall, and the quickness of foot which enables him to reach or cover the ball so often skimming away to third man when less skilfully dealt with, are the outer causes which one would assign as essential features in the mere mechanism and outer semblances of this great genius. He is all compounded, so to speak, of wrist and eye, full of faith in the latter. His execution of every stroke is superb, as powerful as it is graceful. Scarcely has the ball left the bowler's hand ere he has determined its length and moved his feet accordingly. Balls which many are happy enough if they can merely play, oblivious of scoring, are forced by him with wristy swing to the boundary. Such is the power of his strokes, that the race of the fieldsman whom the ball passes is hopeless. Trumper does not seem to have to watch the ball from the pitch, and then to flick it away by wrist and body turn, as does Ranjitsinhji. He divines what the ball will do and where it will be while it is still in the air, and can consequently put the whole force and swing of his body into his strokes. Such an one is scarcely to be written about, however, with a recipe book in hand, or with a bundle of statistics at one's elbow. The really highest manifestations of an art so emotional as well as technical as batting, have little relation to time or to quantity. Perchance the statistical expert will yet have many pages to fill with the first-class records of Victor Trumper. Probably not, for such eye and wrist, such lightning celerity, such risk, is for youth alone. Perchance the cold winds of ill-health have already swept across the stream on whose surface lies the glory and the gleam. Howsoever transient his career, none who have been privileged to see him play a great innings will ever forget that spirit, so self-forgetful, so manly, and so true. More than many a long summer of consistent scoring shall we revere this Sydney light which revealed magnificent possibilities of batsmanship, never before incarnate.

From *The Complete Cricketer* (1906)

Hobbs – and a 'Bad Trot'

JOHN ARLOTT

At the start of the 1905 season Jack Hobbs became a qualified Surrey player. At that time there were twenty-two professionals on the Oval staff; while, of eighteen amateurs, five had virtually irrefutable – and three more, reasonable – claims to selection when available. Twelve of them played Test cricket for England; and Surrey finished fourth in the Championship that season. So, although the 'new' player had batted impressively against Norfolk when he was watched, he was by no means an automatic first team choice.

Once again events fell into a happy pattern for him. The county's first match was a pipe-opener against the Gentlemen of England beginning on Easter Monday. By historic coincidence, the Gentlemen's side was captained by W. G. Grace, now nearing the end of his mighty career; and Surrey by Tom Hayward. They were the first two batsmen, as Jack Hobbs was the third, to reach a hundred centuries in first-class cricket. It was fitting, too, that the first appearance of the man who was to inherit the position of the finest English batsman, should be in a match with his two predecessors, for, between Grace's decline at the end of the century and his own, Tom Hayward stood at the top of the English game. Similarly, Jack Hobbs was to play with and against Walter Hammond and Donald Bradman in another historic overlapping.

His name was posted among the fourteen 'from whom'; and remained there when two amateur batsmen, for reasons possibly not unconnected with the atrociously cold weather, intimated that they were not available. None of the four men who had generally opened the innings with Tom Hayward in the previous season was playing. The ageing Bobby Abel was on the verge of retirement and did not relish so bleak a day; neither Albert Baker nor Fred Holland was fit; and John Raphael, who had been the most successful of them, was not available until after the University match. Still Ernie Hayes, an established batsman who had gone in first, was in the side. By the final stroke of fortune, in the absence of the new captain, Lord Dalmeny, the decision fell to Tom Hayward. He, probably out of consideration, certainly more wisely than he knew, and much to the young man's grateful relief, took Jack Hobbs in first with him. He cannot have dreamt that he was initiating a great opening partnership.

Each got away with a quick single in the first over, but the pitch was awkward and the Gentlemen's opening bowlers, George Beldam and Walter Brearley, were admirably equipped to exploit it. They put out Surrey for 86. Jack Hobbs was caught at slip off Beldam for only 18; but that was enough to make him joint top scorer of the innings with Ernie Hayes. When the Gentlemen batted Neville Knox, in his turn, made the ball lift awkwardly and Surrey went in again only 29 behind.

Overnight – 44 in an hour – and next morning, Jack Hobbs batted with a commanding ease which was a revelation to those who had not seen him play before. He seemed to be taking a century as he willed when he pulled a ball from Walter Brearley that was too near his legs for that stroke and skied it to Frank Crawford at square leg. As he passed Brearley on his way out, that hearty extrovert growled, 'I should drop that stroke if I were you.' He did not drop it; in fact, as he grew older, he scored an increasing proportion of his runs with it; but as he said, 'I learnt to play it properly – to a short ball outside the off stump.' His 88 was the highest score of the game – on either side – and *Wisden*'s report ended with 'the feature of the match was the batting of Hobbs whose first appearance in first-class cricket was an emphatic success. He scored his 88 in two hours and only made one real mistake.'

A week afterwards Essex, the county that refused Hobbs a trial, came to The Oval. He made 28 in a small Surrey first innings but, in the second – with a borrowed bat – 155 at almost a run a minute. This was the authentic Hobbs; and both spectators and players were moved by the dashing certainty of his batting. At the end of the match he caught his fellow-Cambridge man, Bill Reeves, in the deep; the crowd raced across the ground, cheering and calling his name and, in the spontaneous fashion of earlier times, as the players came off the field, his captain, Lord Dalmeny, gave him his county cap.

The following match was against Hampshire and, after scoring only 6 in the first innings, he made a valuable 43 – more than the margin of Surrey's narrow win – in the second.

Next day the Australians came to The Oval. This was undeniably a strong side, beaten in the Test rubber only by, arguably, the most powerful of all English teams. Captained by Joe Darling, they had Victor Trumper, Monty Noble, Clem Hill, Warwick Armstrong, Reggie Duff, Jim Kelly and Frank Laver. Jack Hobbs rated their opening bowler, 'Tibby' Cotter, on that tour, the fastest bowler he ever faced. He had some uneasy moments against him, but he made 94 before Clem Hill, with only a single stump to aim at from the third man boundary, hit it and ran him out. It was not a flawless innings, but it was an aggressive one; no other Surrey batsman scored more than 24 of their 225; but that run-out grieved him all his days: so deeply that he never quite knew whether he resented it out of disappointment, or because he thought it an inaccurate decision. He was caught off Cotter for only 1 in the second innings: and, no doubt, learnt much from watching Hayward make a century.

No newcomer could be expected to continue in such fashion. The tangle of new experiences, impressions, excitement, were bound to have a disturbing effect on concentration. He did little in the following four matches apart from a serviceable 40 against Warwickshire; indeed, returning to Cambridge for the first time as a Surrey cricketer, he was caught at the wicket for nought. Then, at the beginning of June, in the return with Essex, he made a confident and fluent 102. So far from re-establishing his confidence, that innings was followed by a run of poor scores. Briefly at the end of July he seemed to recover his zest and touch with a competent 58 in the second match with the Australians. Immediately afterwards he made a bright 75 not out, when he and Hayward gave Surrey a ten-wicket win over Middlesex with a fast-scoring, unbroken opening stand of 168 in what had been, until then, a bowlers' match. Apart from those two occasions, however, he did not play an innings of as many as 40 in the two months between the second century against Essex and the end of the season.

The truth was that he had no reserves of strength or stamina and, as he had done at Bedford School, he became easily and deeply fatigued. Thirty years afterwards the young Len Hutton found the strain of the six-day cricketing week unsupportable; and he, too, had to be 'rested'. He, though, never lost form as Jack Hobbs did in 1905 when he scored only 150 runs – 72 of them in three innings – in eight matches.

This was the worst time he ever had in cricket, and always afterwards the memory of it coloured the advice he gave to young men who wanted to take up cricket as a career. He had 'bad trots' subsequently but never one so protracted nor which caught him so unprepared: and later, of course, he was established beyond question. Until now his cricket had been a steady progression, a series of mounting achievements. Now came this quite bewildering setback for which he knew no remedy. Technically, weariness had affected the co-ordination of eye, mind and muscles sufficiently to make that minute but crucial difference between the timed and middled stroke and one which was mistimed or edged. The margin of error between middle and edge of a cricket bat is, after all, only two inches. That is a truth which never enters a batsman's mind when he is in form; when he is off, it can become an obsessive hazard. In a real 'trot' the problem rapidly becomes more psychological than technical. This is something the casual part-time player or the follower of cricket often does not understand. For several reasons only the professional cricketer – or career amateur – can experience this feeling; first because his livelihood – which seems like life – is at stake; secondly, it goes on, unrelieved, day after day.

Indeed, the stress is magnified for the man in the first-class game when he has to wait two or three days – perhaps more, over a match-free period – before he has the chance to try again. Nets may help, but they are no substitute for confidence – nor for the luck the out-of-form player needs. At a time like this the cricketer recognizes his loneliness. Cricket is loosely described as a team game; yet in essence it is the most individual combat of all. There is no other isolation in sport so complete as that of the batsman as he faces a bowler supported by ten fieldsmen. The starkest form of that loneliness is suffered by the opening batsman.

Once distress infects a player it intensifies; anxiety and weariness feed on one another; worry-tensed muscles exaggerate difficulties, investing normal stroke-reaction with peril at once, what had seemed as natural as breathing becomes impossible. Luck, too, invariably is involved. Bad fieldsmen catch the uncatchable; the victim gets the one ball of the day that lifts, squats or moves; a good umpire nods; a movement behind the bowler at the moment of delivery breaks concentration. One modern player put it – 'On this tour I have been out in every possible way except 'top hat fell on wicket.'

The 'bad trot' is a batsman's disease. The case that is talked of is invariably one that is cured. If it is not, the player simply goes out of the game. Then no one speaks of a 'bad trot'. It is said 'he was not good enough', 'he could not stand the strain of the first-class game', 'he simply was not sound' or even 'he did not try'. All those may be half-truths. Too often a combination of ill luck and psychological pressure exaggerates relatively unimportant flaws of method. Certainly instances can be recalled of players who seemed to have all the qualities for success but whose self-belief was so undermined by a bad trot that their technique visibly deteriorated . . .

While, ultimately, only the player himself can pull out of one of these spells, it can affect an entire team, especially when a key batsman is afflicted. Some of the happiest and most convivial occasions of any county cricket season celebrate the occasion when a batsman pulls out of a 'long trot'.

Jack Hobbs found the process cruelly cumulative. 'Sometimes after I was out I would go and sit down in the dressing-room without taking my pads off, and think, and I thought I should never make another run.' His arm ached from throwing – the boundaries at The Oval are the longest in the country – he lost his eagerness in the field and, when he fumbled out of weariness, there was always some spectator quick to jeer. Until the end of his playing days he was deeply sensitive to unfriendly crowd reactions. Eventually his batting was so affected that he was twice out – most uncharacteristically – 'hit wicket', which only happened to him three times in the next twenty years. The Surrey club were confident of his ability, but they became worried, not only by his loss of form, but by the effect it had on him. In the attempt at rehabilitation he was moved down the order, reinstated as an opener, dropped, and then recalled for the last match of the season. It was to be played at The Oval with its good batting wicket, against Leicestershire, one of the weaker bowling sides; and there was nothing 'in' it for either county. Jack Hobbs was to bat in the 'easy' position of number five. It was all therapeutically intended; but, with the savage irony of the 'bad trot', he was bowled by an indifferent change bowler named Whitehead for 9 – out of a Surrey total of 549 for six. His ill fortune was underlined, and his winter preoccupations were increased, by the fact that Fred Holland went in first and shared an opening partnership of 112 with Tom Hayward.

Wisden, reviewing the Surrey season, observed encouragingly:

At the opening of the season it was known that a good deal was hoped of him. His early play exceeded all expectations and by the end of May he had firmly established his reputation, his scoring for three or four weeks being extraordinary; it cannot be said that he kept up his form.

No one appreciated the validity of the final phrase better than he. In comparative terms his 1,317 (at 25·82) in all matches put him seventh in the Surrey batting averages: in Championship matches, though, his 1,004 at 24·48 placed him ninth. In six matches, including his first four, he had scored 638 runs, in the remaining twenty-four, 679. He would not have been the pragmatist he was if he had not recognized that the question for him – and Surrey – was whether the true Hobbs was the batsman of the six matches, or the twenty-four.

There was no parent or older man to counsel or reassure him that winter in the lodgings in Fentiman Road that he shared with another ground staff lad, the cheerful Joe Bunyan. Jack Hobbs was thoughtful and anxious: clear-sighted enough to recognize cricket for a perilous career. He did his utmost to keep fit, walking long distances across London, playing badminton and football; once experimenting with a 'body building' system. Even then, the philosophical strain which was so important a part of his character in later years was strong in him. Above all, and for all his modesty and quietness, his resolve was firm, as was to be reflected over the years in his outstanding performances on difficult wickets and in apparently losing situations. He was undemonstratively, but highly combatively, resilient against odds. So he proved now.

From *Jack Hobbs: Profile of the Master* (1981)

Philadelphia in the Golden Age

ROWLAND BOWEN

In the United States, this was the hey-day of cricket in and around Philadelphia – cricket which sustained the game in Boston and Baltimore, in New York and even in an almost typically English country-house form in Virginia. Cricket in America is so much regarded now as a joke or a curiosity that it is difficult to realize that it was in this period that the prospect of Philadelphia actually playing Test matches one day was not to be laughed at. Let us just consider a few of the events of the Golden Age of cricket as they affected Philadelphia: for four years around the turn of the century, there were two competing monthly cricket magazines in that *city* – two! Few countries are able to support one nowadays. One of them – the old *American Cricketer* – revamped itself at the turn of the century to become one of the best *productions* that has been seen amongst cricket magazines at any time. There was an annual which ran right on until the First World War began, sponsored for the latter half of its life by Spaldings, much as Wisden's firm sponsored one in this country, and replete with detailed statistics (F. Fitzmaurice Kelly, its editor in its latter days, was second only to F. S. Ashley-Cooper in his time as a cricket statistician and historian). So much for the literature, which was no new feature of the game in Philadelphia. Look at the tours: from 1896 to 1914 Haverford College undertook five tours to England to play other schools, and clubs. It was many years before any English school toured abroad. The Gentlemen of Philadelphia came here three times, and each time their record was good and some of the play remarkable. Three of the constituent clubs each made tours here to play clubs and county teams and Service teams. There were six trips to Bermuda and to Jamaica. Twelve teams from these islands made tours to North America and chiefly to Philadelphia, and these included Kent, the first county to tour abroad, the MCC, and many of the leading players of the time, Ranji among them. It was an extremely pleasant ending to a cricket season to cross the Atlantic in early or

Cricket in the USA also had its 'Golden Age' and international standing. Above is the famous picture of John Barton King, a fast bowler who maintained his speed and effectiveness over twenty years and topped the English bowling averages in 1908.

mid-September and play on till October in the marvellous surroundings to be found there. There were three Australian tours, official in 1896 (when again they managed to lose to Philadelphia in one of their matches by an innings) and 1912, and unofficial, but hardly less powerful, in 1913. And Philadelphia was never found to be playing above its class.

The leading clubs in Philadelphia were found in this period mostly rebuilding, either after a fire, or for expansion, and provided amongst the world's best settings to play and to watch the game: crowds of twenty thousand could be found on occasion watching an international match. Domestically, cricket was highly organized with any number of different leagues and cup competitions. Domestically too, it was progressive, experiments being made with eight-ball and ten-ball overs whilst English first-class cricket was still dallying with five-ball overs. Indeed, eight-ball and ten-ball overs were adopted officially for certain competitions though the general opinion was that ten-ball overs were too long. Although it cannot be proved it seems likely that the Philadelphian eight-ball overs must have made their impress on the Australian cricketers who visited the city.

Philadelphia had one very great player, of world class – John Barton King: a fast bowler who maintained his speed for twenty

[45]

The picture of cricket at Manheim, Philadelphia, in 1903 shows the Germantown side in the field in a Halifax Cup match. Reproduced from *A Century of Philadelphia Cricket* by J.A. Lester

years, and had perfected a controlled swerve which he used but rarely and then with deadly effect. He headed the English bowling averages in 1908* with a figure not to be achieved or beaten for another fifty years, and never since approached by a touring bowler. (He was not the captain in 1908 as is sometimes stated.) He was also a fine batsman and set up the North American record. He was not a wealthy man, as so many of the Philadelphian cricketers were, and was subsidised discreetly by them. The Americans eschewed professionals: how they swallowed King is something to wonder at! American cricketers regarded professionalism as the potential ruin of cricket, as it had been, in their view, of baseball, leading inevitably to arrant commercialism, and warnings were uttered occasionally about England's professionalism. Only in our own time, half a century after, can we see the bitter truth of those warnings, as commercialism seizes and manipulates cricket to advertise itself.

Why did all this wonderful scene collapse? Partly because it was amateur and depended on the leisured and wealthy amateur for its existence and after the Wall Street crash years later there were few enough of these: partly because the magnificent cricket clubs turned themselves into all-sport country clubs, and a time came when a majority of members were found to prefer the shorter and quicker game of lawn tennis: partly because there was very little real junior cricket, without which the senior game could hardly thrive naturally: partly because the great Philadelphian Eleven of the 1890s was, with only a few changes, still playing twenty years later, not so much because no one else had come along as that the team was all-powerful

---

* 1894 T. Richardson (Surrey), 196 wickets, average 10·33.
  1908 J. B. King, 87 wickets, average 11·01.
  1958 H. L. Jackson (Derbyshire), 143 wickets, average 10·99.
King does not appear in the record books as the line is, for some reason, drawn at 100 wickets, but you would have to find someone who took less than 40 wickets to beat King's figures in that sixty-four-year period!

in itself. There were one or two who saw the portents, but they did not speak up enough nor were their somewhat muted voices heard by others. One thing is certain – that the entire hey-day of Philadelphian cricket fits into the span provided by the Golden Age.

Nowhere else in the United States was cricket so popular, nowhere else was it played to such an extent by native-born Americans (this was one of the great boasts of the Philadelphians) : that it was far more widespread than now is true, with inter-State and inter-city matches and many interesting tours not confined to the eastern half of the country. But rarely was it outside Philadelphia a truly American phenomenon.

From Cricket: A History of its Growth and Development throughout the World (1970)

Charlie Macartney

JACK FINGLETON

I still recall the intense thrill I knew one Sydney day when, passing between two of the Members' stands, I caught a glimpse of the middle and saw Charlie Macartney. He stood erect in the popping crease, his guard just taken, his bat aloft and twirling vigorously in his hands as if seeking a charge of electricity from the air – and many a bowler and fieldsman often thought it had been super-charged.

Charlie Macartney in the middle was a defiant, dogmatic, domineering imp of a batsman. He had a strong, jutting chin. He had alert, brown, twinkling eyes that roved the field to pin-point the openings. He had thick, hairy wrists – tremendously strong – that enabled him to crack his bat at the ball as if it were a whip. He was chockful of batting impertinence and the very sight of him at the wickets was one of the beauties of the cricketing world. He was artistic in his conception of what strokes could be played; he was a wizard at executing them.

They called Charlie the 'Governor-General'. I asked many of his contemporaries how he got the name but none could tell me. Surely, it arose from the lordly mien with which he came to bat. He entered the field with the air of one about to inspect the ranks, conscious of his own top-rank and not prepared to put up with any nonsense from anybody.

He played his first series against England in Australia in 1907–08, but he was no sensation then, nor was he when he made his first tour of England in 1909. He was then a member of the chorus, not a *prima donna*, and he once batted as low as No. 10. Nevertheless, everybody knew whom Victor Trumper meant when, returning from England in 1909, he said: 'We are to lose the "Governor-General". He's going to New Zealand.' ... Luckily for Australia, Macartney stayed in

Australia and that, possibly, was for the good of cricket also, because Macartney might not have blossomed on the dubious pitches of the Isles across the Tasman. Even so, he was slow to blossom in his homeland. Some seventeen years were to pass before he reached the zenith of his career. That occurred in England, in 1926, when he was forty years of age.

Australia has had three individual batting triumphs of the highest magnitude in England. They were achieved by Trumper (1902), Macartney (1926) and Bradman (1930); and an interesting point is that in their vintage years, Trumper was twenty-five and Bradman twenty-two. It is curious, therefore, that Macartney should have known his English triumph at forty, an age when a player is fast tumbling down the hill, if he has not already reached the bottom.

In Macartney's case the apparent anomaly was a consequence of what the cricket world missed from him owing to the First World War and the various illnesses and injuries Macartney suffered when Englishmen were in Australia after that war. He played in only two Tests against J. W. H. T. Douglas' side in 1920–21 – making a scintillating 170 at Sydney. He did not play at all in the Tests in Australia four years later.

Macartney went to England with the unhappy Australian team of 1912 – the side that went without the Big Six (Trumper, Carter, Cotter, Armstrong, Ransford and Hill) – but there was no edge to that tour. Macartney played the outstanding innings of the series, 99 at Lord's, and the manner of his dismissal typified the man and his outlook on cricket. Most Test batsmen, on 99, would creep towards their century like a cat-burglar towards his objective. Not so Macartney. He tried to hit F. R. Foster into St John's Wood Road.

'And I should have done, too,' said Macartney afterwards. 'Damn full toss. Made a mess of it.'

In his halcyon days, Macartney's stroking was pungent, crisp, deliberate. It was not always so. His cricket seems to have undergone violent evolution, for he was noted as a stonewaller when he entered Sydney grade cricket. A critic of those days, Frank Iredale (who had Test experience behind him) wrote that Macartney had an ugly, defensive style. That amazes those who saw him at his greatest, but that it should have been written of him is proof that his batting underwent a vivid metamorphosis.

In the beginning, he was a better left-hand bowler than a right-hand batsman. Whereas he averaged only 18 in Tests in his first tour in 1909, he was second in the bowling with 16 wickets, averaging 16. At Leeds, where he was to win immortality seventeen years later, he took 7–58 in the first innings and 4–27 in the second. Nor did he have any accepted position in the batting order. He went up and down, like a painter on a ladder. He was chosen against A. O. Jones' team in 1907–08 as an all-rounder and batted No. 7. About this time, Duff was lost to Trumper as an opener – no doubt they were Australia's best opening pair of all time – and Macartney opened with Trumper in

WET CRICKET AT THE OVAL

The joys of rain. A characteristic Tom Webster cartoon of the rain-interrupted match between Surrey and the South Africans in 1924

the next Test. He was moderately successful and again opened in the last Test; but in 1912 he found his position-by-right in the batting order and to the end of his Test days he batted first-wicket-down for Australia.

I asked him once which batting position he liked best. Back cracked the answer, snapped in his usual aggressive manner of speaking: 'Opening up. If you get on top of an attack early, you are on top for the rest of the innings. And if the first ball of the Test asks to be hit for six, why you just hit it for six.'

That was his pugnacious philosophy, but he was expounding it long after his Test career had ended. It's not a philosophy one would recommend to a young batsman beginning a Test career as an opening batsman. I know how selectors would react if a batsman was out trying to hit the first ball in a Test for six!

Macartney held that every ball had a look on its face as it came down the pitch to him. 'It was labelled,' he said, 'either 1, 2, 3, 4 or 6. I leave out the 5. Too damn far to run.'

He left out, too, it will be noticed, the defensive stroke for none. Charlie did not believe it even existed. He held that every ball bowled was punishable.

I once opened an innings with Charlie and I walked out on air. A grand old character named Jimmy Searle, every finger and thumb broken and gnarled from years of wicket-keeping, was the New South Wales coach and Jimmy ran mid-week matches on the Cricket Ground No. 2. His team would play against the various Junior teams of Sydney. Many a Test player came up through these games and they were all the more enjoyable for the young in that Macartney, Kelleway, Kippax, Oldfield and other retired or active Test players would often turn out for the 'Colts'.

This particular day I was transported into delight, awe and reverence as I walked out with the great Macartney to open an innings. It was, for me, a most sacred occasion.

'I'll take strike, son,' said Charlie. 'And keep your eyes open for the first ball.'

I did, indeed. I thought the Great Man meant that he would be off for a quick, stolen single and I was doubly anxious to do his bidding. I was just leading down the pitch when the ball came back like a meteorite. I fell to earth; the bowler fell to earth; the umpire did likewise. We were all prone on the ground, as if in an air-raid, as the ball crashed into the pickets.

I picked up my dishevelled self and walked down the pitch to Mr Macartney. 'It's always a good idea,' he told me, tapping his forehead in the middle, 'to aim the first ball right here at the bowler's head. They don't like it. It rattles 'em.'

It was the same man who rattled Macaulay – and England – at Leeds in 1926.

Unknown to the English, the Australians that year held a very high opinion of G. G. Macaulay, the Yorkshire spinner and seamer. He did not play for his country against the Australians (he played instead in a Test trial), and the Australians were apprehensive about him when he was chosen for the third Test at Leeds, Macaulay's home ground.

It was seldom Macartney feared a bowler, but he did Macaulay. 'This bloke,' said Macartney, on the eve of the Test, 'could go through us. There's no better bowler in England. I want permission to "murder" him immediately.'

Collins, the captain, was ill and Bardsley was the Australian skipper for the Test.

'You don't often talk like this, Charlie,' said Bardsley.

'No, but I know just what Macaulay can do to us if we don't nobble him first.'

So Bardsley agreed to let Macartney have his way against Macaulay.

It is well to know this background because it gave rise to one of the most brilliant innings in the history of cricket.

There were storms during the night and the groundsmen switched to a new pitch next day because the original one had been flooded under the covers. The Australians gathered in an anxious band around the pitch while the English were having trouble in the pavilion finalizing their team – and also discussing with Carr, no doubt, what he should do if he won the toss.

The three Australian selectors – Bardsley, Macartney and Ryder – locked themselves in a bathroom while they finalized their team. They, too, had to discuss what they would do if they won the toss. Carr won the toss and put Australia in. That decision by Carr was to become one of the most criticized in Test history this century. I do not think Carr ever lived it down – although he would have been very consoled had he known that Bardsley would have sent the English in had he won the toss.

What made Carr's decision seem illogical was that, although he sent the Australians in, the left-hand bowler, Parker, had been dropped from the English side. Perhaps the Englishmen gambled on losing the toss!

The sun was out as the match began but it soon withdrew, which didn't help Carr. He probably thought that sun on the wet pitch would cause it to 'bite'. It never did.

Bardsley was out first ball of the match – something that had happened only once previously when, thirty-one years earlier, MacLaren fell to Coningham in Melbourne. Sutcliffe caught Bardsley low at first slip off Tate. I can well imagine how the excitable Yorkshiremen would have greeted that!

In strode Macartney. He glided Tate's third ball through the slips for two, but then, horror of horrors for England, he snicked the fifth ball of the opening over to Carr in the slips – and the English skipper muffed the catch! Poor Carr! That became the most publicized missed catch in all Test history by the day's end. Australia, instead of being two down for two in the first over, didn't lose the next wicket until 235.

Had Carr taken that catch, it was not inconceivable that Australia could have been all out by lunch. And the missed catch, following upon Carr's decision to send Australia in, made Carr the most miserable cricketer in all England at the day's end. . . .

Macaulay, playing his first Test against Australia, opened the bowling from the pavilion end. His first delivery was a no-ball, which Woodfull hit for a single. Up came Macartney. He took guard, studied the field, twirled his bat, cocked his front foot to the bowler, as was his wont, and hit Macaulay for two to the off. The next ball he slammed almost for six, over mid-off. The 'murdering' of Macaulay had begun.

The Leeds crowd, which had uttered an agonized 'Oh' when Carr dropped Macartney, now began to exclaim 'Ah' as Macartney unfolded his artistry. He smacked Macaulay for two more fours next over and in 40 minutes, Australia had 50 up – 40 to Macartney. The 100 came up in 79 minutes, Macartney's share being 83. In only 103 minutes, Macartney scored a century, the first batsman since Trumper to hit a Test century before lunch. (Four years later, and also at Leeds, Bradman was to hit a century before lunch, a century before afternoon tea and end up with 309 before stumps.)

At lunch, Macartney was 112 and Woodfull 40. After lunch, the 'Governor-General' went on and on, using his bat like a merciless flail. A field that had closed in on him in the first over of the day and had been expelled in the second, didn't close in again for three hours. Macartney dominated the English attack and none so more than poor Macaulay.

At 151, Macartney lofted Macaulay to Hendren and was out. The crowd rose and cheered him all the way in. In the pavilion, Archie MacLaren said: 'We have been looking at Victor Trumper all over again!'

That was the only wicket Macaulay took. He bowled 32 overs (8 maidens) at a cost of 123 runs. Macartney set out intentionally to 'murder' him, because he feared him, and the sad fact was that Macaulay was never again chosen to play for England against Australia, despite his tremendous feat in top-scoring for England at No. 10 with 76, his sensational partnership of 106 for the ninth wicket with George Geary saving England from defeat.

So, too, in thinking of Carr's decision to field and Carr's dropped catch – no matter how sympathetic one could feel towards him – there is also the thought of what could have been Macaulay's career, in Tests against Australia, had Macartney been dismissed for two runs at Leeds in 1926 and not 151. . . .

This score by Macartney was the middle of three Test centuries in succession. He charmed a Lord's crowd with 133 ('By cripes,' he was reported to have said when he came to breakfast the morning of his Lord's century, 'I feel sorry for the poor coots that have to bowl at me today') and he followed his Leeds 151 with 109 at Old Trafford. And in those three Tests he also bowled 86 overs – not bad work for a man of forty! . . .

Leeds was for Macartney (as it was to be for Bradman) a happy scalping-ground. Yet possibly his most remarkable innings in England was in 1921 when he hit 345 against Nottinghamshire at Trent Bridge. He was missed in the slips at nine, and then stayed at the wicket for four more hours. That's not a bad lacing of the clock – by almost a hundred minutes!

Seeking a comparison, it could be said that had Macartney batted at the same rate as at Nottingham and for as long as the South African, Jackie McGlew, did against the Australians at Durban in January 1958 – 572 minutes for 105 – Macartney would have rattled up something like 860. It is colossal – impossible – but interesting!

Bert Collins, the Australian captain of 1926, said he saw Macartney play a nigh-miraculous stroke in 1926 at Nottingham. The ball was on its way and Macartney had taken his bat back for a cover-drive along the ground. The ball, however, changed direction off the pitch and Macartney, as quickly, changed direction in his down-swing. He hit the ball clean out of the ground, into the street behind the pavilion, over long-off!

In that innings of just on four hours, Macartney hit four sixes and 47 fours. Australia made 675, and Notts, demoralized by a bat 'as crooked and as wicked as original sin', could manage only 58 and 100 – losing by an innings and 517 runs.

In 1926, at Old Trafford against Lancashire, Macartney played a dazzling innings of 160. It sent the spectators into rhapsodies. Many of his runs were made against the great Australian fast bowler, E. A. McDonald, who had an engagement with the county. Then, with the ball, Macartney had 27 overs (16 maidens), taking 4–15 in the first Lancashire innings, and in the second innings taking 1–19 off 19 overs.

How good was Macartney as a bowler? I have a pretty fair idea of that as I played club cricket against Macartney in Sydney. In the opinion of one English critic, Macartney was the best left-arm bowler Australia sent to England. This was before Australia had Bill Johnston, a really high-class left-hander; but they were different types, Macartney spinning and Johnston using the new ball. Macartney clean-bowled – clean-bowled, be it noted! – MacLaren (twice), Fry, Hobbs, Hirst, Warner, Rhodes and Chapman in Tests. That's a pretty distinguished haul to be clean-bowled.

Macartney had a graceful, slow run to the line of about seven yards. With his powerful wrists, he put a terrific amount of spin on the ball and he had a luring, curving flight with adroit changes of pace. Perhaps his best ball was one that came from the off with speed from the pitch. I found that he invariably delivered this ball (he bowled around the stumps) from wide on the line. He cut his biggest finger across the seam with a quick flick, and this, with the angle of delivery, gave it an almost incredible whip and seaming break from the pitch.

Once, in a Sydney grade match, he clean-bowled Tommy Andrews with it, and Andrews, who had made two tours of England with Macartney, should certainly have known his wares.

'You won't get me with that one again, Charlie,' said Andrews, before play began again on the second day. Macartney grinned.

'Now, Tommy,' Macartney called down the pitch when Andrews came to bat, 'you're sure you know it?'

'Yes,' said Andrews, 'I'm ready for you this time.'

'Right, off we go,' said Macartney – and in that very over he clean-bowled Andrews again!

Bert Oldfield told me that story. He kept wicket to Macartney in club, inter-state and Test matches and rated him very highly as a bowler. In addition, 'Little Mac' was a brilliant fieldsman, with sure hands and a quick flick of a throw to the keeper.

In all Tests, Macartney made 2,132 runs at 41 an innings. In all first-class cricket, he made 14,217 runs at 47 and took 366 wickets at 21. A remarkable feature of his career is that, of his 48 first-class centuries, not one was scored at Melbourne. Twenty were made in Sydney and only one in Adelaide. But England saw the best of him, not Australia.

Charlie Macartney had no coaching when young. He watched the giants of his youth and then applied his own methods. In the summer he never varied his habit – not even when he was playing in a Test – of arriving at Chatswood Oval (in Sydney) at 6·40 and leaving at 7·50 on five days a week. Some seventeen Gordon members went to this early-morning practice and Macartney found that the pace of a composition ball skidding off a dewy pitch was ideal for sharpening up his eyesight and his strokes. It was the strength in his wrists that enabled him to play so late – a short, sharp backswing and then a convulsive whip at the ball that led you to believe you were watching magic.

Not only was Macartney the terror of cricketing bowlers. There was also apprehension on the Chatswood bowling rink of a Saturday when Macartney was batting on the local oval, over the railway line from the bowling club. Macartney rarely failed to lift a few out of the ground, clean over the double railway lines and on to the bowling clubhouse roof or on to the bowling green itself.

Because of his audacity, because of his all-round competence, the little Governor-General will never be forgotten by those who knew him. . . . To see him standing in the middle, as I did when a young boy that day on the Sydney Cricket Ground, was to conjure up a tingling vision of artistry soon to be unleashed.

From *Fingleton on Cricket* (1972)

C. H. Parkin – Bowler Extraordinary

C. S. MARRIOTT

At one time the most extraordinary bowler I had ever seen was C. H. Parkin. It is true that eventually he limited his efforts mainly to bowling big off-breaks round the wicket to a leg-trap, but it is not for that comparatively dull, stereotyped form of attack that I like to remember him. What I recall with enjoyment in his earlier seasons was his astonishing versatility, of a rich abundance such as I have seen equalled by only one other English bowler – P. G. H. Fender. There similarity ends: although Fender brought a keen sense of humour to the game and showed it, he never went in for clowning on the field or playing to the gallery. For Parkin was not only a brilliant natural cricketer but a born comedian. He had about him something spontaneous and infectious, an exuberant flair for the comic, which raised him at moments into the ageless tradition of laughter-makers from Shakespeare to Grock and Danny Kaye.

It was at Whitsun 1919, playing in my first Lancashire *v* Yorkshire match at Old Trafford, that I had my first astonishing sight of him at close quarters. I was pretty keyed up in any case; I do not know how many people were packed into the ground, certainly well over thirty thousand, and the atmosphere was electric – the nearest thing to that of a Test match I have known. When Yorkshire went in, Parkin embarked upon a performance I shall never forget. He took fourteen wickets in the match. He bowled every possible variety of ball from fast-medium away-swingers to the highest of slow full-tosses; he swung it both ways, he spun it like a top, producing out of the hat leg-break, off-break, top-spinner and googly, with an occasional straight ball for good measure. If it had been possible to deliver it over-arm and make it reach the other end, I believe he would have bowled the counter-googly, which I have only seen done on a table playing twistygrab.

In Yorkshire's first innings he was comparatively serious, content with raising an occasional laugh and a general expectation of things to come. But when they batted the second time needing 294 to win, he flung off all restraint. Had it been possible, he would have bowled more than six different balls per over. In his continual startling variations of pace he actually gave the illusion, at the end of one over, of having brought his right hand over empty and served up a lob with his left. In another, he played the farcical trick already referred to, when he suddenly stopped dead three yards behind the bowling crease and delivered a high slow donkey-drop which, of all people, foxed out George Hirst, LBW. My word, the crowd rose to that one! They roared and yelled in great gales of laughter, egged on by Parkin with some clown's gesture. Eeeh, Our Cis were making a reet bit o' fun for us! He even did Learie Constantine's famous juggling turn when the next wicket fell, throwing the ball high over his head and catching it one-handed behind his back without looking. And once, when he bowled up into the sky a monstrous balloon designed to drop on the bails, like Spedegue's Dropper in Conan Doyle's story, Herbert Sutcliffe, sheet anchor of the Yorkshire innings, narrowly escaped being caught off the maker's name in awkwardly steering it clear of his wicket. When Parkin did get Sutcliffe caught off a vicious leg-break, that settled it: soon afterwards Yorkshire were all out for 153 runs and Our Cis had bagged eight of them for 53. What a performance! And for myself, after all the hilarious excitement was over, I felt a quiet contentment at having bowled out Roy Kilner in each innings.

From The Complete Leg-Break Bowler (1968)

Wilfred

MICHAEL PARKINSON

Wilfred Rhodes is in his nineties and still a young man. It was my grandfather who first told me about him. He once walked the thirty miles to Bradford to see Rhodes play and he never forgot it.

Rhodes didn't let him down: 'He took six or seven wickets that day without breakin' sweat and I said to a bloke sitting next to me: "How's tha' reckon he'll do in t'second innings?" and he says, "T'same," and I said "How's tha' know?" and he said "If Wilfred does thi' once he'll do thi' aggean. He's spotted thi' weakness tha' sees and if he's done that tha' bound to be Wilfred's next time round," And he was right tha' knows. Next innings he did t'same. Ah, he was a good 'un Wilfred. Tha' could walk thirty miles and reckon on him doing summat.'

Throughout his career Wilfred Rhodes specialized in always 'doing summat'. When he retired from the game he had scored 39,802 runs and taken 4,187 wickets. Only ten batsmen in the history of the game have scored more runs and no bowler has come within a thousand wickets of Rhodes. Only George Hirst is within two of his sixteen doubles of 1,000 runs and 100 wickets in the same season, only Tich Freeman within six of his twenty-three years of taking 100 wickets and no one else has ever twice made over 2,000 runs in a season and three times taken over 200 wickets.

As Sir Neville Cardus wrote: 'The man's life and deeds take the breath away.' His career began with him playing against W. G. Grace in Victoria's reign and ended in the thirties when he played against Bradman. He played first-class cricket for thirty-two years surviving every changing fashion in the game, shrugging off every potential challenger to his crown. Even today, at the age of ninety, the crown is still his.

There are, I suppose, more stories about Rhodes than any other cricketer. He has attracted many faithful chroniclers. My favourite, because it reveals the rare respect which Rhodes commanded from his fellow-professionals, is told by Cardus. To illustrate Rhodes' known mastery of exploiting sticky wickets Sir Neville tells of Charles McGahey, the old Essex player, going out to bat on a sunny day at Bramall Lane, Sheffield. As McGahey walked out to face Rhodes and Yorkshire the weather changed. Looking over his shoulder at the darkening sun McGahey said, 'Ullo! Caught Tunnicliffe; bowled Rhodes . . . o.' And so it was, both innings.

I never saw Wilfred Rhodes play cricket. He had been retired seventeen years when I saw my first Yorkshire game but I fancy I knew more about his deeds than I did of the other players who took the field that summer's day in 1947. My grandfather and my father

Wilfrid Rhodes, also photographed by G.W. Beldam. When, later, he was called back at the age of forty-nine for the Oval Test of 1926 against Australia, he was asked whether he could still pitch his old immaculate length. He replied: 'Oh, well, I can keep 'em there or thereabouts.'

had crammed my young head with tales about him. I first saw him at the Scarborough festival. Play had not started when he entered the ground. He was blind and being led. As he walked by the crowd stood and doffed their hats and said, 'Ayup, Wilfred lad' and he nodded and said, 'Ayup.' I measured off my youth with visits to Scarborough to see the festival and gaze in awe at Wilfred Rhodes.

And later, much later, when my job gave me the excuse, I dared to sit with him. He was listening to the cricket and talking to Bob Appleyard. Jackie Hampshire was batting and he struck a ball massively over the square-leg boundary, his bat making a sound like a hammer hitting an anvil. Wilfred stopped his discourse. 'I'll bet that went some way,' he said.

Appleyard said: 'Six over square-leg. Jackie was sweeping.' Wilfred said scornfully, 'Sweeping. That nivver was any sort of shot. Once I was listening to television and a cricketer was coaching youngsters how to sweep. I had to switch if off.'

I remembered that Rhodes, after retiring from the county game, had coached at Harrow and asked him if he enjoyed it. 'It was all right,' he said, 'but them young lads were over-coached when they came to me. Tha' could always tell what they'd do, allus forward, ever forward. I used to run up to bowl and not let go and theer they'd be on t'front foot, leg stretched down t'wicket. And I'd walk up to 'em and say, "Na' then, lad, wheers tha' going? Off for a walk perhaps."'

He shook his head sorrowfully, 'Tha' knows one thing I learned about cricket: tha' can't put in what God left out. Tha' sees two kind of cricketers, them that uses a bat as if they are shovelling muck and them that plays proper and like as not God showed both of them how to play.'

I remarked how strange it seemed that he, the quintessential Yorkshire professional, the man who 'laiked proper' and not for fun, should teach cricket at one of the temples of the amateur game.

'Lads were all right,' he said. 'I liked them, we got on well. It was t'others, t'masters I couldn't get on with. They allus thought they knew more than me. I told one of 'em one day he'd been interferin' and I said, "Tha' can't know more about this game than me, tha' knows," and he said, "Why not?" and I said, "Because if th' did tha'd be playing for England and I'd be doing thy job teaching Greek."'

Listening to Rhodes one is transported to a world where cricketers wore sidewhiskers and starched the cuffs of their shirts; a game of gentlemen and players, separate entrances, attitudes as different as night and day. Because his mind sees them clearly he introduces you to Trumper and Ranji and Grace and Gregory and Armstrong and Plum Warner. He can conjure up cricket in Victorian England, in the first world war, through the depression years to the 'Golden Thirties'. He is a walking history of the game, blessed with a fabulous memory and the unequivocal attitude of one who is certain of what he says for the simple reason that he was there when it happened. When Wilfred Rhodes tells you that Bradman was the best bat that ever lived and that S. F. Barnes was the best bowler only the foolish would dare argue.

'It's a thinking game is cricket. If tha' doesn't use thi' brains tha' might as well give up. When I took up batting serious and opened wi' Jack Hobbs in Australia, a lot said I couldn't bat. But I thought about it and decided that t'best way to go about t'job in Australia was to play forward. In that trip I made one or two (including a record opening partnership of 323 with Hobbs which still stands) and one day I'm going on t'tram to t'ground and Duff, t'Australian cricketer, sits next to me and starts chatting. He said, "Tha' knows tha' baffles me, Wilfred," and I said, "How come?" and he says, "Well tha's got all these runs on this tour and yet tha' can't bat. Tha's only got one shot." And I said, "Ay, and that's all I need out here." Same with bowling, too, although you could say I was more gifted than most at it. But I still used to think 'em out. Batsmen used to say about me that I could drop a ball on a sixpence. Now that's impossible, no one can do that. I could probably hit a newspaper, spread out at that. But point is they used to think I could hit a sixpence and I used to let 'em keep on thinking and that way they were mine.'

During our talk he riffled through the years, illuminating forgotten summers with his yarns, breathing life into cricketers long dead. About M. A. Noble, the great Australian all-rounder who captained his country at the turn of the century, he said: 'That Noble was a good 'un. Used to bowl his quicker one with his fingers straight up t'seam. He nivver got me.' On Geoffrey Boycott, who played for England seventy years later: 'I said to him one day, "Does tha' cut?" And he said, "A bit," and I said, "Remember not to do it until May's finished".' . . .

He doesn't miss a trick. I once wrote a story for the *Sunday Times* about an incident concerning W. G. Grace. During a Gentlemen versus Players fixture at Lord's Schofield Haigh, the Yorkshire player, asked the good doctor's permission to leave the field early on the last afternoon so that he might journey back to Yorkshire. Permission was granted. On that last afternoon as the time for Haigh's departure and Grace's century drew nigh Grace hit an easy catch toward Haigh. As Haigh awaited the ball the Doctor shouted: 'Take the catch and you miss the train.' Not being daft Haigh missed the catch and in consequence was home in Yorkshire when he wanted to be.

Shortly after writing the story I received a letter. It simply said: 'That story you told about Schofield Haigh was true. I know because I was the bowler.' It was signed: Wilfred Rhodes. I still have it. I wouldn't swop it for gold pig.

It's not everyone who gets a letter from the gods.

From *Cricket Mad* (1969)

Watching Hammond

DUDLEY NOURSE

Where Herbie Taylor would hit the ball effortlessly to the fence as though he was persuading it on its way, I found personal satisfaction in thumping it good and hearty with a resounding smack. I had to feel that I had got some punch into the stroke. It was perhaps the biggest difference to our approach of the game at the crease. I did not envy Taylor his style but I often gloried in his exquisite touch. I knew full well my results would have to come via a different medium . . .

Although I did admire many cricketers and the runs they made I did not ever actually envy any his manner of stroke production until I saw Walter Hammond one sunny day in November 1927.

As a member of Captain Stanyforth's MCC touring side to South Africa, Hammond made a deep impression on me. For the first time I felt I would like to be able to bat 'like that fellow in the middle'.

Sitting with a group of friends I forgot for once to add my voice of criticism of the players in the middle. The scene before me was all-absorbing. The MCC had three ru s for two wickets when out walked Walter Hammond. He made 41 and Ernest Tyldesley compiled 161 that afternoon, yet it was Hammond's innings which remained with me in memory afterwards.

I can see him now, right foot travelling across to meet the half-volley. There was power, yet accompanied by grace. One did not immediately become conscious of the force of the shot until it hit the rails. Just as a single stroke can outlast in memory the many in an innings of mammoth proportions, so that one stroke, the cover-drive, refused to be erased from my memory. Grace and power had become intermingled. Timing was a new theme to me. The ability to persuade the ball on its way adding to the impetus imparted by the bowler's arm became a new discovery.

My admiration knew no bounds when next I saw the great batsman make 90 in the Test match at Kingsmead some time later that season. Yes, here was a man to be copied. There was not the obvious dancing footwork with Hammond in command. It was as though he knew beforehand what the bowler's intentions were and would forestall his hopes almost as he delivered the ball. One would be flicked round the corner, off his body, the next would be deftly picked off his toes to be dispatched out of reach of a cordon of fielders as though he dissected the field deliberately.

The greatest joy came when Hammond shaped to play a shot, found that the ball was not the length he had at first anticipated, and he would change his mind at the last second to play another stroke. This split-second thinking was fascinating. I had not thought it possible to change my mind about a stroke halfway through its execution. Having been shown the way to play the ball at the last possible minute I set to work on that as a means of improving my play. It was only much later that I realized what a profound influence Walter Hammond had upon my game.

From *Cricket in the Blood* (1950)

Australia v. England, 1928–29

Fourth Test at Adelaide, last day

P. G. H. FENDER

Australia, needing 349 to win, ended the sixth day's play at 260 for 6, Oxenham and Bradman not out, 'with the game considerably in England's favour,' wrote Fender, 'provided either of Tate, Geary or Larwood were sufficiently recovered in the morning to be able to bowl at their best.'

The last day was one full of thrills. Two mistakes, both amounting practically to tragedies, were made – one by each side. Oxenham and Bradman started well, and kept going, and neither Tate nor Geary were really fit. Larwood did his utmost, as did the other two, so far as they were able, and produced two or three fast overs in a supreme effort, but not only was he unsuccessful, but Bradman seemed to find him so much to his liking that he was too expensive to be kept on in that critical stage of proceedings.

Although the day was again really hot, the wind had freshened, and was quite strong and was blowing at an angle from cover and extra cover to the batsman. This impeded White when bowling 'against' it, and Tate was too often finding the ball go away to the leg side when bowling 'with' it. He and White changed ends at one period, but only for one over, and White tried bowling over the wicket in another effort to get at his spot. It took a very long time – nearly an hour – for the bowlers to settle down that morning, and all the time runs were coming slowly but surely.

In the hope that White would get one to jump off his spot again, Chapman persevered with two slips to the bitter end, but they had served their purpose, those slips, and nothing further came their way. White found both batsmen bothering him by frequently standing in front of their wickets and gliding the ball to fine leg for one or two, and while he had two slips, he had no man to cover that position. It seemed to me very unwise of him to take away Tate at forward short leg and put him fine, about twelve yards from the wicket, to cover that glance, for not unnaturally the batsmen immediately proceeded to play the much more easy and safer shot, pushing the ball to the umpire for one. So long as it was deemed necessary to keep two slips, both short-leg positions could not be covered, and it was a choice between covering one leg shot and keeping two slips, or one slip and covering both leg positions.

No other strokes of any account were being attempted by either batsman, and right up to lunch we sat watching this duel over those placings of the field. No ball all the time, even to the end of the innings, jumped the tiniest bit that morning, but, of course, the happenings of the previous day could not be forgotten. Up to lunch, out of the 66 runs which were scored, 29 came from taps and defensive strokes which went for singles and twos through the forward short-leg position! – a tremendous proportion.

I am afraid I did not agree with Chapman's policy in this matter. I should probably have kept my two slips for a time – a long time after what had happened; but during that time I should have covered the shot which was easiest for the batsman to make – the forward short-leg shot – and left open the more difficult and more risky leg glance. Leave the difficult shot open rather than the easy one if you are forced to choose. After half an hour or three-quarters, however, and not a ball jumping at all, I think one might well have left the two slip positions in the care of such an artist at the job as Hammond, and taken the second slip to the fine-leg position, if runs were continuing to come there. At least this would have stopped up the leakage and forced the batsman to look elsewhere for safe runs. That would not have been too easy.

It was one o'clock and the total was 308 (42 wanted) before the first success came to the Englishmen, and it was again a grand catch, this time at silly-point by Chapman, which brought the sorely needed wicket. White had by now settled down properly at his old end, and Tate and Larwood had each had a turn the other end as well as Hammond. The latter seemed to be giving the best assistance to White, for while none looked really like getting a wicket, Hammond was making the batsmen 'fetch' their runs more than the other two. Geary did not bowl at all.

At the moment when Chapman dived to his right and held the ball a few inches off the ground to dismiss Oxenham, the game looked to be very nearly lost for England. Forty-one runs only were then needed, and only six wickets were down, with two batsmen going pretty well. Oxenham played a hard forward stroke at White, much as he had often done before, but this time he lifted the ball a foot or so off the ground, and Chapman did not fail to take advantage of the chance. More grand cricket.

All this time, however, we were worried by the run leakage on the leg side off White. Oldfield played an ordinary forward stroke to White the first ball he received; it trickled a few yards to where short leg ought to have been and they got a single for it. It was worrying, that gap, and almost amounted to a tragedy.

English hopes, however, were very soon raised sky-high, and again by a tragedy, a bad error of judgement. It does not need that I should write about the nervous tension which was obvious all around by now, runs coming slowly but surely, and everyone keyed up to the highest pitch of enthusiasm. I think there can be no other explanation for the Australian tragedy, however, than the warping of judgement under a big nerve-strain.

Oldfield played a ball from White fairly hard, straight to Hobbs' right hand, not very deep, at cover and called Bradman, who responded. That ought to be enough to convey the result. Bradman was well out. Such a run would probably never have been contemplated again, and certainly never has been before, without the same penalty. Bradman out, eight wickets down and 29 to win (the total was 320), still anybody's game, but the odds were no longer favouring Australia as they had been doing more and more all the morning.

Grimmett joined Oldfield, and the atmosphere was even more electric than before. A few singles, all through that awful short-leg position, an equal number of maiden overs, and no one could guess which way the game would go. While White had that leg-side weakness, runs were always coming, and still the gap was not closed. White bowled to Grimmett, who suddenly tried a wild swing at the ball, hoping for four on the now open leg side; he missed the ball, and somehow the ball missed the wicket, the expression of both bowler and keeper indicating clearly how near it had been. Oldfield faced Hammond and patted the sixth ball of the over to Larwood in the gully – and the tension broke, for Larwood let the ball roll by and two were run.

Then lunch.

The special joy of the late cut —
Alan Kippax

What an interval! Two wickets in hand and 23 wanted to win. Many forgot the needs of the inner man in the excitement of that three-quarters of an hour.

When the game re-started, I saw to my relief that Chapman had brought Tate back to forward square leg and was chancing the more difficult fine-leg shot. Still not a ball from White rose above normal height, still Hendren and Hammond in those two slip positions strained without result in their places at every ball. Grimmett lashed out at White, attempting an off-drive, and mis-hit the ball, which flew high between those two slips. One alone could never have caught it, and two or even three could have had no better chance. Two runs. Five times in three overs did Tate, now at square leg pick up the ball slowly rolling towards him and thus save what before had been always an easy single. All very good, yet, in spite of all, the score was creeping up. Thirteen to win and two wickets in hand, the great thought at the back of my mind was one of thankfulness that those singles at square leg were now being saved.

Well as Hammond had bowled before lunch, Tate had opened after the interval, opposite White. He seemed to be full of fire and was putting every ounce into every ball, yet more than once Duckworth had to save byes on the leg side. Tate was not fit, but working with all that was in him, and giving the best he could in the circumstances. Tate did more, however, White bowled a short one, and Grimmett, scenting four in the direction of the square-leg boundary, hit it hard. Tate shot out a hand, the ball stuck – dropped – and was caught again at the second attempt! Wise had been Chapman's move in bringing Tate square!

Thirteen to get and Blackie, last man, facing White. The danger, if

[63]

any, seemed to me to lie in the fact that Blackie bats left-handed. In my mind I pictured the possibility of a short one from White, and a left-hander trying to pull it for four; he was hitting *with* the spin, not against it, as a right-hander would be doing, making the same stroke to the same ball. White, after 120 overs in such heat and excitement, might well be tired, and accidently drop a short one.

Blackie played forward safely to the last four balls of that over from White. Oldfield, really the one in whom Australia placed the hopes she may still have retained, faced Tate. Tate fairly hurled himself into the attack, but failed to discomfort the Australian keeper. He saw to it, however, that the single at the end of the over, which Oldfield was looking for, was not forthcoming, and Blackie had to face White again.

Perhaps the same thought was in Blackie's mind as was in mine. 'Wait for that short one, wait for—' And Blackie did. He pushed forward safely again at the first four balls, and then sure enough along came that short one. Blackie laid back and hit really hard – perhaps too hard – for instead of the ball going direct to the square-leg boundary, it went up and up in the air. In the right direction, but a high, not a long hit.

Larwood, who had been fielding two-thirds of the way to the boundary about where a left-hander might be expected to drop a half-volley which he was attempting to on-drive, ran like a hare for the ball. Realizing that it was out or not out, the batsman trotted an easy single, while Larwood raced for the ball. He just reached it, and, though having time to slaken his pace, did not have time to really steady himself.

Still, he hung on to the ball, and having held it safely for a couple of seconds pushed it firmly into the depths of his trouser-pocket and sprinted for the pavilion.

A grand game, and a wonderful tribute to the gripping ability of cricket.

Who shall say that cricket is dull, dead, or decadent, when such games and such finishes can still be produced, quite irrespective of winning or losing?

From *The Turn of the Wheel* (1929)

Bradman at Leeds, 1934

IRVING ROSENWATER

Bradman did not rest after the third Test at Manchester, but played at once in the Australians' following two games immediately before the Headingley Test. Not at his best, he made the top score of the match – 71 – against Derbyshire at Chesterfield. And then against Yorkshire at Bramall Lane he scored his first century for nearly two months, with a really brilliant innings reminiscent of his hundred against Middlesex in May. In front of a 12,000 crowd, and against bowlers including Bowes, Macaulay and Verity, he went in *after* lunch and was out *before* tea for 140. He scored his second fifty in twenty-six minutes, and his last 40 in twenty. Two sixes and twenty-two fours (i.e. 100 runs in boundaries) were hit in the single session by Bradman, who went from 50 to 100 by means of one six, ten fours and four singles. His final 90 runs, in only forty-six minutes, were made up as follows, at one stage 46 out of 47 coming from boundaries:

444164444444411144216441244.

It was clear that when Bradman *was* able to score hundreds, he wasted no time over them. In fact at this point his last five centuries in first-class cricket had been reached in the following splendid times:

86 mins.	253 v Queensland, Sydney	1933–34
87 mins.	128 v Victoria, Sydney	1933–34
104 mins.	206 v Worcestershire, Worcester	1934
77 mins.	160 v Middlesex, Lord's	1934
100 mins.	140 v Yorkshire, Sheffield	1934

Thus the stage was set for Bradman to appear again at Leeds, where in the only previous innings of his life he had scored 334. Hitherto, the style of play he had adopted in the Tests – deliberately, one must assume – had brought poor results and much criticism. 'He almost gave the impression of having made up his mind that a rate of scoring of anything less than eight runs an over was beneath his dignity,' said Douglas Jardine. 'Fortunately for his captain, his side and himself, he ultimately abandoned this creed. The instantaneous success which rewarded his return to his more normal methods at Leeds, served not only to place him on his former pinnacle, but to convince him himself of the error of his previous ways.' Jardine could well have reflected on the ironies of life. In a scrupulously prepared – and bitterly carried out – programme against Bradman in 1932–33, after three Tests Bradman's average was in the 50s. Now, with no special plan against him by England, after three Tests his average was in the 20s.

That average could hardly have prepared Headingley spectators for a second triple-century from Bradman's bat, though people were inevitably saying that one of these days Bradman would make another of his mammoth Test scores. 'We will make a big error if we indulge in pleasant fancies that Bradman is a spent force.' So C. B. Fry had written at the beginning of July, just before the Old Trafford Test. He had not been right on that occasion, but he was to be so now. And what had R. C. Robertson-Glasgow said after Bradman's second innings at Lord's? 'He is still rather inexplicable, but I still fear him.' When the second day of the fourth Test began, Australia were 39 for three (in reply to England's total of 200), with two balls of an uncompleted over by Bowes to be bowled. Bradman had not gone in overnight. That was the night that Neville Cardus invited Bradman to have dinner with him in his hotel. Bradman declined, wishing to go to bed early. 'Thanks,' he said, 'but I've got to make 200 tomorrow – *at least*.' Cardus could not resist the reminder that in his last Test innings at Leeds he had passed 300. 'The law of averages is against your getting anywhere near 200 again.' Firmly enough Bradman replied: 'I don't believe in the law of averages.' Here was not only unshakeable confidence but positive evidence indeed of the new Bradman mentality of 1934.

A quarter of an hour before the resumption on Saturday morning, Bradman had a few minutes' practice against the boundary posts just inside the playing area in front of the old dressing-rooms. He then went out to resume the proceedings with Ponsford. The two balls of Bowes' overnight over were both driven by Bradman past the bowler for four. 'I knew he had got me,' was the reaction, later freely admitted, of Bowes. And the day was certainly to be Bradman's. The runs flowed just as they had from the real Bradman of 1930. The 'playboy' cricket of earlier in the season was gone. The old relentless and merciless mastery was back. The more orthodox that was Bradman's cricket, the more likely he looked to make runs. He was 271 by the close on Saturday night, with Verity's analysis this time standing at one for 100. That one was Ponsford, who had shared with Bradman a titanic fourth-wicket stand of 388 at 68 an hour between 11 o'clock and 5·51 p.m., setting a new record for any wicket in Test cricket. The two Australians – and it was the ultimate fear that at last engulfed England – simply wore out and devoured the England bowling. It was the day that the stentorian voice of a spectator cried out: 'Put on Dolphin!' (He was one of the umpires.) It was the day that J. C. Laker, aged twelve, had his first sight at the crease of Don Bradman, to whom of course he was to bowl on that very ground in Test cricket fourteen years, almost to the day, later. It was the day that Bradman made 76 before lunch, 93 between lunch and tea, and 102 between tea and the close. It was the day that J. M. Kilburn, in the *Yorkshire Post*, described him as 'the champion of champions . . . He is a text-book of batting come to life with never a mis-print or erratum.' When stumps were drawn the Yorkshire police had to race to the middle to protect Bradman from the hysterical crowd. 'What they would have done to him,' said Kilburn, 'I really do not know (the policemen won the race) but no honour could have been too high for the incredible cricketer.'

At the Prince of Wales Hotel, Harrogate, that Saturday night, Bradman told Tom Clarke (who was accompanying the Australians for the *Daily Mail*) that when he got back to the Australian dressing-room after his undefeated 271, the whole Australian team gathered round him with a bottle and a toast 'To Don'. It was perhaps an act of relief as well as of homage. But Bradman would not have it. 'I am listening to one toast,' he told them, 'and that is "To a victory".' 'I am not out to make personal records,' he told Clarke. 'My side required the runs. I am not going out on Monday with the intention of breaking

The power and purposefulness of
Bradman

my former record. I am going out in the spirit that we Australians
want to win this match.'

Bradman went on to 304 on Monday morning before his leg stump
was knocked out of the ground by Bowes. The last time Bowes had
dismissed Bradman in a Test it was for 0! Bradman left the field
wreathed in smiles, his side's score 550 for six, and cheered every step
of the way back. During the innings he had exceeded Clem Hill's
record 3,412 runs by an Australian in Test cricket. He had batted for
seven hours and ten minutes and hit two sixes and forty-three fours.
Ferguson's scoring chart showed hardly a spot on the Headingley field
to which he had not sent the ball. He was back again on top of the
Test averages, for both sides.

Bradman still remains the only cricketer in the world who has twice scored a triple-century in Test cricket (and he was only a single run short of another such score in 1931–32). Both his triple-centuries, moreover, were scored in matches limited to four days, and were compiled respectively at 52 an hour and 42 an hour off his own bat.*

From *Sir Donald Bradman: A Biography* (1978)

McCabe – Specialist in Blood Transfusion

RAY ROBINSON

In an era studded with batting triumphs, it was given to one man, Stan McCabe, to play the three greatest innings seen on Test fields in the decade before the Second World War.

Any one of the three would have been a fitting crown to the finest batsman's career, but it was no accident that all of them were the handicraft of McCabe, not of other master run-makers of the Hobbs-to-Hutton period, such as Bradman, Hammond, Ponsford, Headley, Nourse or Amarnath.

In fact, none of McCabe's contemporaries attempted such batting – in Test matches, of all places – because nobody else thought it could be done. None had the blend of imagination and skill to feel capable of it; by all the standards of the times none would have dared to hope for enough luck to carry it through. The drama of these exploits by McCabe fascinated the crowds. Their delight at his graceful and venturesome stroke-making was sharpened by the piquant feeling that each moment might be the last, as if they were watching a bolting horse or a runaway train.

First of these breath-catching innings was his lone-hand 187 not out against England in 1932, the boldest innings ever played on the Sydney Cricket Ground, or any other ground. The situation when the twenty-two-year-old McCabe walked in to bat was dispiriting. The Australians had entered the valley of the shadow of bodyline. Illness had robbed them of their outstanding batsman, Bradman, on the eve of their first encounter with the fast leg-side assault. Only 82 runs were on the board when McCabe, No. 5 in the batting order, came in to face Larwood, who was in the middle of a bout in which he took three wickets for seven runs.

McCabe immediately showed his determination not to die a death

* Every later triple-centurion in Test cricket, without exception, has not been so enterprising: Hutton's 364 was made at 27·40 an hour; Hanif Mohammed's 337 at 20·84; Sobers' 365 at 35·66; Simpson's 311 at 24·48; Edrich's 310 at 34·96; Cowper's 307 at 25·33; and Rowe's 302 at 29·60. The two remaining triple-centuries are Sandham's 325 at 32·50 an hour and Hammond's 336 at 63·39 an hour – which puts Bradman's two scores into second and third place in the table of runs per hour. No one would pretend, however, that Hammond's innings at Auckland in 1932–33 was scored against a particularly potent attack.

of shame on a day of dark disgrace, though Jardine, Larwood and Voce were trying to set a noose about his neck. Without a flinch, he stood up to the fearsome bowling; he hooked the short balls as if there were no danger to his ribs or skull, and as if he were unaware of the battalion of catch-awaiting fieldsmen, covered by outer scouts lying in wait for the lofted ball. When the direction of the bowling changed, flowing drives and crisp cuts kept him gliding along. Nobody thought it could last for long, yet when those daring hooks were lifted they continued to fall beyond the fieldsmen's reach. By the day's end he had scored 127 in a little more than three hours, with seventeen boundary hits.

Fifty-five minutes on the second day brought the end of Australia's innings. In that time McCabe took command, manoeuvred to keep the strike, and scored 60 while four wickets fell for 10 at the other end. In going for the bowling bald-headed (or almost, for one so young) he was debited with a nominal chance at 170, when he cut Larwood behind point with such stinging power that it would have been captious to blame Voce for not making a catch. At an average rate of 47 an hour, McCabe scored his 187 while his seven partners made fewer than 90. It was like a blood transfusion for a sinking innings. Boundary hits brought him 100 of the runs. Nineteen of the fours were leg strokes, thirteen of them hooks which rapped the fence between wide long-on and square-leg.

For audacity, skill, effortless power, and courage against the bowling that beset him, no other batsman on the active list could have equalled his performance.

In size, dominance and value to a team in difficulties, it ranks with three epic innings by Victor Trumper, Clem Hill and Ranjitsinhji in the period which men over sixty describe as the Golden Age of cricket. After England had led by 292 on the first innings at Sydney in 1903, Trumper made 185 not out for Australia while seven partners fell for 95. He hit twenty-four fours; his scoring rate was 49 an hour. At Melbourne in 1898, in an innings in which Australia's sixth wicket fell at 57, Hill scored 188 while seven team-mates were making 94. The left-hander made twenty-one boundary strokes and his hourly rate was 37. When England followed on 181 in arrears at Manchester in 1896, Ranjitsinhji made 154 not out (twenty-three fours) at the rate of 48 an hour, while nine partners were dismissed for 112.

No amount of debate will ever determine which of the four magnificent innings was the finest. McCabe's was played on a pitch of modern excellence, but he was up against a method of attack more unsettling than the other three had to face.

If McCabe's 187 was a blood transfusion for his side, his 232 in the Nottingham Test, 1938, was a heart-massage innings which revived the patient after hope had been given up. The Englishmen had led off by amassing the overwhelming total of 658 for eight wickets before Hammond declared the innings closed. After Fingleton had gone for 9, Bradman for 51 (after an unsuccessful appeal against the light) and

Brown for 48, the Australians' position was desperate.

McCabe, who was vice-captain, had been out of touch for weeks. A few days before the Test he had raised the question whether it would not be better to choose another batsman instead. With about half an hour to go to complete the Saturday's play, he began in the gloaming, yet batted more firmly than his predecessors and scored 19 before stumps were drawn. On Sunday night he had a slight cold, but O'Reilly assured him: 'You'll sweat it out by 3 p.m. tomorrow.'

When two more wickets fell in the first quarter-hour on Monday, it seemed as if the innings would peter out before McCabe could work up a single bead of perspiration. Half the side was out, with Australia still more than 500 behind. Farnes was bowling at keen speed, and Wright was making leg-breaks snap from a boot-worn patch. McCabe's way of countering the menace of that patch was to skip forward smartly whenever Wright tried to pitch the ball on it. He played watchfully for more than half an hour until the downfall of Badcock (9) left only the tail-end division of wicket-keeper and three bowlers to come.

That was the signal for McCabe to take the match in his own hands. For the next couple of hours his batting was enchanting. It held every one under its spell, bowlers as well as spectators. From the players' balcony, Bradman called to a few of his team who were inside the pavilion: 'Come and look at this! You've never seen anything like it.' In the Press box, Woodfull was moved to write: 'It is a pity that the whole cricket world could not see this double-century scored.'

The 30,000 who were lucky enough to be there watched wonderingly as the vice-captain added 170 while his last four partners scored 38. When he was 123, he gave a sharp chance to square-leg, but Edrich did well to get a hand to it and save a four.

The arrival of Fleetwood-Smith as last man was accepted as an infallible sign that the innings was drawing its last breath. Instead, his advent inspired McCabe to unfold the most dazzling half-hour's batting of the match. Hammond spread five fieldsmen around the boundary, yet could not prevent fours – McCabe had so many strokes and guided them so surely. The Englishmen fared little better when, near the end of overs, they drew in to encircle him with a net of infielders, trying to block the singles he needed to get the strike at the other end instead of his vulnerable partner. While Fleetwood-Smith rose to the occasion by surviving 18 balls and collecting five runs, Stan scored 72 in the last enthralling 28 minutes – something unheard-of in Test cricket, even in the days when Bonner and Jessop were denting pavilion roofs. McCabe's 232 in 235 minutes (thirty fours, one six) is the fastest double-century in Test history. His 213 on the second day came up in 200 minutes, his last 127 after lunch in only eighty minutes.

For all the speed of his scoring – he skimmed through his last 100 at the dizzy rate of 109 runs an hour – each stroke was made with the artistry natural to him, each was properly chosen for the ball it had to meet. Despite the urgency of the chase for runs there was not one

McCabe — a specialist,
according to Ray Robinson, in
blood transfusion for sinking
innings

slogging hit, in fact no show of force, because of the precision of his
timing. It was power without violence, dash without slap.

McCabe made his 232 while eight partners were scoring 58 – an
achievement without parallel in international cricket. When at last
Ames caught him off Sinfield, Australia's arrears had shrunk to 247
and the match had been plucked from England's grasp. He had taken
the steam out of the English bowlers and given the Australians fresh
heart to face the follow-on, justifiably hopeful of keeping England
from victory in the $8\frac{3}{4}$ hours before the time-limit expired.

When McCabe returned to the pavilion, Bradman greeted him
with: 'If I could play an innings like that I would be a proud man,
Stan.' Surely the highest tribute ever paid a batsman.

Two former English captains, A. E. R. Gilligan and R. E. S. Wyatt,
agreed that it was the best Test innings they had seen, and their
opinion was shared by a renowned cricketer of an earlier generation,
S. F. Barnes, as this dialogue between Neville Cardus and the mighty
bowler showed:

Barnes: 'The finest innings I have seen,'

Cardus: 'Think again; you saw Trumper.'

Barnes: 'I can only repeat it is the greatest I ever saw.'

Cardus: 'I'd have liked to see you out there bowling to McCabe.'

[71]

Barnes (after a moment's thought): 'I don't think I could have kept him quiet.'

The other striking instance of McCabe's indomitable spirit in adversity – for his deeds were as much a triumph of character as of skill – was his 189 not out at Johannesburg in December 1935 against the South Africans, who had won their first Test rubber in England earlier that year.

After a fine 231 by A. D. Nourse in South Africa's second innings of 491 the Australians were in a corner. To win, they needed 399 runs in the fourth innings, on a wicket worn by the traffic of three days' play. In Test history no team which had been set the task of getting more than 340 in the fourth innings had ever won, in England, Australia or South Africa. Precedent held out no hope for victory when the Australians began batting after tea interval on the third afternoon, and, as another day remained for play, the South Africans had ample time to get them out. When the first wicket fell for 17, the Australians were in a tough spot.

The common policy at such times is to attempt a dogged, back-to-the-wall struggle in which the full weight of the task bears incessantly on the batsmen, taxing their nerves until every over is loaded with tension, every run becomes an effort. This psychological pressure and the wearing of the wicket are the two reasons why, dozens of times, 300 in the fourth innings has been beyond the power of Test teams. That was not McCabe's way of meeting the crisis. He never believed that the best defence was defence, anyway. He refused to give the bowlers the advantage of holding the initiative because he had the vision to perceive that it made the task more burdensome. That afternoon and next day he carried the fight to the enemy, not in a desperate, headlong sortie, but measuring each blow with cool judgement and delivering it with polished skill.

He sped to his first 100 in ninety minutes, despite the class and variety of the attack by Langton (a great medium-pace bowler), Crisp (fast), Mitchell (googly), Robertson (ultra-slow off-spin) and Bock (medium-pace). Several times McCabe had to use his pads to fend off wide-turning balls. Before a sharp leg-break got past the patient Fingleton (40) McCabe made 148 of a second-wicket partnership of 177. He scored 100 before lunch on the last day. By then he had been joined by Len Darling, a kindred spirit in putting side before self, and in inclination for free strokeplay.

Thunderclouds were banking up from the north-west. Whether the coming downpour would wash the match out or would doom the Australians to finish their struggle on a sticky wicket the batsmen did not know. They pressed on boldly in failing light. Vivid lightning was flashing in the gloom as McCabe, at 166 and 186, cut Crisp's fast bowling above ground and was missed behind point by a fieldsman who had little chance to sight the ball properly. Once Darling edged Langton to the left side of second slip, who groped for the catch without touching the ball. An appeal against the light came at 2·45 p.m., not from the batsmen but from South Africa's captain, H. F.

Wade, who said it was dangerous for the fieldsmen. Soon after play had ceased the thunderstorm broke, so soaking the field that the game was abandoned two hours later, with Australia 274 for two wickets, McCabe 189 not out and Darling 37 not out.

McCabe's brilliance had so transformed the situation that, instead of struggling to stall off defeat, the Australians were playing like winners, with 125 more runs to get and eight wickets in hand. He batted $3\frac{1}{4}$ hours for his 189 while 66 were scored at the other end. He hit twenty-nine fours, probably a record for a Test innings under 200. As at Sydney and Nottingham, he won his Johannesburg triumph by tackling a depressing situation in a way that the few other living batsmen possessing enough skill for it would have regarded as too venturesome, even foolhardy. There was something Churchillian in his spirited resistance to his adversaries: he fought them in the crease, and he fought them up the wicket.

McCabe's scores in those three innings were big – so big that they were within the range of only the first flight of the world's batsmen – but size was far from being the only element in their greatness. Other batsmen have made more than a dozen Test scores larger than his highest, but nobody had made so many so quickly to rally sides that have been beaten to their knees. As a saver of lost causes he has no rival.

From Between Wickets (1946)

Headley: Nascitur Non Fit

C. L. R. JAMES

I write of George Headley purely as a cricketer. And I do so contrary to the pattern of this book, because, first, this West Indian narrowly escapes being the greatest batsman I have ever seen. Pride of place in my list goes to Bradman, but George is not far behind. In fact, it is my belief that if he had lived his cricketing life in England or Australia he would not be behind anyone. Everyone is familiar with his scores. On a world scale his average is, I believe, exceeded only by Bradman and Merchant. His average of one century in every four Test innings is second only to Bradman. In those days there were no Test matches against India and Pakistan and New Zealand. George had to meet the full strength of England and Australia. The second reason why I write about him is that he is a remarkable individual. I believe that every great batsman is a special organism; it must be so, for they are very rare, as rare as great violinists – I doubt if I have known many more than a dozen.

There is a third reason, but that I shall reserve.

I saw George in 1930, I saw him in 1934, I played cricket with him

[73]

in Lancashire. He had to a superlative degree the three cardinal qualities of the super batsman. He saw the ball early. He was quick on his feet. He was quick with his bat. The most important of all, in my view, is seeing the ball early. In 1953 George told me that from the time he began to play cricket he saw every ball bowled come out of the bowler's hand. He added that if he did not see it out of the bowler's hand he would be at a loss how to play. The conversation began by his telling me of a bowler in league cricket, of no importance, who had bowled him two balls in succession neither of which he saw out of the hand. The experience left him completely bewildered.

He was as quick on his feet as any player I have seen except Don Bradman. To see Bradman get back, his right foot outside the off-stump, pointing to mid-on, and hook a fast bowler was to witness not cricket but acrobatics: you knew he had got there only after he had made the stroke. George's speed of foot was of the same kind. He was as quick with his bat as any. Bowlers, seeing the ball practically on his pad, appealed against him for LBW, only to grind their teeth as the bat came down and put the ball away to the fine-leg boundary. Any single one of these three qualities makes a fine batsman, and courage and confidence are the natural result of having all three.

What I want to draw special attention to here is George's play on wet or uncertain wickets. Here are his scores on such wickets in England.

		Other high scores in the innings
1933		
v. Northamptonshire	52 out of 129	32 and 15
v. Yorkshire	25 out of 115	25 and 16
v. Nottinghamshire	66 out of 314	54 and 51
v. Lancashire	66 out of 174	29 and 18
v. Leicestershire	60 out of 156	22 and 19
v. Leveson-Gower's XI	35 out of 251	70 and 44
1939		
v. Surrey	52 out of 224	58 and 52
v. Yorkshire	61 out of 234	72 and 28
v. England	51 out of 133	47 and 16
	5 out of 43 (4w)	13 and 11
v. Somerset	0 out of 84	45 and 17
v. Gloucestershire	40 out of 220	50 and 28
	5 out of 162	43 and 26

In those thirteen innings George passed 50 seven times. Three times only he scored less than double figures, and in his other three innings his scores were 25, 35 and 40. I believe those figures would be hard to beat. Look at a similar list made for Bradman by Ray Robinson in his fascinating book *Between Wickets*.

	Match	*Total*	*Bradman*	*Top Scorer*
1928	Brisbane Test	66	1	Woodfull 30 n.o.
1929	Sydney	128	15	Fairfax 40

1930	Notts Test	144	8	Kippax 64 n.o.
	Northants	93	22	Bradman 22
	Gloucester	157	42	Ponsford 51
		117	14	McCabe 34
1932	Perth	159	3	McCabe 43
	Melbourne	19 (2w)	13	
1933	Sydney	180	1	Rowe 70
		128	71	Bradman 71
1934	Lord's Test	118	13	Woodfull 43
1936	Brisbane Test	58	0	Chipperfield 36
	Sydney Test	80	0	O'Reilly 37 n.o.
1938	Middlesex	132	5	Chipperfield 36
	Yorkshire	132	42	Bradman 42

In fifteen innings Bradman passed 50 only once, 40 only twice and 15 only four times. His average is 16·66. George's average is 39·85. You need not build on these figures a monument, but you cannot ignore them.

Bradman's curious deficiency on wet wickets has been the subject of much searching comment. George's superior record has been noticed before, and one critic, I think it was Neville Cardus, has stated that Headley has good claims to be considered *on all wickets* the finest of the inter-war batsmen. I would not go so far. It is easy to give figures and make comparisons and draw rational conclusions. The fact remains that the odds were 10 to 1 that in any Test Bradman would make 150 or 200 runs, and the more the runs were needed the more certain he was to make them. Yet if Bradman never failed in a Test series, neither did George. I believe Bradman and Headley are the only two between the wars of whom that can be said. (Hammond failed terribly in 1930 in England and almost as badly in the West Indies in 1934–5.)

But there is another point I wish to bring out. Between 1930 and 1938 Bradman had with him in England Ponsford, Woodfull, McCabe, Kippax, Brown and Hassett. All scored heavily. In 1933 and 1939 West Indian batsmen scored runs at various times, but George had nobody who could be depended on. In 1933 his average in the Tests was 55·40. Among those who played regularly the next average was 23·83. In 1939 his average in the Tests was 66·80. The next batsman averaged 57·66, but of his total of 173 he made 137 in one innings. Next was 27·50. It can be argued that this stiffened his resistance. I do not think so. And George most certainly does not. 'I would be putting on my pads and sometimes before I was finished I would hear that the first wicket had gone.' This is what he carried on his shoulders for nearly ten years. None, not a single one of the great batsmen, has ever been so burdened for so long.

He had characteristics which can be attributed to less than half a dozen in the whole history of the game. He has said, and all who know his play can testify, that he did not care who bowled at him: right hand, left hand, new ball, old ball, slow, fast, all were the same. He loved the bad wickets. And his reason is indicative of the burden he carried. 'On a bad wicket it was you and the bowler. If he pitched up you had to drive. If he pitched short you had to turn and hook. No nonsense.' I sensed there a relief, a feeling that he was free to play the only game which could be successful under the circumstances, but this time his own natural game.

George was a quiet cricketer. So quiet that you could easily under-estimate him. One day in 1933 West Indies were playing Yorkshire at Harrogate, the wicket was wet and Verity placed men close in, silly mid-off and silly point, I think. The West Indian players talked about bowlers who placed men close in for this batsman and the other batsman. George joined in the reminiscences. Someone said, 'George, if Verity put a man there for you—'

A yell as of sudden, intense, unbearable pain burst from George, so as to startle everyone for yards around.

'Me!' he said. 'Put a man there for me!'

They could talk about it for other players, Test players, but that anyone should even think that such fieldsmen could be placed for him – that was too much for George. The idea hurt him physically.

George was a great master of the game in many senses. He landed in Australia (1931–2) a boy of twenty-one who had never played or seen cricket out of the West Indies. As he has told me in great detail: 'I was an off-side batsman, drive, cut and back-stroke through the covers. Of course, I also could hook.' Australian critics were startled at his mastery of batting and of an innings of 131, played at Victoria in less than even time, one critic who had seen all the great players of the previous thirty years said that no finer innings had ever been seen on the Melbourne ground. An innings of 82 against New South Wales evoked the same admiration. Then, as he says, the word went round: keep away from his off-stump and outside it, you will never get him there. Henceforth in every match, on every ground, it was a leg-stump attack and an on-side field. George was baffled and I remember how anxious we were at a succession of failures. What he did, under fire, so to speak, was to reorganize his batting to meet the new attack.

This is what happened to George in Australia: 25, 82, 131, 34. Then he failed steadily: 27 run out and 16; 0 and 11 (Test, to Grimmett both times); 3; 14 and 2 (Test); 19 and 17. Nine successive failures. It is only by the Third Test that George is once more in control of the situation: 102 not out out of 193 (next highest score 21), and 28 out of 148 (again top score); 77 and 113; 75 and 39; 33 out of 99 (top score) and 11 out of 107 (Fourth Test); 70 run out and 2; 105 and 30 (Fifth Test).

He had so mastered the new problems that Grimmett considers Headley to be the greatest master of on-side play whom he ever bowled against, and he bowled against both Hobbs and Bradman. Yet of George's 169 not out in the Manchester Test of 1934, A Ratcliffe, reviewing modern cricket (*The Cricketer Annual*, 1933–4), says, 'His cuts off the slow bowling were a strange sight to see and I had only seen such strokes once before when Woolley cut Roy Kilner's slow deliveries to the boundary time after time.'

George Headley, this West Indian, would be my candidate for a clinical study of a great batsman as a unique type of human being,

George A. Headley (right) with E.A. Martindale. Headley was the first player to score two centuries in a Test match at Lord's (1939), and he virtually carried West Indian batting in the 1930s. Sir Pelham Warner said that his second name, which was Adolph, should be Atlas

mentally and physically, So far as I know no one has probed into this before.

Mentally. George is batting against an Australian slow bowler, probably Grimmett. To the length ball he gets back and forces Grimmett away between mid-wicket and mid-on or between mid-wicket and square-leg. He is so quick on his feet and so quick with his bat that Grimmett simply cannot stop ones and twos in between the fieldsmen. Every time Grimmett flights the ball, out of the crease and the full drive. Grimmett, that great master of length, cannot even keep George quiet. He has a man at fine-leg. He shifts him round to square and moves square to block up the hole. Next ball is just outside the leg-stump. George, gleeful at the thought that fine-leg is no longer there, dances in front of the wicket 'to pick up a cheap four'. He glances neatly, only to see Oldfield, the wicket-keeper, way over on the leg-side taking the catch. The two seasoned Australians have trapped him. That sort of thing has happened often enough. Now note George's reaction.

'I cut that out.'

'What do you mean, you cut it out?'

'I just made up my mind never to be caught that way again.'

'So you do not glance?'

'Sure I glance, but I take care to find out first if any of these traps are being laid.'

'Always?'

'Always.'

And I can see that he means it . . .

Similarly with placing. For George, to make a stroke was to hit the ball (he had a loud scorn for 'the pushers') and to hit it precisely in a certain place. He could not think of a stroke without thinking of exactly where it was going. Whenever he had scored a century and runs were not urgent, he practised different strokes at the same ball, so as to be sure to command the placing of the ball where there was no fieldsman. Those who know George only after the war do not really know him. In 1939 he was, in addition to on-side play, a master of the cut, both square and late, and though he was, like Bradman, mainly a back-foot player, half-volleys did not escape him. This placing to a shifting field must also be to a substantial degree automatic. Having taken a glance round, *and sized up what the bowler is trying to do*, the great batsman puts the ball away more by reflex than conscious action . . .

Now physically. Headley has told me that the night before a Test he rarely slept more than an hour or two. (The night before the second century in the Test at Lord's in 1939 he never slept at all.) But he is not suffering from insomnia, not in the least. This fantastic man is busy playing his innings the next day. The fast bowler will swing from leg. He plays a stroke. Then the bowler will come in from the off. He plays the stroke to correspond. The bowler will shorten. George hooks or cuts. Verity will keep a length on or just outside the off-stump. George will force him away by getting back to cut and must be on guard not to go too greedily at a loose ball – that is how in Tests he most fears he will lose his innings (a revealing commentary on his attitude to bowlers). Langridge will flight the ball. Down the pitch to drive. So he goes through every conceivable ball and makes a stroke to correspond. This cricket strategist obviously works on Napoleon's maxim that if a general is taken by surprise at anything that occurs on a battlefield then he is a bad general.

Morning sees him in the grip of processes he does not control. He rises early and immediately has a bowel motion. At ten o'clock he has another. And then he is ready. He is very specific that these automatic physiological releases take place only on big-match days. He is chain-smoking in the dressing-room. But once he starts to walk down the pavilion steps he would not be able to recognize his father if he met him halfway. Everything is out of his mind except batting. Bumpers? Bodyline? He is not concerned. He gets out to good balls (or bad), but such is his nervous control that no bowler as such has ever bothered him. Near the end of an English tour he is physically drained except for batting. He has a few days' leave, he sits and smokes. His companions plan expeditions, make dates to go out with girls. George sits and smokes. From where he sits he does not want to budge an inch. But when they return to the tour, as soon as he has a bat in his hands, he is as fit as ever; fit, however, for nothing else except batting. When the season is over the fatigue remains and it takes him weeks to recover his habitual self. I watched the West Indians in the nets at Lord's in 1933 before the tour began. George never to my knowledge practised seriously. He fooled around playing the ball here and there. It was his first visit to England; but he was as sure of himself as if he were in Jamaica. In 1933 he ended the season with scores of 79, 31 (run out),

167, 95, 14 and 35. He was third in the averages for the season, Hammond and Mead averaging 67 to his 66. If he had thought about it in 1933 he would have made the runs needed. With him batting was first, not second, nature. In 1939 he was 72 with Hammond next at 63. He was a fine fieldsman and of the great batsmen of his day only Bradman was faster between the wickets . . .

No, I have not forgotten the third reason why I wanted to write about George Headley. And note it well, you adventurous categorizers. I know Constantine and Headley pretty well, as cricketers and as human beings. Contrary to all belief, popular and learned, Constantine the magician is the product of tradition and training. It is George the maestro who is an absolutely natural cricketer.

From Beyond a Boundary (1963)

Grimmett – The Old Fox

JACK FINGLETON

Thomas Carlyle once declared that genius was an infinite capacity for taking pains. No cricketer I knew could better illustrate the truth underlying the dictum than Clarence Victor Grimmett. It does not deny that 'genius must be born and never can be taught', as Dryden insisted. It breathes the absolute necessity for cultivation if high reward is sought.

Grimmett had immense cricketing talent and he had, moreover, which is imperative if a cricketer is to scale the heights, an innate love of and obsession with cricket. Without incessant and assiduous concentration, however, his mere devotion to the bowling art would never have earned him his lofty seat among the cricket mighty.

C. T. B. Turner, the 'Terror' of the 1890s, who once spread-eagled and nonplussed 314 victims in an English season, ascribed much of his success to constant early practice with the object of gaining mastery of length and spin. He marked the spot on the county wicket at Bathurst where he used to practise before Sheffield Shield and Test honours came his way, and kept pegging away until he was satisfied with his control of the ball. It was said of the Victorian Albert Trott, who subsequently became a consistent all-rounder with Middlesex for a decade, that it was his early custom to place a fruit case in front of the stumps to develop a capacity to turn around it into the stumps.

Grimmett possessed a similar tenacity of purpose. Born in New Zealand, he says he played no game other than cricket until he was twenty-two. He tinkered with baseball on migrating to Sydney, a migration brought about by a hankering for good cricket and opportunity, but Grimmett gloried in the fact that he lived almost exclusively for cricket. Even through winter, he practised assiduously.

Grimmett's practice was never aimless. It was always with a set purpose, and the fitting manner in which to greet this warm, smiling little man after a winter's hibernation was not to inquire after his health or his family, but to seek knowledge of what new bowling mystery the winter had yielded.

'You'll find out soon enough,' Grimmett would say, enigmatically.

Neville Cardus once told me of how, during Hitler's war, he met Clarrie in Rundle St, Adelaide. The conversation, to two such lovers of cricket, was understandably lugubrious.

'This is a terrible thing, this war, Neville,' said Clarrie.

'It is, indeed,' readily agreed Neville, 'when we think of all the art and culture it has left in ruins throughout Europe. The lovely old historic buildings, the –'

'Yes, yes,' hastily cut in Grimmett, 'I know all about that. I was thinking particularly of a new ball I had discovered. I'll never have the chance now to try it out against class batsmen.'

Grimmett lived to perfect something new in the bowling art. He was forever experimenting, his wrist, his body, at this and that angle at the moment of delivery, his shoulder at varying heights. The last particular delivery he produced took him some twelve years to perfect before he would bowl it in a big game. This was known as the 'flipper', because of the click of his fingers as he released the ball. He bowled it with a leg-break action and the ball, making pace from the pitch, would come in from the off (Pepper, Dooland and Benaud copied Grimmett's flipper). Batsmen in neighbouring states, alert to the little man's magic in the off season, would warn one another of the 'flipper'. 'You can't very well miss it. You'll hear it from Clarrie's flick of the fingers.'

Sometimes, you might feel sorry for this frail little chap, whose perpetual service at the bowling crease over the years had given him a rounded right shoulder. It seemed such a pity that so persevering a disciple should labour for twelve years to produce a 'mystery' and then have it betrayed by the flicking sound of his fingers. There was something unfair, too, about the quick passing of Grimmett's secrets from batsmen to batsmen. Poor old Clarrie!

Not for nothing, however, was my dear friend Clarrie known as the Sly Old Fox of Cricket. He knew well what batsmen said about him, that they thought they had unravelled his mysteries.

So, then, with his picturesque little hop and skip at the beginning of his run, he jogged his few yards to the crease to bowl against the knowing batsman. Grimmett's right arm took its little swing back; the ball went on its way with a low trajectory and on the air was the unmistakable sound of the fingers flicking.

From the pavilion, you could almost see the comfortable smirk on the face of the batsman as he went forward confidently to meet the ball. The flicker, indeed, he seemed to say! 'Just watch how I deal with this.'

The ball, however, has not turned from the off. It is an ordinary leg-break – if Grimmett ever did bowl an ordinary leg-break – and the batsman's legs are spreadeagled in a sorry mess. The ball beats the bat, Grimmett turns to the umpire with his appealing finger up, and the umpire agrees with him. Off trudges a disillusioned batsman to the pavilion. Who told him that Grimmett's flicker came from the off?

You were fortunate, in such circumstances, if you were on the fielding side and working close to the stumps. The little chap would trudge over, his right foot pigeon-toed in a distinctive manner, and across his face would spread an impish smile of huge delight. Then it would dawn on you.

'Why, you old fox, Grum,' you'd say. 'I do believe you bowled a leg-break then and flicked the fingers of your left hand.'

Grimmett would hug himself in convulsive delight, but would not admit anything. He loved bowling against batsmen who 'knew' all his tricks, 'knew' how to pick his flicker. It was their wits against his. He had been in this bowling business a long, long time and he had to learn the hard way. Bowling was like the game of life, hard. . .

When you were on tour with Grimmett, he would never bowl to you in the nets. There were several reasons for this. He wanted to concentrate upon control of length and direction without distraction from other players and not against batsmen, as often happens in the nets, who chance their eye and play strokes they would not attempt against him in a match. This practice had no appeal to Grimmett. Moreover, looking into the future, he was too long in the head to give practice to a Test fellow who, upon returning to Australia, would be an interstate opponent.

He was a migratory soul. He came to Sydney from New Zealand, left there for Melbourne and found his permanent residence in Adelaide. It was while he lived in Melbourne that he got a load of Merri Creek soil, with which the Melbourne Cricket Ground pitch is made, and built his own pitch in his back garden. He practised on his home-made pitch at every opportunity, his sole fieldsman a fox terrier.

Grimmett used a number of cricket balls and taught the dog to lie down until he wanted them back. On Sunday mornings, neighbours came for a regular practice and it was interesting that one who came to bat on Grimmett's pitch was Ponsford, then on the verge of breaking into big cricket.

Grimmett had one paramount idea at his self-imposed and self-conducted practices – the attainment of length and direction as the solid foundation of his bowling. He experimented with all types of spin. He often used a tennis or ping-pong ball, observed the results of spin and came to the conclusion that speed off the pitch was the ideal to strive for. With characteristic thoroughness, he decided to discard, except for demonstration purposes, those spin deliveries which did not fizz off the pitch.

He learned how a ball swerved according to the kind of spin imparted and how the arm movement also had its effect upon the flight of the ball. While he was experimenting, he was building according to his own solid specifications what he calls his 'stock ball'. His practices always ended with ten minutes of two deliveries and nothing else, a slight leg-break of perfect length and direction, and an ordinary straight through delivery with leg-break action. At any time, Grimmett could pick up a ball and pitch it where he wanted. A batsman with a few runs on the board and, therefore, settled to his job with confidence, welcomes the advent of a slow bowler because there is almost sure to be a few full tosses or long hops until the bowler feels his fingers and settles into his job. No such helpings came from Grimmett. It was incredible how his very first ball came down on a perfect length, causing the batsman's feet to twitter.

As a young boy, I was watching my first Test when Grimmett played his first Test against England in Sydney. He was an immediate sensation. Coming on after Mailey, who got only five overs (and none in the second innings), Grimmett, as he was often to do for Australia in the years ahead, took up almost permanent occupancy of one bowling end. He took 11 wickets off thirty overs at a cost of 82 in the two innings.

Hobbs, whose wicket Grimmett took in the second innings, completely under-estimated Grimmett's potential when, after this game, he predicted failure for him on English pitches. Mailey had been the slow spinner for Australia in the four preceding Tests but here began a long reign for Grimmett, which, had it not been for a fault in Bradman's judgement in 1938, might have been even longer. . . .

Grimmett could get through an Australian eight-ball over, assuming it was a maiden, in under two minutes. There was no time-wasting with the little man. He moved smartly, he wheeled quickly and over would go his cunning right arm, a devious mind behind everything he did. . . He loves to tell of the time when he appealed for LBW against a prominent New South Wales batsman. The appeal was refused. The batsman called out 'Clarrie', and with index finger drew an imaginary straight line up and down the pitch, suggesting that Grimmett's appeal was a bad one.

There was not a flicker of a smile from the Fox. He wheeled again into the next delivery. Again the ball hit the pad.

'How's that?' said Grimmett, turning to the umpire.

This time the finger went up. As the crestfallen batsman left for the pavilion, Clarrie called out to him, 'Excuse me.' The batsman turned and saw Grimmett's index finger suggesting a straight line up and down the pitch.

With infinite relish, Clarrie told O'Reilly and me about his last club match in Adelaide.

'As I walked on to the ground,' said Grimmett, 'I was surprised to see the umpire come back to me. He held out his hand. I shook it with feeling. "Mr Grimmett," he said, "this is the greatest honour I have had in cricket – standing umpire to your bowling."'

'I made sure I bowled at his end,' continued Grimmett. 'I told him I would show him every ball I could bowl. So I went through them –

leg-break, googly, flipper and so on, naming them to him before I
bowled. I said, "I will bowl two faster leg-breaks on the off-stump,
going away, and then I will bowl my flipper the third ball and get him
leg before." I did just that. As I turned to appeal, the umpire had his
arm in the air, shouting "How's that?"'

A wonderful cricketer was my old friend, Clarrie Grimmett.

From *Fingleton on Cricket* (1972)

Hammond in Command

RONALD MASON

The Lord's Test of 1938 attracted a vast and absorbed crowd, as it
always does when Australia are there; the sun shone gloriously upon
the opening overs, the excitement was tensed beyond any that had
been felt in that place for four years or more. Perhaps it was screwed
a point higher by the obscurely sensed international unrest; Austria
had gone down before Hitler in the early spring [... and in] the
background of many minds must have lurked the doubt, even as the
immemorial plane-trees rustled in the June heat and the great ground
lay open to the sunshine, packed as it had hardly ever been packed
before, whether this might be the last time for years or for ever that
the English would be permitted the deep pleasure of this classic rivalry
and contest. It was an unvoiced doubt but was not silenced for being
buried; it gave the occasion an added edge, awakened the common
perceptions to a more than common keenness. Hammond won the toss
and expectation quickened.

McCormick began as he began that other time in Brisbane, prancing and fearsomely hostile ... and at the outset of this Test Match he found a little answering greenness in the wicket and made his slightly short-pitched deliveries whip and sing round the apprehensive ears of Barnett and Hutton. Barnett, a straightforward, true batsman who liked straightforward true bowling, was prone to fence and swish at this kind of thing, while the Hutton of June 1938 on a sporty pitch was neither the Hutton of August 1938 on a shirt-front nor the Hutton of 1950 on anything that was offered. Accordingly, there was a tentative air about the batting, and a dangerous tendency to prod; and the score was only 12 when Hutton prodded once too often and spooned a feeble dolly catch. Edrich, who followed, was defeated almost before he was in, missing a blind scared hook before being devastated trying a blind scared pull; and with the score at no more than 31 Barnett was bullied into giving just such another dolly catch as Hutton's. England 31 for 3 with the game barely forty minutes old and the shine still on the ball. The bottom fell out of all England spectators' hopes; or would have fallen out but for the emergence of the assured cocky figure of Eddie Paynter to assist the calm, detached authority of Hammond, playing the fiery imponderabilities of McCormick with apparently minutes to spare.

In these frightening straights Hammond proceeded to one of the greatest innings of his life: greatly set, greatly prepared for, greatly executed. Before he had been in twenty minutes it was clear, and to nobody was it clearer than to Bradman, who was master in this business. McCormick, in face of this impassive contempt, shrivelled into insignificance in a couple of overs. Fleetwood-Smith came on and was instantly thrashed twice for four in his first over, deadly murderous calculated blows off good-length balls, menacingly certain. The dangerous spinner wavered in his length, and Hammond drove another half-volley straight past his boots for four. Even the great O'Reilly found he could not spin the ball as he wished in face of such aggression. Paynter was every bit as calm, and once hit Fleetwood-Smith for six over fine-leg with engaging impudence. The initiative was taken right away from Australia. Against all probability and out of the unpromising depths of initial disaster, Hammond and Paynter took England's score to 134 for 3 before lunch. Hammond had made 70, beautifully in command, relaxed and serene, untroubled by the early disasters. In the interval he and the rest of the players were lined up and presented to King George VI, with Earl Baldwin in attendance; a gracious if distracting ceremony, but failing, one is happy to remember, to turn Hammond's concentration from the matter urgently in hand.

A man I know saw every ball of this day bowled, and for every ball he stood, packed in the overflowing crowd high at the back of the stands behind long-off as you face the pavilion; he was young then and he had an important examination pending, and he should have devoted his day to his books, but he left them on an impulse and came

The majesty of Hammond: a big
hit to leg

to Lord's. He stood there on his hot and aching feet all day and focused
his gaze on the mastery unfolding before them; out of the fogs and
frustrations of middle age he says he would gladly, ever so gladly, go
through the whole of that day again, for he has remembered it in
peace and war, in alien city and alien continent, through tension and
tranquillity all his life. He remembers Hammond coming in with
squared grim shoulders to the chaos and by the very force of skill and
personality raising the England innings on those shoulders to
honourable levels again; how after the first sighting minutes he settled
compactly to the central task, how soon he flexed his shoulders in an
experimental cover-drive, and how for several overs he would ever
and again unship one of his great patent off-drives and tingle the

[85]

palms of cover or extra-cover or mid-off; how Bradman dropped a man back on the crowd's toes at deep extra-cover and how Hammond off the back foot cracked good-length ball after good-length ball at this man in the deep, great reverberating drives that whistled and thrummed with the power of his wrists and shoulders, drives my friend remembers for their individual beauty and power after nearly a quarter of a century – then how as he came to certainty of timing and found at last his effective direction one drive at last cracked clean through the ringed field out of all possible reach and was followed at once by others like it, until the off-side seemed as full of holes as a colander and though the fielders never abated their energy and courage he seemed at the end able to place the ball, and place it at intimidating speed, precisely where he chose. 'It was a throne-room innings,' said Cardus, watching enraptured. 'He played greatly and deserved better bowling.'

McCormick on his return was as good as useless; Fleetwood-Smith and O'Reilly at least kept a length; but not a ball beat the bat for hours. Paynter's crusading lightfoot impudence well matched the crushing authority that Hammond had once and for all triumphantly assumed; he suddenly burst into brilliance, driving and late-cutting to charm the world. Hammond got to his hundred, one of the outstanding Test centuries of his own and his contemporaries' time, in just under two and a half hours; by this time he was playing at will from anywhere in his own half of the wicket, mobile and well-balanced, on the easy hunt for runs. 'He only gave one chance,' says my friend reminiscently, 'and that broke Chipperfield's finger' – and he stifles a cheerful smile, for he is a kindly and humane man. Paynter was a sudden and unexpectedly LBW for 99, a sad oversight to end a glorious attacking innings and a record stand of 222. Denis Compton, chafing at the long wait, was fatally over-impetuous and underestimated the tiring O'Reilly; and at tea England had lost five wickets for 271 and Hammond, steady as Gibraltar, was 140 not out – 70 before lunch, 70 after, an excellent symmetry.

The last two hours were a duel between him and O'Reilly, bowling great-heartedly in the heat and intensifying his accuracy when he might have been expected to relax it. Never so O'Reilly; he plunged venomously to the crease with formidable aggressive energy never abating; he contained Hammond, though leg-stump tactics did not noticeably daunt him from on-drives and leg-hits. The cool reliability of the well-tried Ames supported him refreshingly for the whole of this session; no chance was given, no risk was taken, the day proceeded gravely to its appointed close. A symmetrical one, too; for in this last period he added precisely one more 70 to the other neat 70s of his day's compiling; it was as if he added to the artist's grace a mathematician's native precision. Hammond faced the last over of this racking day and played it coldly and forcefully as a maiden, laying the ball dead under his nose with uncompromising finality. 'All day he had carried a burden,' said Cardus, 'and with a calm which hid from us the weight and magnitude of it. He came to his 200 as easily and as majestically as a liner coming into port.' My friend on the terraces, resting his throbbing feet and stretching his paralysed muscles, took comfort in the reflection that Hammond was probably more weary than he, and saluted him as he cheered him home with the rest of the packed crowd, for uplifting not only the corporate spirit of all England's supporters but a weary student's flagging morale, and for lightening not only his path to the examination-room but his memory for the rest of his life.

And next day Hammond climbed to greater heights; he began where he had left off. He unloosed on the now indifferent bowling a violent barrage of his finest scoring strokes. Cardus threw all his hand on to the table and reported the last brilliant phase of his innings in terms of music, declaring that when the game is lifted into music by the art of a glorious cricketer he could not deny the habits of a lifetime. He added 30 in twenty magnificent minutes, making his total 240 in all and England's 457, and then played forward at McCormick and was bowled leg-stump. The enormous Saturday crowd began their applause before the bails had even come to rest; the roaring acclamation continued and intensified as he receded from the wicket; and then occurred the rare, spontaneous and extraordinarily moving gesture with which very few are ever honoured and which signs for them the day and their subsequent life alike – the Lord's pavilion rose as one man and gave him the standing ovation that no one dictates but that is simply the instinctive corporate tribute of an admiring company to a performance that their blood has told them is worthy of this very special and distinguished accolade.

From *Walter Hammond* (1962)

Hutton – the Immaculate Stylist

JOHN ARLOTT

Sir Leonard Hutton was the second professional cricketer to be knighted. The first was Sir Jack Hobbs; and the two had much in common; more, probably, than any other two comparable great batsmen. Both came from homes where cricket was a cherished part of the domestic atmosphere. Both were instinctive batsmen, emerging, virtually uncoached, as natural stylists; complete in technique in all conditions, and consistently heavy scorers. Each was, too, albeit in Hutton's case for a shorter period, the finest batsman of his time. They were both modest, temperate men; never flamboyant, in the manner of some outstanding performers. Although they were both quiet, undemonstrative competitors, they were utterly firm and unyielding in face of any opponents.

Essentially they were both sensitive batsmen; they might play forcing – but never violent – strokes. Both invariably produced the sympathetic response; not merely understanding and dealing with the ball, but harnessing its pace, line, swing or spin so that their strokes had an air of inevitability.

The fundamental difference in their performances lay more in attitude, which was created by the period, atmosphere and setting of their cricket, than in any other aspect of their play. Jack Hobbs, growing up into the Edwardian period, set out to compete with the other leading batsmen of the period, many of whom were amateurs. So he, too, played forcing and attacking cricket making exuberant strokes and taking his place in a winning English team.

No one who saw Len Hutton's vividly brilliant innings in the first Sydney Test of 1946–47 could doubt his ability to flay a Test attack. No more than 37 in twenty minutes, but a display of driving pace bowling never forgotten by those who watched it. For that matter, his onslaught on the West Indian pace bowlers at Lord's, and again at The Oval in 1939, were the innings of a man who could rout the most hostile bowling. From time to time in the county game, too, he would permit himself a virtuoso performance. Even his Yorkshire team-mates were first amused and then amazed when, as quite a young man, in his very next innings, after his first sight of a major performance by Hammond, he, not once, but many times, reproduced perfectly that splendid cover-drive in all its majesty.

In the main, though, he was shaped by growing up and into a strongly resistant Yorkshire team; and an England side which for many years was not merely beaten by Bradman's Australians, but harried and battered by their post-war bowling, which was not merely fast but punctuated by bouncers delivered with high and menacing skill. Hutton was a patient man and a brave one. He held on purposefully; wavered only once; and, because he added that strain of character to his skills, he lived to captain an England team to beat Australia in both countries.

Like Jack Hobbs, he was of little more than average height and, by comparison with such as Hammond, of slight physique. Like Hobbs, too, he lost what might well have been the most profitable batting years of his life to a world war. In that same war an injury shortened his left arm sufficiently to render him – for a season or two until, with immense skill, he made the necessary adjustments – vulnerable to off-spin. Like Hammond before him, he virtually eliminated the hook from his repertoire – except on one of his virtuoso forays – and became, it seemed, invulnerable to all but exhaustion – and that rarely beat him.

An unmistakably great batsman from the start, he began, ironically, with 'ducks' at all levels, but rapidly justified himself. He played for Yorkshire 2nd XI at sixteen; the first team in 1934, when he played an innings of 196 against Worcestershire, but had regularly to be rested because of the strain of three-day play on a slight physique –

The grace, and power, of Hutton

and his opening partner, Herbert Sutcliffe, declared him certain to go in first for England. At twenty-one he did, and scored a century. A year later, at The Oval, he made his historic 364 – in 13 hours 17 minutes – against Australia. Across the years the memory remains of Hutton walking in at the end of that innings, drawing his weary body straight, but unable to conceal the drawn face and hollow eyes of a man so exhausted that he looked as if he were ravaged by fever.

He was, too, tired when, at thirty-nine, he decided to retire. He had been much battered by injury, operation, illness; his pale, broken-nosed face was weary. In twenty-one years, less six lost to war and most of another (1935) to illness, he had made 40,140 runs, with 129 centuries at an average of 55·51. In June 1949 he scored the record aggregate for a month, 1294 (including three noughts!) and followed it with 1,050 in August. He was a better leg-spinner (173 wickets at 29·42) than some recall and, if he was not a spectacular fieldsman, he was sound, and an utterly safe catcher, especially at crucial moments.

Apart from his immense technical skill – expressed through immaculate style – Hutton's highest quality was a quiet tenacity. He was

England's main batsman (only Compton challenged him for ability in the immediately post-war years) and as such he became the prime target for those relentless competitors, Keith Miller and Ray Lindwall, arguably the finest and most hostile pair of fast bowlers in cricket history. In the Lord's Test of 1948, he was undoubtedly disturbed by their short-pitched pace and, at Old Trafford, for the first time since his Test debut in 1937, the selectors left him out of the England team. Recalled for the next two, he stepped conclusively back into his rightful place with 81, 57, 30 (last out and top scorer in a total of 52) and 64, in a losing team.

He reeled off runs against South Africa (1948–49) and New Zealand (1949) and, in the end, the 1950 West Indies. He was in no doubt, though, that his true challenge lay in Australia in 1950–51. In terms of individual batting performance, that was his finest period. In a losing side (beaten 4–1) he had an average of 88·83, 45 runs higher than that of any other batsman on either side. Then, too, he played his historic 62 not out in a total of 122 on an 'unplayable' Brisbane sticky.

During the next year it was suggested that, like Hammond before him, he might become an amateur and take over the England captaincy. With characteristic determination, he insisted that, if he captained England, it would be as a professional and, in 1952, he became the first professional officially to be appointed captain of England. He was immensely proud of the office; but he was also aware, sensitive, and not a little resentful of the fact that some of the reactionary fringe of the Establishment thought his appointment an unhappy break with tradition. He gave no outward sign of his feelings except, perhaps, to become a little more withdrawn. He proved a master tactician: perceptive, dogged, ruthless, successful.

Under him England beat India (1952); and at last (1953), after a record period of almost nineteen years, they took The Ashes from Australia. Hutton himself, with innings of 189 and 205, ensured that England came back from two-down to draw the 1953–54 series in West Indies. Selectorial aberrations meant that the 1954 home rubber with Pakistan was only drawn; and then Hutton faced his closest examination as a captain; Australia in Australia. Once again he made a bad start; put Australia in at Brisbane, saw Morris, who went on to 153, dropped in the first over, lost Compton, injured; and England were beaten by an innings and 154. Hanging on grimly; directing Statham and Tyson – the kind of pace weapon he had always longed for – with cool ruthlessness, he led England to wins in the next three Tests and their first rubber in Australia since the Bodyline series of 1932–33.

He was satisfied. He had taken a physical and psychological hammering over the years and he was ready to go. His knighthood was fitting reward for the man who had changed his country's standing in its national game.

It is sometimes – indeed, often – alleged that Len Hutton was responsible for two lamentable trends in the modern game. Undoubtedly he deliberately slowed the over-rate to reduce his opponents' scoring opportunities. In 1954–55 in Australia, too, he would walk across to speak to his fast bowlers, Statham and Tyson, during overs, in order to conserve their energy so that they could bowl through most of a session. Secondly, he has been blamed – as the outstanding player on whom so many young cricketers modelled themselves – for eschewing the classical concept of footwork and playing spin bowling defensively from inside the crease. This may have been dictated by his attempt to compensate for the shortening of his arm. In any event, he was realist enough to employ the soundest method he could devise; and it resulted in one of the most secure defences of recent times.

Beyond all criticism, Len Hutton's was a splendid record of run-scoring; while his captaincy was unequalled by any other Englishman of modern times. He derived immense, if undemonstrative, satisfaction from it all: and from seeing his son Richard play for England. Neither was he so dour as some thought him, for he had a dry, wry – sometimes almost surrealist – sense of humour. Moreover, if he was a cautious cricketer, he was not afraid to gamble with investments. By shrewd dealing, some years of astute and conscientious operations as a business executive, and as a newspaper commentator on Test matches, he amassed sufficient of this world's goods to settle and enjoy life in the effete south of England; that struck him as the best joke of all.

From *Wisden Cricket Monthly* (September, 1981)

Compton

NEVILLE CARDUS

Denis Compton was a master batsman who allowed no bowler to enslave him. Whenever he ceased scoring quickly we knew that the bowling was unusually good. He enjoyed his own cricket, played the game on his own terms. His technique, though comprehensive and reliable, never tyrannized him. He was a great improviser, instinctive and free. For example: in August 1947 Kent, on the third afternoon, invited Middlesex to score 397 to win at the speed of more than ninety an hour. And Middlesex lost by only 75. On a dusty Lord's pitch in glorious sunshine, Douglas Wright bowled at his cleverest, which meant that in his every other over, the batsman needed to cope with at least one almost unplayable spinner. Compton scored 168 before getting out to a deep-field catch off Wright.

One of his strokes I can see whenever I close my eyes and wish. He danced out to drive with the spin to the off, anticipating a leg-break. Not until the ball pitched was it revealed as a consummately disguised 'googly', whipping off the pitch viciously. Compton had to readjust his entire physical shape and position at the last split second. As a consequence he fell to the earth flat on his chest; but he found time to sweep to the leg-boundary the fizzing spin from the off. It was a case of delayed science.

The fact is that Compton at bottom batted with respect for and knowledge of rational law, though frequently he appeared to be playing according to law of his own, and making it up as he went along. He was, like George Gunn, eccentric and original; but George did his stuff with a mature cynicism, Denis pulled science by the beard like a cheeky schoolboy. No cricketer has ever been more of a schoolboy's hero than Compton. Schoolboys crowed like cocks as Denis walked out of the Lord's pavilion on his way to the wicket. They adored him because in him they saw the cricketer they themselves would have wished to be. Compton's cricket was always young of impulse. He ran his runs with a most likeable waddle; when he broke his 'duck' he would scamper along the pitch for dear life, as though, like any schoolboy, he was afraid he might not get another run.

Sir Jack Hobbs used to open his score by placing the ball to an inch, then running his single at his leisure. In Compton's longest innings he was continually eager and adventurous, 'daring' himself to do this or that thoroughly unacademic thing. But no discerning student of cricket was for a moment blind to the fact that Compton, for all his sportiveness, was fundamentally a sound, even a correct batsman: no matter how he seemed to make shots on the spur of the moment, no matter how unconventional his preliminary physical motions, when his supple blade made contact, his feet were rightly placed, his body was over the ball, his nose 'smelling' it. In Australia, he was at first somewhat nonplussed by the bowling of Iverson for Victoria. At the other end of the wicket David Sheppard was batting steadily, but runs were not being scored quickly enough. So David, between overs, approached Denis for instructions, 'You go on just as you are', was Compton's advice, 'I'll attend to the antics.'

In point of genius he stood above all batsmen of his period. He, the most animated and brilliant stroke player, also has to his credit one of the greatest defensive innings ever achieved in a Test match. At Nottingham, in June 1948, England began a second innings 344 behind and lost two wickets for 39. Compton proceeded to discipline himself wonderfully. In a dreadful light often, against Miller at his fiercest, he stayed at the wicket six hours fifty minutes, scoring 184. Then a brutal ball from Miller reared shoulder-high, Denis shaped to hook it but slipped on the wet grass, and fell on the stumps. Long and spartan though the innings must have seemed to Compton himself, not for a moment did it try the patience of anybody peering through the recurrent encircling gloom. It was a classic innings in style, reserve power and easy unselfconscious bearing.

While Compton was still adorning English cricket, it was his colleague and contemporary Sir Leonard Hutton who usually was

Denis Compton — that characteristic sweep — Middlesex *v* Worcestershire, 1957

called 'The Master'. But Sir Leonard many times had to suffer to be dictated to by bowlers, Denis seldom, if ever. If he occasionally defended, cutting out his boldest, most individual strokes, the reason was that the situation of the game demanded that he should temporarily play for Middlesex or for England. Whether doing as he liked with an attack, or denying himself 'for the cause', he was always personal, inimitable and fascinating to eye and cricket sense, never merely efficient, never anonymous.

After taking guard at the beginning of an innings, he would twiddle his bat as he surveyed the fieldsmen and their placings. As with all truly great batsmen, his bat looked as though it possessed sensitiveness, as though it were tactile, and as though some current of his own nervous system were running from him, via his fingers, into the blade. He moved to the ball on light fantastic toe. Now and again he would skip out of his crease as the bowler was more than halfway through his run. If he found that the ball, when pitching, was too short for a forward stroke, he would skip back to his crease and perform a neat late-cut through slips which, having expected to see him drive to the off, had stood up and relaxed.

Again, like all great players, he made bowling adapt itself to his own extraordinary notions of what is a hittable length. 'He sometimes makes a bowler look silly,' said a master-spinner who was a contemporary of Compton; 'but it is grand fun to bowl at him.'

His 'wonderful year' happened in the summer of 1947. He scored 3,816 in this season, a record, with eighteen centuries, also a record. His batting average for fifty innings, eight times not out, amounted to 90·85 – breathtaking figures to the credit of a batsman who collaborated so frequently with the bowler in his own dismissal. In 1947 summer sun blessed England, which was still licking war wounds. Never have I been so deeply touched on a cricket ground as I was in this heavenly summer, when I went to Lord's to see a pale-faced crowd, existing on rations, the rocket bomb still in the ears of most folks – see this worn, dowdy crowd watching Compton. The strain of long years of anxiety and affliction passed from all hearts and shoulders at the sight of Compton in full sail, sending the ball here, there and everywhere, each stroke a flick of delight, a propulsion of happy sane healthy life. There were no rations in an innings by Compton. Men, women, boys and girls cheered him to his century, running all his runs with him. The gods had been good to him, endowing him with the ideal cricketer's looks and the ideal cricketer's delight in the game. But, in his prime, the gods treated him churlishly; they crippled him almost beyond repair. Nothing could daunt his spirit, though.

Knee-cap or none, he remained an artist-batsman, beyond the powers of assessment of the scoreboard. I doubt if any cricketer has been so much loved as Denis in his heyday. All eyes at once were fixed on him as he came into the field, padded or with his team-mates.

Round about 1947–48 I sometimes took Kathleen Ferrier to dinner in the Ivy Restaurant. Not many of the people at the tables knew who she was. But once, when Denis was my guest, one diner after another came to him asking for his autograph. 'Next time I invite you out to dinner,' I told him, 'I'll book a private room.' His face was known to thousands never present at a cricket match. His portrait was to be seen on hoardings everywhere, advertising a hair-cream – and on the field of play, at any rate, Denis' hair was unruly beyond the pacifying power of any cream, oil or unguent whatsoever.

He was always 'in the game', not a virtuoso batsman exclusively, in the eyes of the public. The crowds followed all his movement wherever he fielded; sometimes he was placed near the wicket and he would bend, hands on knees, like a schoolboy playing leap-frog. As a bowler, he could spin the ball left-handed from the back of the hand; what is more, he was really a dangerous bowler of his kind whenever he found the right length. He sent down his overs at quick motion; no time-waster here. (Imagine Compton wasting his precious moments of fun on the cricket field!) He brought his arm over after a few steps, and frequently was bowling another spinner before the batsman had resumed 'position' again.

He might have won a Test match at Leeds in 1948, the game in which Australia in the fourth innings scored 404 for three wickets, and achieved one of the most remarkable victories in cricket's history. The pitch was dusty – no use to seamers, no use to Laker; but 'made' for leg and 'googly' spin. Norman Yardley, the England captain, put Compton on to bowl straightaway; and Compton straightaway caught and bowled Hassett. He span really viciously and, as I looked on, I expected him to take a wicket every over. Arthur Morris, who eventually amassed 182, was goaded into running out of his ground to cope with Compton; and Godfrey Evans missed a difficult stumping chance. Then – lo and behold! – Bradman, baffled by a swift leg break, sliced to first-slip, where Jack Crapp dropped him. During the lunch interval the Australians decided that Denis had to be knocked out of action, and when play was continued a fierce assault on his slow spin was made by the left-handed Morris. Denis, taken off, did not bowl again until Australia had virtually won the match. If Compton had been given licence to bowl all through that astonishing afternoon, I fancy Australia would have lost. Compton's analysis might have worked out at something like 7 for 200. But England, with 400 runs to play with, could have 'closed' one end of the wicket with the length attack of Alec Bedser and Pollard; and Compton would, as certainly as anything in cricket can be certain, have sent along one pretty unplayable ball every three or four overs. To this day Denis regrets that he was not trusted at Leeds in 1948 to win a Test by his bowling – after getting rid of Hassett, and having both Morris and Bradman missed off him in his opening overs. Not that Denis is given to regrets. His temperament is happy and resilient. It is absurd that he had to grow up into middle age; in his case growing up was against nature.

Some cricketers – especially batsmen – are born old; some have old age thrust upon them, while in the act of batting. Compton at one time threatened to keep the advancing years at bay indefinitely, so the fates had to do something about him; and they crippled him. Whom the gods love . . . .

From *Playfair Cricket Monthly* (June, 1960)

'No, you be Denis Compton — I'll be Neville Cardus.' Cartoon by Bernard Hollowood

III

Interval Talk
The Joys of Cricket

'I bowled three curates once
With three consecutive balls.'
Norman Gale : 'The Church
Cricketant'

How I got Compton Out Twice in an Innings

JOHN CLEESE

'So why should we listen to your opinion on the subject of cricket?' you ask. Well, I'll tell you why. Because I once got Denis Compton out twice in an innings, *that's* why. '*Twice* in an innings?!' you cry.

Now, I should make it clear that I believe that getting Denis out once in an innings would not be that much to write home about. A cause for momentary joy certainly, particularly in 1947, but not something that one would necessarily want on one's gravestone. After all, a lot of people have done it. Lindwall, Miller, Bedser, Laker and Bertie Buse, to name a few. But to dismiss the brilliantined genius twice in one knock is something else. Here is how it happened.

Denis came down to play against Clifton College, a West Country sports academy, in 1958. His son was a pupil there. So was I, I was in the team as a slow off-spinner, because during June I was more or less unplayable. This was because for these four weeks the pitches were in line with a huge red-brick building called School Hall. Being six foot five, my arm cleared the sight-screen easily and so if I bowled the ball from the right end with the right trajectory the batsman was lucky to get so much as a late glimpse of it. During June, this was. Compton came in July.

He'd been in about ten minutes when I was called upon to bowl. He'd not had much of the strike and needed about four for his fifty. He was coming down the wicket in a way I'd never seen before. In first-class cricket I'd seen him leave his crease as the bowler bowled. On this day he was setting off at about the same moment that the bowler commenced his run-up. There was a danger with the quickies that he was going to strike the ball before it left the bowler's hand. I'm very sorry, I'm exaggerating. Let's just say he was as non-creasebound as it is possible to be.

As an off-spinner I had one advantage over and about School Hall. That was our coach, Reg Sinfield, ex-Gloucs and England. He was quite my favourite person at Clifton, funny and wise and kind. I'm afraid he showed most of the masters up dreadfully. Anyway, Reg had told me to bowl very wide at any batsman running down the wicket, so just before my first over I said to the wicket-keeper, one Pickwoad, '*Third* ball, I'll bowl him a very wide one. Be ready for it, we might get a stumping.' 'You can bowl him a wide one if you like,' said Pickwoad, 'but I'm not stumping him. I want to watch him bat.' This was a blow.

I don't remember what happened to my first two deliveries, but they were eventually retrieved. I ran up to bowl the third ball. Denis

Vicky in the News Chronicle

Compton left his crease and I bowled him a wide one; so wide that it surprised him, passing him yards down the wicket. It pitched, leaving him stranded, and proceeded at a gentle pace and comfortable height towards the waiting Pickwoad. Pickwoad calmly rotated his wrists through 180 degrees, and thrust the back of his gloves at the ball. The ball shot up in the air. 'Damn!' cried Pickwoad towards the master-in-charge, umpiring at square leg. But to my amazement the ball landed, span sideways and bumped against the stumps, dislodging a bail, with the King of the Sweep still yards out of his ground. I'd got him.

Time passed. I became aware of a strange stillness. It occurred to me that no one had appealed. Denis had wandered back to his crease and now stood there, slightly puzzled, Pickwoad was replacing the bail. The other fielders seemed absorbed in their personal problems. Pickwoad picked the ball up and tossed it back to me. 'Bad luck,' he called.

Then I realized I'd blown my chance. If I'd appealed straight away it could have been put down to youthful excitement. But to do so now was cold-bloodedly to spoil everyone's afternoon. I'd got Compton out and no one would ever know. It was a sad moment. I turned, walked back to my mark, ran up and bowled the next ball, a slow high full toss on the leg stump. Spectators started taking cover.

Whether Denis was distracted by the sight of a bowler openly weeping in his delivery stride, or whether he took it upon himself to right this particular wrong, I shall never know, but painstakingly he hit a catch to mid-on. Mid-on was Ken Whitty, playing in his first match for the XI, and consequently the only other man in the ground

[99]

with an interest in the catch being taken. Had the ball been edged to Pickwoad, it would no doubt have been thrown over the sightscreen for six. Whitty grabbed glazedly at the ball and suddenly stood there triumphant, the ball securely wedged between his chin and his forearm. Compton, D. C. S. c White b Cheese, the *Bristol Evening Post* later announced. . . .

P.S. Pickwoad now lives in Canada. Serves him right.

From *The Ashes Regained* by Mike Brearley
and Dudley Doust (1979)

The Church Cricketant Here on Turf

NORMAN GALE

I bowled three sanctified souls
　　With three consecutive balls!
What do I care if Blondin trod
　　Over Niagara Falls?
What do I care for the loon in the Pit
　　Or the gilded Earl in the Stalls?
I bowled three curates once
　　With three consecutive balls!

I caused three Protestant 'ducks'
　　With three consecutive balls!
Poets may rave of lily girls
　　Dancing in marble halls!
What do I care for a bevy of yachts
　　Or a dozen or so of yawls?
I bowled three curates once
　　With three consecutive balls!

I bowled three cricketing priests
　　With three consecutive balls!
What if a critic pounds a book
　　What if an author squalls?
What do I care if sciatica comes
　　Elephantiasis calls?
I bowled three curates once
　　With three consecutive balls!

From *Cricket Songs* (1896)

I *Landscape with Cricket Match in Progress:* Paul Sandby

II *Cricket at Moulseyhurst*, by an anonymous artist

III *Thomas Hope of Amsterdam* (1792): J. Sablet

IV The charm and spirit of this watercolour by Diana Sperling (1791–1862) overcome any doubts one may harbour about its accuracy, for example of the two-stump wicket, which was superseded before she was born. But perhaps this survived, in her sheltered country-life existence, spent principally at Dynes Hall near Halstead in Essex, which was her parent's home, and Tickford Park, Buckinghamshire. Reproduced in *Mrs Hurst Dancing and Other Scenes from Regency Life 1812–23.*

V *Cricket on College Field, Eton:* William Evans

VI *England v Australia at Lord's* (1887): George Hamilton Barrable and Sir
Robert Ponsonby Staples, Bart.

VII Charles Crombie: two cartoons from his 'Laws of Cricket Illustrated'

Firing in the Quick One

C. S. MARRIOTT

The finest gambit I know is to fire in your quick one immediately after a batsman has played back to a good length leg-break ... I have always got a special kick out of this stratagem because it was entirely my own discovery. Nobody taught it to me: I learnt the secret by means of a deliberate experiment while bowling against Kent at Old Trafford in June 1919, my first season with Lancashire.

This match started on a rain-sodden wicket, which took a long time to cake a bit on top under a hot sun. Kent won the toss and batted; Hardinge and Collins settled down to play themselves in. The wicket was too slow for the faster bowlers, nothing much happened for a while, and after a time Jimmy Heap was put on at the Stretford end and myself at the other. The ball was turning, but slowly. I started with two overs of leg-breaks to Wally Hardinge, well pitched up. I was struck by the fact that he was playing back to almost every ball, taking no chances, and presenting a bat that looked extremely wide, backed up by a vast expanse of pad. Then it occurred to me, next time he played back to a good length leg-break, to fire in the quick one next ball. I pitched another leg-break well up to him and sure enough, he played back to it; then I let go a quick one, putting all I had into it, a half volley right on the middle stump. It went thump against his pads before his bat was half way through the stroke; I emptied my lungs and up went the umpire's finger.

From *The Complete Leg-Break Bowler* (1968)

A Tale of Hendren and Three Bouncers

IAN PEEBLES

Alf Gover remembers his first visit to Lord's, which was in 1929. He tells his own story with becoming modesty, so I will pass it on as nearly to his version as I can get.

Alf arrived at the professionals' dressing-room in good time and had no difficulty in recognizing the only occupant of the downstairs room. Pat Hendren greeted him very civilly and, having ascertained his name, asked him what he did. 'I'm a fast bowler,' said Alf. 'Are you very fast?' asked Pat. 'Yes, I am,' replied Alf. 'Well,' said Pat, 'be careful how you bowl at me. I'm not as young as I used to be, and I don't like fast bowling so much.' Well, thought Alf, I've got one in the bag.

When Alf had his first bowl at Pat he had three balls to go to finish the over. The first was naturally a bouncer and it not unnaturally landed in the Father Time stand. The young Alf attributed this to blind panic and tried again, and this time it only cost him four. The third bouncer went the way of the first for six, the umpire called over, and Jack Hobbs stopped to speak to Alf.

'Why are you bowling bouncers at Pat?' he inquired. 'Because he doesn't like fast bowling,' replied Alf.

Jack's expression of mild surprise turned to blank astonishment. 'Who on earth told you that?' he asked. 'He did,' said Alf. At that Jack smiled. 'Then *I* am telling you,' he said, 'that Pat is still as good a player of fast bowling as anyone I know.'

From *Patsy Hendren* (1969)

Tragedy at Thunderpore

IAN PEEBLES

One winter's evening while following the fortunes of the MCC in India my eye fell on the venue of their next match – Thunderpore. That's not the real name of the place but near enough to awaken poignant memories.

When I went to India the side was captained by Lionel Tennyson, one of the richest characters of his age. He is lovingly remembered by a vast number of people as a great personality, who by his enjoyment of life gave great enjoyment to all who met him. He belonged ideally to another age, as even the now spacious-seeming days of the twenties and thirties hardly offered full scope for his infectious gusto and gaiety. His heart was in proportion to his sturdy frame and stuffed full of courage and kindness. His conceits were enormous, unaffected, and endearing, a sitting target for the shafts of his friends, whose unrestrained badinage was the sincerest gauge of their affection. If he should occasionally appear in a somewhat undignified light in what I have to tell, I can truly say it stems from the same source.

As the good ship *Viceroy of India* was nearing Bombay our captain convened a meeting in order to arm his inexperienced team against the perils of the Orient. The first part of his address was devoted to the appalling consequence of any indiscretion in diet or other matters in tropical countries. This message, endorsed by the resounding medical terms the speaker had filched for the occasion from the surgeon's manual, made a most powerful impression.

The ensuing part of the talk was a timely reminder of the standard of behaviour expected of us as a touring team in a foreign country.

A country cricket match in the mid nineteenth century, by an unknown artist

There would be mistakes on the part of umpires, said our leader, but these must be accepted with the traditional stoicism of the sportsman and a big happy smile. His sixteen listeners almost longed for an opportunity to exhibit these manly qualities.

As the tour went on, however, the mistakes in umpiring were singularly few, while the health of the side, although jealously guarded, at times gave much cause for anxiety. Later on when we arrived in the fateful field of Thunderpore strains and dysentery, in varying degrees of severity, had robbed us of half our numbers, and we were hard pressed to raise eleven mobile, if not able, bodies. But the die being cast, that is having lost the toss again, we tottered into the arena, and the match got under way.

The first few overs delivered by Alf Gover, then recently risen from a bed of sickness, were uneventful. During the third only the most acute observer would have been alarmed at the tense expression on his face as he started on his long, hustling run. It was when he shot past the crouching umpire and thundered down the pitch with the undelivered ball in his hand that it became obvious that something was amiss. The batsman, fearing a personal assault, sprang smartly backward, but the flannelled giant sped past looking neither to right nor left. Past wicket-keeper, slips, and fine leg in a flash he hurtled up the pavilion steps in a cloud of dusty gravel and was gone. That he has never received full credit for this record is due to the lack of timing apparatus and the distance, from the start of his run to his uncomfortable destination, not being a recognized one.

As, in the tight-lipped precipitation of his flight, he had been unable to give any hint of his future movements, fine leg, after a moment's thought, followed up the steps and, having rescued the ball from the bowler's convulsive grasp, announced that we had better start looking for a substitute.

The choice fell on a junior groundsman, and there followed another pause while he was forcefully persuaded to wear boots. Whether pigskin offended his religious tenets or whether he just objected to the discomfort of wearing any type of footwear for the first time, we never did discover.

During this pause another disaster befell us. I was idly bowling the ball to and fro with George Pope, our one remaining bowler of any consequence, when unfortunately something distracted his attention. The ball took him rather below his grievously upset tummy, and to my horror he went down with a terrible hissing sound. When I reached the other end he was in the arms of several helpers who had heard the thud, sweating in a fearful manner and showing the whites of his eyes.

When at this moment the Lord turned to ask him to bowl he was astonished and infuriated to see his one remaining hope apparently writhing in his last agonies. As the victim couldn't speak and no one else had seen the incident, no answer was forthcoming to his testy demand as to what the hell had happened now. Personally I thought that a tactful silence would be best in the circumstances, so without more ado poor old George was carted off to be erroneously treated for a sudden heat-stroke.

Just when it seemed that we might as well pack up altogether, mingled sounds of applause and primitive plumbing announced the heroic reappearance of Gover. At this the game was resumed and he bowled jolly well, admittedly aided by the batsman's uncertainty as to what he was going to do on arrival at the crease.

But they say that misfortunes come in threes, and we didn't have long to wait.

The Lord, bent with sorrow, was standing in the gully in a somewhat broody attitude when a brilliant piece of play lit the gloom like a fork of lightning against a sombre sky. Alf, slightly depleted but ever game, sent down a ball of whizzing speed outside the off stump of India's fairest cutter, Mushtaq Ali. The bat flashed in those blued-steel wrists to catch the ball 'twixt wind and water' and send it ray-like to the paling – but no, that's not quite right. The captain's leg happened to be in the way.

The ball caught him a smack on the shin that would have snapped off a lesser leg like a piece of rotten matchwood. As it was, the results were spectacular, and we beheld another record burst asunder. With a shrill trumpet of agony our captain's mighty bulk rose vertically to a height of eleven feet nine inches, where it appeared to remain suspended for several seconds. It was the nearest thing we saw to the rope trick in India, and on regaining terra firma his agility and eloquence completely eclipsed the efforts of all the nautch girls and impassioned orators we had endured in the course of our travels.

The minor setbacks of the rest of the innings were but pin-pricks against this majestic background, but old Miss Fortune had not yet

ceased to leer.

When we started our innings in chastened mood, for the first time
in India Umpire Blunder raised his hideous head, or rather his
disrupting finger.

Things were indeed desperate when the Lord hobbled out to save
the day. Four stinking decisions had easily counterbalanced a friendly
attack, and feeling ran high or low according to temperament. But
here was the man for the occasion. He had taken just about as much as
any man ostensibly engaged on a day's pleasure could be asked to
endure, apart from being in some pain. What of it? Had he not made
63 in a Test Match with one hand?

The first ball he saw bowled was met by Smith (P.) in the middle of
the bat and deftly deflected to fine leg. Up went a great shout, and
simultaneously Umpire Blunder's finger. The batsmen had changed
ends when this diabolical decision was eventually borne in on them.
Smith left stunned, and after a moment's stupefaction his partner
advanced on Umpire Blunder. Now was the supreme test. Remembering his teachings on the ship, we awaited the outcome breathlessly.
Would it be the big happy smile? If the same thoughts crossed the
captain's mind he brushed them aside for something a whole lot better.

He made Umpire Blunder a short address which blew him backwards, bow-legged.

I cannot give you the exact text of that immortal message, that is Umpire B's copyright, but stripped of its stupendous embellishments, it boiled down to a straightforward enquiry as to whether, having started blind, he was now also bereft of his hearing.

It is not surprising how long the recipient took to find his voice, considering how small it was when found. The snag was that the next striker had arrived by the time he had reversed his decision, so the point was lost.

But when all is said and done, I doubt if even a smile as happy as Lionel's would have helped in the circumstances. Anyway, every psychiatrist will tell you he done right.

From *Talking of Cricket* (1953)

First Game of the Season

JACK BRAITHWAITE

In the Yorkshire League we always seemed to start the season with a game at Bramall Lane, Sheffield, and Bramall Lane in early May is hardly the place to start anything except an anti-air-pollution campaign.

But they were good games because it *was* Bramall Lane and you can never have a dreary game there – the crowd won't let you.

The best ones were played in a Wagnerian half-light with the clouds banking black and steep over the football stand and Ellis Robinson and George Pope in opposition. Robinson was our professional. He had played for Yorkshire and Somerset and was an off-spinner of imagination and tremendous natural skill. George Pope was one of the great line of Derbyshire seamers, a line including such bowlers (and characters) as Gladwin, Copson and Les Jackson.

The classic Robinson-Pope meeting came the Saturday after Blackpool had beaten Bolton in the Cup Final. Bramall Lane that day was a seductive, lush strip of turf with the clouds hanging heavy and low, sitting on the chimney pots like plump pigeons. It was a day made to measure for George Pope and his art and he didn't conceal his delight when Sheffield won the toss and sent us in.

'Fancy thi' chances then, Ellis,' he yelled through our dressing-room door.

'I'll gi' thee some stick this afternoon Popey. Ah can bat thee wi' mi' cap neb,' replied Ellis.

But it was Popey's day and not all of Robinson's optimism or skill could prevent it.

Ellis came in about fourth wicket down with few runs on the board and Popey swinging them like boomerangs.

He walked slowly to the crease, taking his time, adjusting his eyes to the light, sizing things up. He took guard, touched his Yorkshire cap and looked hard at Popey standing in the slips. 'Na' then Ellis, are tha' going to get any chalks?'

'Reckon on fifty, George.'

'I'm doing a bit today tha' knows, Ellis.'

'Tha' nivver could bowl.'

Robinson settles into his stance. The bowler begins his run. Tap-tap, bat on crease. An outswinger, Robinson forward. Misses. Stumper takes it.

Pope (looking up at heaven): 'Jesus Christ, Ellis. Tha' allus wor lucky.'

'Lucky be buggered. I let the bloody thing past.'

'Nivver. Nivver. Tha' nivver saw it.'

And so on, until Pope was bowling which prevented him from talking, but not Robinson who now conversed with whichever fielder happened to be the nearest.

'Fancy thi' chances does tha' lad? Be careful. I wouldn't like to face meself on this track today. Not today I wouldn't. Oh no.'

Pope approaching the crease. Loose, almost affable action. Not so quick as he used to be but twice as crafty. Right to the far edge of the bowling crease. Immaculate length. Ball pushed diagonally at the leg stump. A lot of cut on it. Hits pitch and snaps back, beats the bat and catches Robinson high on the front pad as he pushes forward. Pope whips around, glowers at the umpire for a second and then lets one go which you could have heard in Manchester.

'Owzat?'

'Not out,' says the umpire.

'And I should bloody well think not,' shouts Robinson from the other end of the pitch. 'It wouldn't have hit a set of stumps six feet high.'

Pope glares at him down the track. Robinson glares back. There seems to be no one else in the whole of Bramall Lane except these two glaring and snarling at one another.

Pope turns on his heel and walks back to his mark. As he passes the umpire, who is still trembling from the blast of the appeal, he says, in a soft, polite voice, 'A little high perhaps, Mr Umpire?'

The umpire nods.

'Perhaps so,' says George, all smooth and buttery, 'but I thought I would enquire, you know.'

And so it went on. There was no holding Pope that day. Everything was right for him: the grass, green and damp and gripping the seam like a lover, making the ball change direction as if it were pitched on to corrugated sheeting.

We were bowled out for under 50 and Pope took eight wickets for less than 20 runs. The only consolation we had was that he would have taken wickets against any team in the world on that track and in those conditions.

But we were in with a chance with Robinson angry and a couple of useful seamers. But it rained during the tea interval and when play recommenced the wicket was wet and useless and Sheffield easily knocked off the runs. It 'was no good talking to Robinson as we changed for home. He kept muttering to himself. 'Bloody weather. I'd have shown Popey. Nivver could bowl. I'd have caused some panic.'

So we went into the bar to drown our sorrows and went home silently, in our special bus through the rain-misty, slimy streets of Sheffield with only a stop for a fish and six and a bag of scraps before we reached Barnsley.

We went to our own club bar where we told the second team just how much Popey had been bending them – exaggerating like anglers – until Saturday night slid away into Sunday morning when we woke up stiff as sergeant-majors, certain now that the season had started. And glad.

From 'Tha' nivver could bowl' (*Time & Tide*, 3 May 1962)

Gamesmanship

BERNARD HOLLOWOOD

I was once talked out by the great Lancashire and England bowler 'Dick' Tyldesley in a match at Burslem against Nantwich. We were in a strong position, ninety-odd for four and needing only about thirty runs to win. That day I was in form and my fifty had been made largely at Tyldesley's expense – occasional fours and a lot of short but safe singles. Every time I scampered home to Dick's end he chatted up the umpire for the kill. 'Only just in that time, just!' 'He'll try that once too often, won't he?' 'Can't get away with that kind of thing for long!' and so on.

And then I pushed a ball from him to mid-wicket for another easy run. Dick stood over the stumps waiting for the fielder to return the ball. 'Come on,' he said coaxingly to umpire and fielder, 'he's done it now; that's put paid to him.' And although I was a yard past the stumps when he broke the bails his 'Owzat!' was supremely confident. Not an appeal, but a statement, the password to his unanimity with the umpire, the key to their abiding friendship. As the finger shot up I could hear, in my mind, umpire and bowler congratulating each other on their perspicacity. 'Silly young idiot,' they were saying, 'we warned him what would happen, and he took not a blind bit of notice. A pity, because he was playing well, but of course we had to observe the Laws. And he was quite clearly run out by a mile.'

When I hear it said that so-and-so 'has the umpire in his pocket' I automatically think of Dick Tyldesley and the day he swindled Burslem out of a comfortable win.

Syd Barnes was another who cowed umpires – though he scorned the obvious stratagems. There are bowlers who, having hit the batsman's pads, pull up smartly and lean over in front of the umpire and take a sight down the pitch. In that position they pause, scrutinizing the situation in a manner to suggest that by withholding an appeal they are being extraordinarily magnanimous. Then they look round at the adjudicator with a pained expression, as if to say: 'Well, it was worth an appeal, but for your sake I won't shout until I'm absolutely certain.' Very comical.

Barnes was always certain that he knew better than the umpire, and his method of registering displeasure with a decision was to stare at the official hard and long, his lean features loaded with disgust and contempt. These staring sessions seemed to last for minutes on end and were acutely embarrassing to everyone except Barnes. I was batting with him in his last match for Staffordshire at Castleford in 1935 when he was given out, LBW, to the Yorkshire fast bowler, Hargreaves. From the other end he looked dead in front, but Barnes stood his ground and glowered at the umpire for so long that I honestly thought he had refused to go. The fielders watched, immobile and fascinated, and the umpire looked distinctly uncomfortable. Then, with the passing of aeons, old Syd turned and marched to the pavilion with a face like that of Mr Hyde.

Thirty years ago I wrote a piece for *The Boy's Own Paper* in which I described Barnes' method of psychological warfare against tremulous batsmen. 'All who have been fortunate enough to play with him,' I wrote, 'are agreed that as a bowler of length and spin, Barnes has no equal. Even one of our youngest cricketers, the record-breaking Len Hutton, has said, "One of my best innings was against Sydney Barnes when I was sixteen; I scored 69 not out." I remember that innings of Hutton's, and I recall the warm praise it received from Barnes. The master, or the "maestro" as he is known in Staffordshire, turns the ball with equal facility from leg or off without ever losing a perfect length. His field placing is a work of art. It is not a matter of "a bit deeper" or "round a little". When Barnes moves him a fieldsman must proceed to an appointed spot, mathematically determined, *and stay there.*

'Denbighshire were batting and near "stumps" on the first day had lost three wickets – all to Barnes. The game had been held up by rain and Staffordshire badly wanted another wicket before the close. The last over was called and the spectators moved to the gates. Barnes was bowling. The batsman defended stubbornly. Five balls were played carefully. Then, in the middle of his long, springy run for the last ball, Barnes stopped. He motioned to me at point (two yards from the bat). His long fingers made some sign which I did not understand, but I

Gamesmanship and S.F. Barnes;
two cartoons by Bernard
Hollowood

'Barnes (S. F.) lbw b Hargreaves . . .'   A. N. Other lbw Barnes 0

moved round to silly mid-off. After all, there was only one ball. Once again Barnes turned to bowl, and once again his eyes swept the field as he began his run up to the wicket. I was watching, my hands cupped. His delivery arm was almost over when he halted suddenly, and looked at me with a face as black as thunder. Then, while the crowd laughed derisively, he walked up the pitch and led me (almost by the hand) to the position he had in mind. "The old buffer," I thought. "How does *he* know what the batsman will do?"

'By this time the poor batsman was in a terrible state. He looked hard at me, and I saw panic in his eyes. Barnes bowled. The batsman prodded forward and the ball popped, so gently, into my waiting hands. It was typical of the "maestro".'

From *Cricket on The Brain* (1970)

Herecombe v Therecombe

HERBERT FARJEON

Sharp practice in our national game is probably a good deal more common than most Englishmen would care to admit. Although it is true that the other side is seldom openly accused of cheating, there can be hardly a pavilion in the country which has not at some time in its existence creaked with dark whisperings against the impartiality of umpires from men who have been given out LBW, or against the honour of wicket-keepers from men who cannot bring themselves to believe that such a ball could possibly have hit the stumps. League cricket in particular produces complaints from batsmen who are convinced that they were not really so much bowled or caught or stumped as tricked out. Yet I question whether any match has ever been conducted in a more thoroughly unsportsmanlike manner than a certain officially 'friendly' match between the old-world villages of Herecombe and Therecombe. In the annals of the game it will, I imagine, stand for all time as the only match in which, although there was not a drop of rain, although play continued uninterrupted through the whole afternoon, and although both sides had a knock, only two balls were bowled. That, I feel sure, must be one of the most remarkable of all the records unchronicled in the pages of *Wisden*.

Herecombe and Therecombe were old antagonists. For some reason, as irrelevant as it is mysterious, there was no love lost between them. The feud, I believe, went deeper (if anything can) than cricket. But after the sensational tie in which a Herecombe batsman, backing up, was run out before the delivery of the ball, and a Therecombe batsman, politely rolling the ball back to the bowler, was successfully appealed against for 'handling', small wonder that each side vowed to win the next encounter by hook or crook. And small wonder, perhaps, that even the winning of the toss by Herecombe was viewed by Therecombe with deep suspicion.

The Herecombe captain elected to bat. Of course, he had no idea when he marched to the wicket to open the innings that it would be over in one ball. It was an astonishing ball, striking a flint – the ground was like that – and skidding at right angles to square leg.

The Herecombe captain slashed at it, missed it, was dumbfounded, and audibly ejaculated 'Well, I declare!' Everybody on the ground heard him, including the Therecombe captain. And the Therecombe captain was not slow to seize his opportunity.

'Come along boys!' shouted the Therecombe captain, and made for the pavilion. His boys followed him. Nobody, with the exception of the Therecombe captain, knew quite what was happening. An explanation was demanded. The explanation was given.

'Didn't your captain say he declared?' asked the Therecombe captain. 'Very well, then. Us to bat, boys, and one run to win!'

A heated discussion ensued. Everybody called everybody else a dirty swindler. Threats were levelled, fists were shaken. The umpires read the Laws of Cricket through three times. In the end they decided that the Herecombe captain had inescapably, if unintentionally, declared. The Herecombe team thereupon proposed to chuck it.

But suddenly the light of battle glinted in the eye of the Herecombe captain.

'All right,' he said to the Therecombe captain, 'we're game! You go in and win *if you can*!'

Then he led his men on to the field, handed the ball to little Smith, who had never bowled in a match in his life but who had once won a local Marathon race, and whispered a few words of command in his ear.

The Therecombe batsmen came out. The umpire called 'Play!' Little Smith began a long, zig-zag run up to the wicket.

But before little Smith reached the bowling-crease, a queer thing happened. He doubled back. Then, like a dog after its tail, he began running round in circles.

What, gasped the spectators, was up with little Smith? Had he gone stark, staring mad? There he was – turning and twisting – twisting and turning – darting this way and that – hopping, skipping, jumping – a most eccentric run, indeed – but never delivering the ball.

'Hi!' growled the Therecombe batsman, 'what's your bowler think he's doing?'

'Oh,' drawled the Herecombe captain, grinning, 'just playing out time, you know, playing out time. . . .'

So that was it! Another heated discussion now arose. Crowds congregated round the umpires, who read the Laws of Cricket all over again, while little Smith kept on running. But they could find nothing in the Laws of Cricket limiting the length of a bowler's run. Apparently a bowler could run all day before delivering the ball, and apparently he meant to.

Hour after hour little Smith kept up his capering – a noble effort – the batsman sternly refusing to leave the wicket lest he should be bowled in his absence. The fieldsmen lay down at full length on the ground. Spectators went away and then came back again, to find little Smith still running. Longer and longer grew his shadow as the sun travelled into the west. The clock on the old church tower chimed five, then six, then seven.

And now a new point of discussion arose. It had been agreed that at seven o'clock stumps should be drawn. But was it legal to draw stumps in the middle of a ball? The umpires got together again and, after much cogitation, decided that it would not be legal.

Then things became really exciting.

Little Smith shouted that if that was so, then dang him if he would deliver the ball till it was pitch dark. Still the batsman stood grimly on guard, determined if possible to make a winning swipe when the chance came at last. Again the spectators departed – this time for supper. Again they returned – this time under a harvest moon.

And there were the fieldsmen still lying on the grass, there was the batsman still standing at the wicket, and there was little Smith, still running.

At ten o'clock came the climax. It was dark. The moon had disappeared behind a cloud. Half a dozen of the fieldsmen had taken up positions beside the wicket-keeper behind the stumps to prevent an untimely bye. Little Smith let fly.

The Therecombe batsman screwed up his eyes to pierce the gloom. He struck. He missed.

'Match drawn!' shouted the Herecombe captain.

It was not quite the end. During his long vigil, the batsman had been doing a bit of thinking. He now protested that if stumps could not be drawn in the middle of a ball, neither could they be drawn in the middle of an over. The umpires started to consider the latest point. But while they were debating, the Herecombe captain put an end to doubt by appealing against the light – a rare thing indeed for a fielding side to do – the umpires allowed the appeal, and the game was over.

Whether the umpires were right in all their rulings may be open to question. I think they were. In any case, it must be conceded that they had some very knotty points to solve, and that on the whole they appear to have discharged their duties conscientiously.

From *Herbert Farjeon's Cricket Bag* (1946)

Play Your Own Game!

A. G. MACDONELL

Ten runs for three wickets and one man hurt.

The next player was a singular young man. He was small and quiet, and he wore perfectly creased white flannels, white silk socks, a pale-pink silk shirt, and a white cap. On the way down in the char-à-banc he had taken little part in the conversation and even less in the beer-drinking. There was a retiring modesty about him that made him conspicuous in that cricket eleven, and there was a gentleness, an almost finicky gentleness about his movements which hardly seemed virile and athletic. He looked as if a fast ball would knock the bat out of his hands. Donald asked someone what his name was, and was astonished to learn that he was the famous novelist, Robert Southcott himself.

Just as this celebrity, holding his bat as delicately as if it was a flute or a fan, was picking his way through the daisies and thistle-down towards the wicket, Mr Hodge rushed anxiously, tankard in hand, from the Three Horseshoes and bellowed in a most unpoetical voice: 'Play carefully, Bobby. Keep your end up. Runs don't matter.'

'Very well, Bill,' replied Mr Southcott sedately. Donald was interested by this little exchange. It was the Team Spirit at work – the captain instructing his man to play a type of game that was demanded by the state of the team's fortunes, and the individual loyally suppressing his instincts to play a different type of game.

Mr Southcott took guard modestly, glanced furtively round the field as if it was an impertinence to suggest that he would survive long

enough to make study of the fieldsmen's positions worth while, and hit
the rate-collector's first ball over the Three Horseshoes into a hay-
field. The ball was retrieved by a mob of screaming urchins, handed
back to the rate-collector, who scratched his head and then bowled his
fast yorker, which Mr Southcott hit into the saloon bar of the Shoes,
giving Mr Harcourt such a fright that he required several pints before
he fully recovered his nerve. The next ball was very slow and crafty,
endowed as it was with every iota of fingerspin and brain-power
which a long-service rate-collector could muster. In addition, it was
delivered at the extreme end of the crease so as to secure a background
of dark laurels instead of a dazzling white screen, and it swung a little
in the air; a few moments later the urchins, by this time delirious with
ecstasy, were fishing it out of the squire's trout stream with a bamboo
pole and an old bucket.

The rate-collector was bewildered. He had never known such a
travesty of the game. It was not cricket. It was slogging; it was wild,
unscientific bashing; and furthermore, his reputation was in grave
danger. The instalments would be harder than ever to collect and
Heaven knew they were hard enough to collect as it was, what with
bad times and all. His three famous deliveries had been treated with
contempt – the leg-break, the fast yorker, and the slow, swinging off-
break out of the laurel bushes. What on earth was he to try now?
Another six and he would be laughed out of the parish. Fortunately
the village umpire came out of a trance of consternation to the rescue.
Thirty-eight years of umpiring for the Fordenden Cricket Club had
taught him a thing or two and he called 'Over' firmly and marched
off to square-leg. The rate-collector was glad to give way to a Free
Forester, who had been specially imported for this match. He was only
a moderate bowler, but it was felt that it was worth while giving him
a trial, if only for the sake of the scarf round his waist and his cap. At
the other end the fast bowler pounded away grimly until an
unfortunate accident occurred. Mr Southcott had been treating with
apologetic contempt those of his deliveries which came within reach,
and the blacksmith's temper had been rising for some time. An urchin

The joys of village cricket: scoring
(at Kenton)

had shouted, 'Take him orf!' and the other urchins, for whom Mr Southcott was by now a firmly established deity, had screamed with delight. The captain had held one or two ominous consultations with the wicket-keeper and other advisers, and the blacksmith knew that his dismissal was at hand unless he produced a supreme effort.

It was the last ball of the over. He halted at the wicket before going back for his run, glared at Mr Harcourt, who had been driven out to umpire by his colleagues – greatly to the regret of Mr Bason, the landlord of the Shoes – glared at Mr Southcott, took another reef in his belt, shook out another inch in his braces, spat on his hand, swung his arm three or four times in a meditative sort of way, grasped the ball tightly in his colossal palm, and then turned smartly about and marched off like a Pomeranian grenadier and vanished over the brow of the hill. Mr Southcott, during these proceedings, leant elegantly upon his bat and admired the view. At last, after a long stillness, the ground shook, the grasses waved violently, small birds arose with shrill clamours, a loud puffing sound alarmed the butterflies, and the blacksmith, looking more like Venus Anadyomene than ever, came thundering over the crest. The world held its breath. Among the spectators conversion was suddenly hushed. Even the urchins, understanding somehow that they were assisting at a crisis in affairs, were silent for a moment as the mighty figure swept up to crease. It was the charge of Von Bredow's Dragoons at Gravelotte over again.

But alas for human ambitions! Mr Harcourt, swaying slightly from leg to leg, had understood the menacing glare of the bowler, had marked the preparation for a titanic effort, and – for he was not a poet for nothing – knew exactly what was going on. And Mr Harcourt

[115]

More village cricketing: 'lost ball'

sober had a very pleasant sense of humour, but Mr Harcourt rather
drunk was a perfect demon of impishness. Sober, he occasionally
resisted a temptation to try to be funny. Rather drunk, never. As the
giant whirlwind of vulcanic energy rushed past him to the crease, Mr
Harcourt, quivering with excitement and internal laughter, and
wobbling uncertainly upon his pins, took a deep breath and bellowed,
'No ball!'

It was too late for the unfortunate bowler to stop himself. The ball
flew out of his hand like a bullet and hit third-slip, who was not
looking, full pitch on the knee-cap. With a yell of agony third-slip
began hopping about like a stork until he tripped over a tussock of
grass and fell on his face in a bed of nettles, from which he sprang up
again with another drum-splitting yell. The blacksmith himself was
flung forward by his own irresistible momentum, startled out of his
wits by Mr Harcourt's bellow in his ear, and thrown off his balance
by his desperate effort to prevent himself from delivering the ball, and
the result was that his gigantic feet got mixed up among each other
and he fell heavily in the centre of the wicket, knocking up a cloud of
dust and dandelion-seed and twisting his ankle. Rooks by hundreds
arose in protest from the vicarage cedars. The urchins howled like the
intoxicated banshees. The gaffers gaped. Mr Southcott gazed modestly
at the ground. Mr Harcourt gazed at the heavens. Mr Harcourt did
not think the world had ever been, or could ever be again, quite such
a capital place, even though he had laughed internally so much that
he had got hiccups.

Mr Hodge, emerging at that moment from the Three Horseshoes,
surveyed the scene and then the scoreboard with an imperial air. Then
he roared in the same rustic voice as before: 'You needn't play safe
any more, Bob. Play your own game.'

'Thank you, Bill,' replied Mr Southcott as sedately as ever, and, on
the resumption of the game, he fell into a kind of cricketing trance,
defending his wicket skilfully from straight balls, ignoring crooked
ones, and scoring one more run in a quarter of an hour before he
inadvertently allowed, for the first time during his innings, a ball to
strike his person.

'Out!' shrieked the venerable umpire before anyone had time to appeal.

The score at this point was sixty-nine for six, last man fifty-two.

From *England, Their England* (1933)

The Cricket Club of Red Nose Flat

JAY HICKORY WOOD

Now, when a man identifies himself with
    certain acts,
It's very rude for any one to doubt that
    they are facts.
There are only two ways for it – you
    believe him, if you're wise;
If you're not, and he is little, then you tell
    him that 'he lies.'

So, as my friend was taller than myself
    by quite a head,
And a toughish-looking customer, I swal-
    lowed all he said.
But when at last he paused for breath,
    and also for a drink,
I thought I'd change the subject, so I said,
    'No doubt you think
That cricket as a sport is very womanish
    and tame
Compared with scalping Indians. Do you
    understand the game?'

'Do I understand the game?' he said.
    'Wall, stranger, you may bet
What I don't know 'bout cricket – wall,
    it ain't invented yet.
Perhaps you ain't aware, my friend, that
    'way down Ole 'Frisco
We had a slap-up cricket club?' I said I
    didn't know.

'Wall, now you know,' he answered, 'and
    I'll tell you 'bout a game
We played there just a year ago as warn't
    so plaguy tame.'
And this is what he told me – of course it
    mayn't be true –
But as he told the tale to me I tell the tale
    to you:

    *   *   *   *

'The boys 'way down in 'Frisco, though
    all a reckless lot, –
They'd most come out from England, –
    and had got a tender spot.
That spot it were the village green, where
    as boys they'd bowl and bat,
So we all made up our minds we'd have a
    club at Red Nose Flat.

We didn't have no captain – leastways
    we elected four,
But some one allus pistolled them, so we
    didn't vote no more.
You see, them captains allus tries to boss
    the blessed show,
Which ain't a healthy thing to do, 'way
    down in Ole 'Frisco.

Wall, we went ahead a-practising, as
    happy as could be,
Till Thunder Jack shot Blood-red Bill for
    hitting him for three.
And we held a general meeting, and we
    passed the following rule:
"A member pistolled on the field by
    members, in the cool,
Providing he is up to date in payment of
    his 'sub,'
Is planted at the sole expense of this 'ere
    cricket club."
We heard as how a lot of chaps from
    Philadelphia
Was out on tour, so we challenged 'em to
    come along and play.
Our challenge was accepted, and one day
    they came around,
All ready for to play us, so we took 'em to
    the ground.

Joe Blazes says to me, says he, "Ole pard,
    I'll tell you what,
There ain't a single shooting iron in all
    the blessed lot.
What do they mean a-coming 'ere,
    expecting for to win?
It ain't half good enough, ole pard, a jolly
    sight too thin."

They tossed for choice of innings, and
    you bet we won at that;
We all was whales on tossing, and we
    started for to bat.
'Twas just as well we won the toss,
    because, I'm bound to say,
That even if we'd lost it, we'd have batted,
    any way.

Wall, first of all I starts to bat, along o'
    Thunder Jack,
The bowler sends his ball along, I makes
    a mighty smack,
But, somehow, 'stead of hitting that there
    ball with that there bat,
I hit it with my leg. The bowler shouted
    "How is that?"

And that there blessed umpire started for
    to answer "Out,"
When he saw my shooting iron – so he
    guessed there was a doubt;
And he'd heard as how the batsman
    always got the benefit,
Which plainly showed as how that blessed
    umpire knew a bit.

You'd have thought as t'other umpire
    would have had some common sense,
But he went and said as Jack were out, on
    the following pretence:

Old Jack had made a mighty swipe, and,
    if he'd hit the ball,
I guess we hadn't never seen that ball no
    more at all.

But, then, you see, he missed it, and his
    wickets they was downed
By the wicket-keeping chap, who said as
    Jack was out of ground,
And 'stead of speaking up and saying as
    there was a doubt,
The umpire said as Thunder Jack was
    very plainly out.

Then Jack he pulled his shooter out; and
    drew on him a bead,
And that there blessed umpire he went
    very dead indeed.

We shouted out "Fresh Umpire," but,
    somehow, no one came,
So we guessed we'd do without one, and
    we then resumed the game.

Wall! after that they took to bowling
    very nice and slow,
And, if a fielder caught a ball, he allus let
    it go;
So Jack and I, we slogged away as lively
    as could be,
Until my score was ninety-seven and
    Jack's was ninety-three.

Wall, we had to close our innings so's to
    give us time to win,
And, as they couldn't get us out, we said
    they might go in;
They didn't seem so anxious for to bat as
    you'd have thought,
But we talked to them persuasive, and
    convinced 'em as they ought.

We told 'em as good cricketers should
    sooner die than yield,
And we loaded our revolvers, and we
    started out to field.
We'd Rifle Bill, a deadly shot, a-fielding
    near the rails,
And when Bill means to shoot a chap he
    very rarely fails;

We'd Blazing Bob at cover point, and
    Mike was near the stand,
And Thunder Jack kept wicket, with his
    shooter in his hand,
And Lord! them Philadelphy chaps, they
    couldn't bat a bit;
I bowls 'em nice and easy just to tempt
    'em for to hit,

But 'stead of smacking at the ball, they
    kept on looking back,
And seemed most interested in the ways
    of Thunder Jack.
One chap did hit a ball to leg, and started
    on a spurt,
But Rifle Bill just fetched him down, and
    he retired hurt.

Of course we beat 'em hollow; why, they
    never scored a run,
But they all admitted freely as it had been
    splendid fun;
So we challenged 'em to come again, and
    play us a return,
And, p'r'aps it may be fancy, but they
    didn't seem to yearn.

However, we persuaded 'em to play it out next day,

But, when the morning came, we found as they had gone away.
We've challenged other clubs since then, but one and all they states,
As, they're very, very sorry, but they have no vacant dates.
So we swept the decks completely, and we calculated that

The boss of all the cricket clubs was ours at Red Nose Flat.'

*   *   *   *

And this is what he told me – of course it mayn't be true –
But as he told the tale to me I've told the tale to you.

A menu for Hampstead Cricket Club reproduced from *A History of Kent C.C.C.* by Lord Harris (1907). The drawing is based on the William Nicholson woodcut 'Cricket — June' from his *An Almanac of Twelve Sports* (Heinemann, 1898). The principal figure is Alfred Mynn, who died in 1861; the wicket-keeper is labelled as Tom Lockyer, but the original was believed to represent Pinder or Edward Pooley

The Way Back

GRAHAM WHITE

For the benefit of those who dislike mysteries it seems only fair to mention, here and now, that this is not only a mystery, but one for which I can offer no fitting explanation.

I make no apology for this, for no one could have tried harder to provide one. Since that amazing evening, now nearly five years ago, I have turned the thing over in mind a hundred times, and still I can find no solution that fits all the facts.

Just a particularly vivid dream, you will say, no doubt, and sometimes I confess I am almost convinced myself.

Almost, but not quite.

For if it was a dream how is it that every detail remains as vivid today as it was when I sat in that pub, scratching my head in bewilderment for the first time? And then again. . . .

But I am merely irritating you with this preamble; let me begin at the beginning – the place, a quiet little lane off the main road to Petersfield; the time, half-past eight on as lovely a June evening as ever mellowed the rolling Hampshire countryside.

I know it was half-past eight, for as I rested on a gently sloping bank by the side of the lane, I heard the sound of a distant church clock sounding clearly across the quiet fields. I glanced at my watch, surprised to find the time had slipped past so quickly, and jumped hastily to my feet; I had planned to reach Broadha'penny before dusk – to get a good look at the old Down, and what seemed equally important, a pint or two of mild-and-bitter in the cheerful atmosphere of the historic Bat and Ball.

To the best of my knowledge, I had never approached Broadha'penny from that direction before, and not being at all sure of the way I was relieved, upon turning a sharp bend in the lane, to see not a hundred yards distant a little thatched cottage, at the gate of which stood an old man, watching my approach with idly curious eyes. He was a very old man, I noted as I drew closer, with a face as creased and lined as a walnut shell. A shapeless felt hat perched above his scanty grey locks, and a clay pipe hung bowl downward from the corner of his mouth.

'Am I right for Broadha'penny,' I enquired as I came abreast of him.

He nodded and withdrew his pipe.

'Ay, you can get this way, sir. Take the second turnin' to yer left and goo straight up. 'Twill bring ye right on to the Down.'

I thanked him and was about to pass on when he halted me with a gesture of his pipe, and spoke again.

'But – jest a minnit, sir. You baint goan' up there tonight, are ye?' he asked, and I thought I detected a note of anxiety, almost of apprehension, in his voice.

'Why, yes – I was,' I answered, curiously. 'Plenty of time to get up there before dusk, isn't there?'

He nodded again.

'Ay – plenty of time. But I wouldn't go up there tonight – not if I was you, sir.'

'But – why on earth not?' I persisted.

'Well, tes Midsummer's Eve, y'now!' he said at length. And then, noting my look of blank astonishment, he continued: 'Mind you, I ain't saying 'tis so and I ain't saying 'tisn't. But they do say there's queer goings on up on Broadha'penny, Midsummer's Eve. Somethin' to do with them old cricketers. Folks as've been up on the Downs've told me they seen 'em with their own eyes, playin' like they used 'undreds of years ago. Spooks, I reckon they be. 'Tis fer you to do as you please, but me, I wouldn't go up there tonight – no, not for a 'undred quid, I wouldn't, and that's a fact, sir!'

For a moment I suspected an elaborate leg-pull, but so obviously in earnest was the old fellow that it would have been churlish even to have appeared disbelieving. I thanked him non-committally, and continued on my way, rather delighted with the encounter.

Ghosts on Broadha'penny! Harris and Beldam, Barber and Hogsflesh, Nyren and Brett replaying the great matches of the past on mystic Midsummer's Eve. A local fable, of course, but what a lovely thing Barrie or E. V. Lucas might have written round such a theme.

'Silver Billy' cutting 'Lumpy' Stevens at the point of the bat, with the dense ring of Hampshiremen baying their immortal 'Go hard – tich and turn, tich and turn!' Or would a 'soundless, clapping host' be more in keeping?

Musing in this strain as I went along, I suddenly realised that I was paying no heed to the old man's instructions. Second on the left and straight up. Had I passed it, I wondered.

A little way ahead a narrower lane led off to the left. I looked down it and saw that it led up to a small wood. As I stood there, hesitating, I saw some distance down the lane, a tall figure with the gait of a countryman, swinging along in the direction of the wood. That decided me. I struck off down the lane at a brisk pace. If I was wrong, I told myself, I could always catch up the man in front and ask again.

In a few minutes I reached the wood, and followed the winding track through the trees. I kept up a good pace, anxious to keep within hailing distance of the stranger, should the necessity arise. And presently came the first signs that something strange was happening.

From the outside, the wood had appeared small, perhaps a quarter of a mile in depth, yet after five minutes' hard walking there appeared to be no immediate prospect of reaching the other side. And a few moments later another extraordinary thing struck me. The light was going; it was growing dark – at nine o'clock on Midsummer's Eve!

I was not exactly scared by these discoveries, but, I confess it, just a trifle uneasy. There was something decidedly eerie in the atmosphere of that wood – an indefinable something that made your scalp tingle, and I felt a distinct sense of relief when the path suddenly straightened, and I saw through the descending gloom the dim figure of the man who had entered the wood just before me. Almost without thinking I called out to him.

'I say, there – is this the way to Broadha'-penny?'

And back came the reply in the broadest Hampshire I have ever heard: 'Ay, that it be, sir. Ahm goan that way meself.'

He halted until I came up with him.

'Tes fuddlin' like, in this yer loight, sir,' he chuckled as we walked on. It was a comforting sound, that chuckle, for the light was now almost gone, and there was still in the air an inexplicable eeriness which made any sort of company welcome. The track, which now led steeply uphill, was hardly discernible, and I remarked upon the fact to my companion, wondering if he, too, had noticed this sudden transition.

'Ah, tes dark enough, sir,' he agreed. ''Twill lighten soon, though. We'm al but through the wood naow.'

And then – a casual but shattering afterthought.

'Tes early in the day for a gentleman to be about, sir!'

Early? I shot a quick glance at the dim figure beside me. Early? What on earth was the man talking about? But before I could pursue the subject further my attention was caught by something else – something near the ground. Something that shone and flickered in the gloom as my companion moved along. And then I saw.

Silver buckles!

'There y'are, sir, tes lightening areddy,' I dimly remembered him saying, but I made no reply: my gaze was still riveted on his shoes.

Silver buckles . . . and white stockings . . . knee-breeches and dark velvet cap! I could see them plainly now, and as swift realization dawned upon me I suppose I must have staggered from the shock.

Ghost or human, this was a Hambledon man! And it was no ghost, for even as the thought flashed through my mind, a powerful steadying hand shot out and grasped me by the elbow.

'Steady, sir. Mortal easy to turn an ankle on these yer ruts.'

A little unsteadily I muttered my thanks, and strove hard to collect my scattered wits. But a second or two later came another and final shock. For suddenly I discovered that I, too, had changed. Gone were my flannels, my old tweed coat and my brown brogues. In their place I was wearing a green, heavily embroidered coat with wide turn-back sleeves, knee breeches and heavy buckled shoes. A stock nestled beneath my chin, and when I raised a bewildered hand to my head I encountered, not the floppy brim of my comfortable old felt, but the stiff, unfamiliar shape of a tricorn hat! To describe adequately my feelings at that moment is beyond me, yet it is important that I make some endeavour. I do remember, for instance, that with this inexplicable change of clothing there came gradually a change of personality. Surprise gave way to the extraordinary sensation of being two different people at the same time. And on top of all this was the dim knowledge that I was at the beginning of something that, long, long ago, had happened before.

The wood was thinning now, and the light was growing stronger every moment. I glanced sideways at my companion, studied his regular, handsome features for a second or two, and instantly knew him.

'Why, heavens alive – aren't you Tom Sueter,' I found myself asking.

He nodded and smiled.

'Ay – that's me right enough,' he acknowledged, and the two people who were me studied him afresh – one with excited interest: the other with the bewildered amazement of one confronted by a miracle.

But gradually the old 'me' was receding into the background, becoming a mere unfeeling recorder of events, while my new personality took charge of the fantastic situation.

'Look – tes a fine sky,' announced Tom, pointing up through the trees. 'Like as not it'll be a great day for the match.'

And quite naturally I found myself replying, 'As it should be, Tom. A great day for a great game, eh? Shall we win d'ye think?'

He laughed, a deep musical laugh that was good to hear.

'Lord, sir – I wouldn't like to say about that. Cricket's a funny game, as you may well know. They're sendin' a good team against us, by all accounts, but I've a fancy we'll win with any luck, sir.'

By now a good deal was clear to me. I knew, for instance, that by some strange means I had accidentally stepped back in Time – stepped back nearly two hundred years – back to the days of Hambledon's greatness. Today Hambledon were meeting all England on Broad-ha'penny Down, and here was I walking up the now historic ground with Tom Sueter, the first wicket-keeper of all time. Who I was it never occurred to me to question; by now all my thoughts were centred on the forthcoming struggle.

'Harris is playing, I suppose?' I found myself asking.

'Ay,' responded Tom. 'What's more he'll be out on the Down by this time, makin' 'is wicket, if I'm not mistaken. A thorough man is David. No leaving things to chance with him. Ay, and there he goes, too – and young Nyren with 'im, by the looks of it.'

By now we had emerged from the wood, and the Down lay in front of us. There was little sign of life, but away to the left a plume of smoke issuing from the chimney of the 'Bat and Ball' indicated that others besides ourselves were already astir. And some distance from the inn two figures were moving across the dewy turf.

'That's them all right,' confirmed Tom. 'Come, sir, an' we'll see what David's got in store for 'em. Ah, but he's a knowin' one when it comes to pitching a wicket, is David.'

His eyes shone with honest admiration as he led me across the Down. As we approached closer I saw that the wickets had already been pitched – two low stumps, set wide apart and surmounted by a longer one. The two men were busily engaged in scooping out a small hole between the stumps, too absorbed in their task to notice our approach.

'Mornin', David – mornin', John!' sang out Tom Sueter when we were but twenty yards away. They looked up and returned his greeting. The older man, thick-set and of medium height, straightened himself, and immediately I recognized the plain, rugged, yet by no means unattractive features of David Harris, the greatest bowler in all England.

He acknowledged me with a touch of the forefinger to his forehead, and then gave his attention to Tom, who was striding up and down the pitch, scanning the rough, bumpy surface with expert eyes.

'A rare 'un, David,' was his verdict. 'She rises nice from that end, too. They'll not score many from you today, if I know anything about it.'

Young Nyren wiped his knife in the grass and joined in their deliberations, and, left to my own devices for a few moments, my eye fell upon a bat lying in the grass. I picked it up and examined curiously the black, twine-bound handle, and the strange curved blade, shaped rather like a primitive hockey stick. Almost without thinking I essayed a stroke or two. The bat was heavy, far heavier than any I had handled before. All right for hitting provided you were accustomed to the strange shape of the blade, I decided, but my attempt at a wristy square cut was laboured and clumsy.

'You have some acquaintance with the game, I see, sir,' observed a voice behind me. Turning, I found Harris regarding me with renewed interest.

A little embarrassed, I flushed and admitted that I had played before – once or twice.

'Then perhaps I may be permitted to send you down a ball or two,' he enquired. From his pocket he produced a ball – a leather ball, rather larger than its modern counterpart, it seemed, and with coarser stitching.

I hesitated, but curiosity overrode caution.

'I should be delighted, Mr Harris,' I replied, 'But I warn you I am a mere tyro at the game. It will be but poor practice for you, I fear.'

I moved to the far wickets, remembering Harris' preference for rising ground, while Tom Sueter, grinning amiably, took up his customary position behind the stumps, and young Nyren moved across to cover.

I was fairly trembling with nervousness as Harris paced out his run, and paused to mark the turf with his heel, yet there was one comforting thought at the back of my mind. Indifferent batsman though I was, I was facing Harris equipped with a batting technique evolved by batsmen over a period of nearly two hundred years. Surely I could not fail utterly?

Harris turned, faced me for a moment, raised the ball slowly to his forehead, rather after the fashion of a bowls player aiming his wood, took a step backward, and then ran up to the wicket.

The ball beat me completely. It was not fast, as we know fast bowling today, but its pace, coupled with the extraordinary method of delivery – the ball appeared to shoot at me from beneath Harris's armpit – found me so unprepared that it had flashed past me and smacked into Sueter's waiting hands almost before I had started my stroke.

Tom tossed the ball back, and Harris paced out his run again. I was better prepared for the second delivery, and by going right forward I managed to play the ball back to him along the bumpy turf. When I repeated the stroke off the next ball, he raised his eyebrows in faint surprise, and there was an encouraging grunt from behind the wicket.

'That's it sir. Get out to 'im!'

Harris bowled again. The same fastish, good length ball. No – not quite the same, I suddenly realized as I played mechanically forward. A shade shorter, the ball hit the turf, whipped up with astonishing quickness, and struck me hard on the back of my left hand. It was a painful blow, but fortunately I took it on the knuckles. A little higher and my fingers would have been ground against the handle of the bat. All contrition, Harris hurried down the wicket as I sucked my injured knuckles, but I made light of the incident and tossed the ball back to him. He apologized with every appearance of concern, but I fancied the corners of his mouth were twitching, as he turned away, a suspicion immediately confirmed by a remark from Tom.

'A beggar for rindin' em, is David,' he observed as I took guard again.

A little nettled, I edged out of my crease as Harris ran up again. Another good length one, but I sighted it early, jumped to the pitch of the ball, and drove it hard along the ground to cover, where Nyren fielded it expertly.

My success was short-lived, however, for the next, a masterpiece of flight and length, utterly defeated me and passed through the wickets. I did my utmost to give as good an account of myself as possible, but a few minutes later I was beaten again. The strangeness of the heavy, crooked bat, and the rough state of the pitch contributed to my downfall perhaps, but I doubt whether in any conditions I should have defied this man for long. A dozen balls were enough to convince me that here was a born bowler – a bowler who would have been great in any age. He bowled steadily, sending down hardly a loose ball, until I turned and offered the bat to Tom Sueter. He smilingly declined, as did the others.

'There'll be plenty o' play for us before the day is out,' prophesied Tom. 'A grand wicket, David; ye've seldom pitched a better. Well' a bite o' food and a drink'll do me, now.'

Together we moved off towards the distant 'Bat and Ball,' Harris, breathing a little heavily after his exertions, walking beside me.

'Your style is unusual, sir,' he observed as we went along,' but with teachin' and practice you would be a difficult man to beat. 'Tis mortal rash to leave your ground, though, if I may make so bold as to say it.'

'Ay, ye'd be a pretty batsman with experience,' confirmed Tom Sueter, 'and you dussent need take much heed o' David, sir. Reach in an' hit 'em away – tes the only way with him. An' better'n gettin' yer knuckles rinded!'

There was a general laugh, in which Harris joined, while I flushed like a schoolboy.

'A mug of ale'll go down well after that; thirsty work bowlin',' observed David Harris. 'An' we'll have it out here, I think. Too good a mornin' to be indoors. John' – he turned to Nyren as we reached the Bat and Ball – 'bring us out four mugs of ale, will you? You'll do us the honour of joinin' us, I hope, sir?'

I readily assented. A few moments later Nyren returned, bearing four mugs. Harris handed them round and raised his mug to me with a courteous nod.

'Here's to you, sir.'

'And here's to Hambledon,' I responded. 'I trust England will fare no better than I, Mr Harris.'

There was a general laugh, and I raised my mug and drank deep. It was the strongest ale I have ever tasted, yet smooth as milk. I drained my mug, only dimly aware of its potency, and called for another round. Nyren disappeared again, and we sat down on a bench overlooking the Down.

'Quiet now,' said Harris. 'It'll look a bit different in an hour or two, though. Ah, thank ye, sir. Your health.'

Nyren handed round the refilled mugs and we drank again. And now I was becoming aware of the ale's effect. My head was beginning to swim. When I spoke I was conscious of slurring consonants. I relapsed into silence, deeming it prudent to listen till the effects of the liquor had worn off a little.

I closed my eyes, and listened to the burring voices of Harris and Sueter, and the occasional interpolations of Nyren.

From a long way off came Tom Sueter's pleasant chuckle.

Ay, Sir Horace'll be cuttin' the daises with a will, before the day's out. 'Twill be a close match, you mark my words, David.' And that was the last thing I remembered.

You will not be in the least surprised to learn that when I awoke it was to find myself lying on the gently sloping bank from which I had risen as the clock struck the half-hour. The clock was still striking but when I sat up and looked at my watch I saw that it was now half-past nine.

I had been asleep I told myself, but even as the thought struck me doubts began to filter into my mind. Could all that have been no more than a dream? Dreams were muddled, chaotic experiences, as a rule, and this. . . .

And yet it must have been; what other explanation could there be, anyway?

A chill breeze blew across the meadows, galvanizing me into action. I jumped hastily to my feet and walked on down the lane, still turning over in my mind the fantastic experiences of the past hour. Yes, it was a dream all right, I decided, but what a dream! How crystal clear every detail of it remained in my memory.

And then, rounding a sudden bend in the road, I stopped dead in my tracks.

A hundred yards ahead stood a small thatched cottage. At the gate stood an old man – a very old man. His face was as lined and seamed as a walnut shell. A shapeless hat perched above his scanty white locks, and a clay pipe, bowl downward, hung from the corner of his mouth.

I passed him with averted eyes, too shaken to venture any enquiry.

A quarter of a mile further on I found the second turning on the left, but the wood, if there ever had been one, had vanished. The lane led straight up on to the Down, with scarcely a tree along its entire length. I passed on. It was now a quarter to ten; Broadha'penny would have to wait till the morrow, I decided. It was only a few minutes later that a little inn hove in sight. I entered the private bar, threw down a shilling and called for a pint of mild-and-bitter.

It was while waiting for the drink that I hit upon what seemed to be the only solution to my strange adventure. I must have come this way before, probably by car, and the old man had been standing at the gate of the cottage when I passed. And though I could not remember it, my subconscious mind had been at work while I dreamed. At any rate, the absence of the wood proved that it could not have been a real experience. And anyway, how else, except in a dream could I have found my way from the 'Bat and Ball' to that grassy bank by the wayside?

'Pint o' mild-and-bitter, sir!'

The landlord's voice broke in upon my thoughts. He slapped down the glass, picked up my shilling, and was about to turn to the till when he checked himself.

''Ullo, that's nasty, sir,' he observed solicitously. 'Like a drop of iodine?'

Following his gaze, I looked down – and found myself staring a little stupidly at the reddened, lacerated knuckles of my left hand.

From Cricket on Saturday (1947)

IV

The Modern Game
Cricket since 1945

'Cricket is always the memory
of cricket.'

*Brian Jones : Cricket
for Christmas*

Part of the crowd at Lord's, 21 June, 1963. West Indian supporters jump for joy as England's first innings closes for 297

Keith Miller

MIHIR BOSE

Even as the Australians took the field for the First Victory Match [in 1945] they were deeply pessimistic about their chances. Richard Whitington, who opened the innings in all five Victory Matches, wrote: 'In their hearts was a deep and haunting misgiving that they might all make fools of themselves'. But, largely owing to Miller, that was to be the last moment of Australian pessimism.

In the First Victory Match at Lord's, after England had made 267 on a 'green' pitch, Miller's 105 in 210 minutes (he hit only six fours and his one and only lofted shot produced a simple catch to Ames) was the core of the Australian reply. His allies were Hassett and Stan Sismey. These efforts were magnified by Stanford and Pepper, who put on 88 for the ninth wicket, resulting in a substantial lead. Then Cec Pepper, using his height to get considerable purchase for his finger spin, converted the lead into a dramatic six-wicket victory with Pepper himself hitting the winning run off the fourth ball of the last over just before seven o'clock.

Now the great transformation in Miller's career that was to lift it to another unsuspected plane was about to take place. Miller the opening bowler emerged.

It happened in the second innings of the Third Victory Match at Lord's. Australia were sixty behind and would be required to bat last; England were playing three schoolboys in the team – Dewes, White and Carr. In the first innings Miller, still No. 5 in the bowling, had taken the wickets of Dewes and Carr. There was also the unrelenting campaign of Bob Crisp – the South African fast bowler turned writer. He had successfully persuaded Miller to settle on a fifteen-yard run and he was determined to get him to open the bowling. So as Dewes came out to bat with Hutton, Hassett gave the new ball to Miller.

This remains one of the significant moments of his career. The pre-war testimonial match apart, he had never opened the bowling in a full-scale representative match. Before this Victory Match he had bowled 44 overs and taken three for 81. At Bramall Lane, in the Second Victory Match, which England won, his pace had impressed the players and enraged the spectators. Washbrook had been hit on the temple, Hutton on the forearm, and the Yorkshire crowd had shouted, 'Go off, Larwood.' Yet he had not been seriously considered as a fast bowler and even at Lord's, as we have seen, it was expediency that guided Hassett.

But whatever the motives, it paid dividends. Miller soon bowled Dewes with an out-swinger. For Dewes it was the start of a less than happy association. He was to become a regular Miller victim. As he told me, 'Miller was just too quick'. Miller took two more wickets, that of Edrich, breaking a threatening stand between him and Hutton, and later that of Pollard. The denizens of the Long Room echoed, in more suitable language, the opinion of the Bramall Lane: fastest since Larwood. In sixteen overs he took three for 42, Cristofani took five for 49, and England were all out for 164, leaving Australia to get 225 in 300 minutes. Miller made 71 not out – the highest Australian score of the match – in just under two hours and Australia won by four wickets.

Just before the fourth match, again at Lord's, Albert Cheetham, who had opened the bowling with Graham Williams, returned to Australia and Miller was confirmed as the regular opening bowler. But there was a problem. At Lord's, while fielding to his own bowling, he had strained a back muscle. From now on his bowling was always to be associated with his back. Over the years it was to cause him considerable pain and earn him snide references: whenever he was reluctant to bowl (and he often was) it was suggested that the real cause was not any physical problems but the Miller temperament.

It is possible that this was not as welcome a moment in Miller's career as is generally supposed. Increasingly his bowling affected his batting – in 1948, as we shall see, most crucially – and he never did recapture his 1945 form. But the argument cannot be resolved. He might have been a more consistent batsman had he never been a bowler, but then some of the most dramatic moments in Test cricket would have been lost.

In the fourth match the Australians were playing to a plan: to place England in a position where Hammond would have to take risks in order to win. In a three-day match the Australians made 388 in a day and a half, with Miller again making the most significant contribution. Using three bats and after overcoming the sharp in-swing of Pope, he made his second century in the series, appropriately in front of the newly elected prime minister, Clement Attlee. His 118 took just under three hours, and with Stan Sismey he put on 121 in two hours. It provided Australia with a valuable advantage. England would have to score heavily and quickly to win. England made 469 but not quickly enough. The plan succeeded and the match was drawn. Australia went into the last match at Old Trafford still leading 2–1.

This match was to see, probably, the most heroic Miller innings of the series. The ground, extensively damaged during the war, had been repaired by German prisoners of war at a cost of three-farthings an hour and the wicket had rolled out a green top. *Wisden* called it a 'natural wicket which encouraged the bowlers and, at times, gave them much assistance'. Hassett won the toss, batted and Australia had lost four wickets for 66 when Miller came in. For the next 135 minutes, while England, using only three bowlers – Pope, Pollard and Phillipson – removed the other six Australian batsmen, Miller made 77 not out while his other colleagues were adding 107 runs to the total. Only two other batsmen made double figures, both of them under 30.

Then, when England batted, Miller with sheer speed tried to right the advantage. He soon removed Fishlock but Hutton and Hammond held firm. The one solidly defensive, the other boldly venturesome saw England first to safety and then to a position from which victory was possible. England led by 70 in the first innings. But at last Miller failed: he made 4. Australia could leave England only 141 to win, and just before the Manchester rain clouds pressed home, England won by six wickets to square the series 2–2.

So at the end of his first series Miller headed the batting with an average of 63·29, his aggregate of 443 was the highest on either side, and his ten wickets were at a very respectable cost of 27 runs each. Outside the Victory Matches his batting displayed its richness in a variety of conditions. Amidst rainstorms and on a muddy Old Trafford pitch he made 52 out of 109 for the RAAF against Lancashire, the only half-century in the match. Against Voce – who took eleven wickets – and on a rain-affected Nottingham wicket he made 81 not out (with two sixes), the highest score of the match between Nottinghamshire and the Australian Services. And on a Sheffield green-top where Bowes took four for 48 he made 111, thrice hitting Booth, the Yorkshire spinner, into the pavilion. None of his colleagues in the Australian Services side passed 30; only Hutton with 111 replied for Yorkshire. Yet Miller's most memorable feat was still to come.

Towards the end of the season England played the Dominions at Lord's. There was cricket diplomacy before the match. Hassett fell ill and a captain had to be found. Constantine, the senior international cricketer, was the natural choice. But this was a Dominions team with Australians, South Africans and New Zealanders in the side, and a black West Indian as captain appeared revolutionary. Sir Pelham Warner went to the dressing-room just before the match. He spoke of Constantine's seniority, the position of the cricket world, the importance of the match; he sensed a slight hesitation, then a senior member of the team agreed. Immediately everybody fell in line and

Constantine got a great reception from the Lord's crowd.

The match itself provided a fitting climax to the season. 1,241 runs were scored in three days: there was a century by Donnelly, two by Hammond, but Miller played probably the greatest single innings of this period. It started on the evening of the second day, Miller finishing with 61 not out, having hit a six to the top tier of the pavilion. Then, on the morning of the third day, came cricket that moved even Sir Pelham Warner to awe. 'In an experience of first-class cricket of nearly sixty years I have never seen such hitting.'

The bare statistics are inspiring. In ninety minutes he scored 124 runs and, at one stage, in three-quarters of an hour he and Constantine put on 117 runs. On a ground that measures 188 yards by 144 yards he hit six more sixes. One of them carried to Block Q on the right of the pavilion and another landed on the small roof of the broadcasting box above the England players' dressing-room. A. E. R. Gilligan was in the box:

> The hit came up over mid-on, rising all the time as it came. On hitting the pavilion it fell into a hole that had been made in the roof of the commentary box by shrapnel and the ball had to be poked out by a stick.

This hit very nearly equalled Albert Trott's record of hitting M. A. Noble, the Australian bowler, over the pavilion, Miller falling short by two feet. Later, experts were to reckon that had the match been played on the more traditional pitch – it was played on an adjoining one with a slightly longer carry – then Miller might have equalled the record. But for Miller 'nearly equal' sounds more appropriate.

Yet this was no indiscriminate hitting. The pedigree of his stroke-

When Keith Miller played, something always seemed to happen. Here he makes an acrobatic catch to dismiss Hardstaff at Nottingham, 1948

play was unquestioned – in the opinion of many it rivalled Hammond – and his command of the bowling quite exceptional. The principal English sufferers were Wright and Hollies, and Miller's 185 was made out of a score of 336 in which only four of his colleagues reached double figures. It also formed the basis of a narrow Dominions victory.

The innings confirmed all the earlier good notices. In English eyes he was established as the 'discovery' of the war years. ... English critics were particularly impressed by his style: it was so peculiarly English. It was based on forward play, crowned with that most supreme of cricket strokes, the drive. His repertoire was extensive. He had a thrilling cut, embellished at times with, for such a huge frame, a very delicate late cut. He played shots on both sides of the wicket but it was the drive, particularly the cover-drive played from an authoritative, upright stance, that was to become his signature tune. Yet his tendency to lunge forward did get him into trouble. Often he lunged so far forward that he overbalanced and fell. Over the years Miller's batting was to change in only one respect: he discarded the hook. And the man who was intimately associated with bumpers was often uncomfortable against them. 'Miller cut rather an inept figure himself against the bouncer. He didn't like them,' as Fingleton wrote years later. But that came much later.

Now Miller was established as the great contemporary hero – that is not too strong a word. It was a happy fusion of technical eloquence and distinctive physical attributes, one in particular: his hair. All cricketers exhibit mannerisms but Miller's hair, and what he managed to do with it, became so intimately associated with his cricket that even in retrospect it is difficult to separate it from his play. It was dark and, for the period, long. It seemed to be everywhere: falling over his face as he batted, tossing in the air as he ran up to bowl. Every now and again he would sweep it back with an elaborate gesture. This, in the final analysis, set his cricket following apart from that of his contemporaries. For young boys he was something out of *Boy's Own* paper, the one cricketer likely to sustain fantasy. The weight of the applause probably never matched Bradman's but the shrillness revealed the anticipatory thrill. For young girls there was his undoubted sexual appeal: they would send him letters, offer him chewing gum (he was an addict by now) and follow his every move. At that time, no doubt, some of his gestures, like tugging at his sleeve as he went out to bat or scanning the sky for aeroplanes as he fielded, were signs of nervousness – he was still unused to crowd adulation – but later they were to become deliberate instruments of crowd control. And like all good and genuine heroes he encountered disapproval: hair clips through the post.

The Golden Boy had emerged, and Nugget was to be his nickname for the rest of his carrer.

From *Keith Miller: A Cricketing Biography* (1979)

Indian Summer, 1946
Merchant's Technique and Mankad's Action

JOHN ARLOTT

V. M. Merchant

His 148 at Lord's v MCC was not Vijay Merchant's highest innings of the 1946 tour, but it was his richest. The air held rain and little light of sun, yet English as the setting was, this Indian batsman showed us there his best. I knew how anxious he was to make a hundred that day and I was amazed to see his stroke-play flowering under his anxiety.

Merchant's physical quality is neither the massive might nor the whipcord leanness of other great batsmen. There is something softly feline about him – at the wicket, shirt and sweater heavy to wrists, thick white muffler at his throat, blue-capped, he moves pad-footed – but the stroke, for all its control, is flash-fast because, ignoring the bowler's hand, he plays every ball strictly 'off the pitch'. An innings by Merchant grows: it sprouts no exotic blooms, but its construction is perfect to the last detail. No chance, no ball which beats the bat, no brutishness of the wicket, no pace or spin or swing can disconcert him: like Herbert Sutcliffe, until he is finally and definitely out, Merchant is the batsman in possession, intent upon tending his, and his team's, score. Day after day, season-long, I watched him, notching off each hour with thirty runs and marking the meal intervals with his cap – when the peak is directly over his right ear it is time for lunch or tea or the close of play.

Not only was he the mainstay of the team's batting in terms of the runs he made himself, but often he nursed the start of a big innings by Modi or Mankad or Hazare, each of whom batted better in his company.

Merchant's batting technique is never violent, he seems to have an unvarying system of ball-valuation which controls his batting reflexes. Bowl an over of balls two feet short of a length and he will hit you for six certain fours to mid-wicket on the leg side: bowl a good-length over on the middle stump and he will play you back a maiden: and this holds good whether his score is 0 or 100. But it is not to say that he cannot, or does not, adjust his batting to the state of the game. If the state of the wicket reasonably permits it, he will start to cut when he has made about fifty, and his cut is the finest in first-class cricket today: more rarely he will use a whiplash cover-drive. Merchant's soundness is vividly illustrated by his methods of dismissal during the tour. He was most frequently dismissed LBW, the in-swinger which straightened off the pitch. That ball is the one for which the seam bowler prays – he can but pray, for no man alive can bowl it at will: that rare, providential delivery came to be regarded as Merchant's weakness – since no deliberately contrived ball could be relied upon consistently to worry him. Merchant, as batsman, captain and man, is well pictured in an incident in the match against the South of England at the Hastings Festival. He was captain of the side, in the absence of Pataudi. On the third day he was in considerable pain from strained stomach-muscles. Believing that changes in the batting order often unsettle batsmen, he decided to go in first as usual, but to get out fairly quickly. Once at the crease he scored at twice his usual pace, but by the same strokes: his deeply absorbed batting-sense allowed him to take a risk only in making the ball into a punishable one, but not in playing it. On his dismissal he returned to the pavilion in increased pain, to shake his head sadly at his inability to sacrifice his wicket.

Vinoo Mankad

His rebellious, straight black hair gleaming, laughter richly present in his deep-set eyes, he bustles powerfully through his short run and bowls with a thick left arm – the orthodox left-hander's spinner leaving the bat, or, when least expected and with no chance of action, the ball that goes with his arm. And, the ball bowled, he is tense to scamper to mid-on or mid-off to stifle the single at conception. Give him the ball, for he wants to bowl again, his over will last little more than a minute and he has so much to do. There is no time for expressions of regret or surprise or disappointment, there are many ways of dismissing a man and he will try them all. Throw a bail-high full-toss, or the spinner, tossed higher but pitching no further up, the in-swinger at almost medium-pace, or spin to a length and watch –but never become automatic, never bowl the aimless ball, never let the batsman rest. And Vinoo Mankad never allows a batsman to rest.

From *Indian Summer* (1947)

Even Bradman had battles to fight

ALEC BEDSER

When I went to Australia in 1946–7 my background was restricted to two years of apprenticeship at The Oval, one full season with Surrey and three Tests against India. County cricket in 1946 was made up of teams of old stagers and young hopefuls, and though I could count my successes against India I knew I was in for a far tougher examination in Australia. It was perhaps as well that the gulf between Australia and England was not realized. So eager was the feeling to resume Tests between the two oldest rivals that little thought was given to the fact that England was ill-equipped for such a venture. The elderly party had an average age of thirty-three, and only Godfrey Evans,

Denis Compton, Jack Ikin and myself were under thirty. There were occasions when I felt I was an unarmed David facing a whole team of Goliaths.

In a different sense Bradman was also feeling his way after a war-time illness severe enough for him to be invalided out of the army. At one point he was hardly able to shave himself, and the general impression was that if he had failed in the first Test against England at Brisbane he would have retired. Only the bowlers and close-to-the-wicket fielders appreciated how near he was to being out on more than one occasion. Yet he clung tenaciously to his innings, and he taught me that even Bradman had battles to fight. To get to the top was one thing, to stay there another, and the only modern sporting comparison I can suggest as the equal of Bradman in dedicated resolve is the South African golfer Gary Player. Bradman had enough difficulty in his first fifty to have tempted a less determined man to concede defeat. Even so the history of two momentous series might have been altered if Bradman had been given out when he was twenty-eight caught at second slip by Ikin off Bill Voce. From my position at short leg I thought it was a fair catch. The delivery was a widish half-volley, and evidently both The Don and the umpire believed the ball scraped the end of the bat and on to the ground before it flew to Ikin. There are still arguments about the justice of the decision, but gradually the real Bradman began to emerge and he ended with 187 and the door wide open for him to carry on for the remainder of the series and on to England in 1948.

Looking back I have to acknowledge that my career would have been infinitely poorer had Bradman bowed out at Brisbane. The more I bowled to him the more I learned, and I would have been denied my most satisfying moment when I was able to produce at Adelaide in 1947 what Bradman sportingly described as the best ball he had ever received. That success was to boost my morale and status, and I was soon to take his wicket in five successive Test innings, including three by the same method. The Yorkshire writer J. M. Kilburn in his book *Cricket Decade* wrote: 'To suggest because of these conquests Bedser was Bradman's master would be to approach the ridiculous, but the moments are not likely to be forgotten by either Bedser or Bradman.'

I would be the last to claim any so-called 'mastery' – an altogether too extravagant thought – but I still savour the compliment The Don paid to me when he said that in certain conditions I was the most difficult bowler he had ever faced. No bowler could wish for more.

The manner of three of the five dismissals, caught by my faithful ally Len Hutton at backward short leg, provoked endless discussion and speculation. One school of thought insisted that the sequence was evidence of Bradman's decline – that it would never have happened in his earlier years. But such an assertion cannot be proved or disproved. All I can say is that the actual method of dismissal did not come about by accident. Also, as far as I know, I was the first to use it which meant that it was new to The Don, either before or after the war. I am still asked if I found a chink in a hitherto impenetrable

armour, or whether it was 'just one of those things'.

But there was a plan. It was based on an accurate full-length delivery on the off stump, my knack of being able to make the ball swing in to the batsman late in flight, Bradman's well-practised habit of searching for a first run with a push to mid-wicket, and the fact that he knew all about my inswinger and leg cutter. The inswinger, I might add, was often despised in English cricket at the time. I agree with this opinion if bowled at the leg stump but the line of the off stump is quite different.

Norman Yardley, who had succeeded Wally Hammond as captain, and I planned to have two forward short legs, instead of the usual one, in the hope of blocking a single to the mid-wicket area. If nothing else, we figured, it might prevent Bradman from getting off the mark with his customary speed, and perhaps (surely a forlorn hope) upset the rhythm of his innings.

More importantly a third fielder was put in an orthodox catching position at an angle of forty-five degrees at backward short leg for the inswinger. The plan was linked to the lessons of the 1946–7 tour, starting with MCC's fixture with South Australia before the first Test. Hammond decided I was not to be 'shown' to Bradman, and when he batted I had John Bradman, then aged seven, on my knee in the dressing-room. Dick Pollard, the Lancashire medium-pace bowler, was managing to keep Bradman relatively quiet with three short legs, but the full significance of the field placings escaped me at the time. Hammond with his vast experience should have been alerted to the tactical possibilities the field presented.

My own inexperience was soon to overtake me. In the Brisbane Test Bradman, still in single figures, lobbed a ball which lifted a little into a vacant space where a short leg ought to have been positioned. In fact my leg-side field was not used until the fourth Test at Adelaide where there was a second important development for me. The first had come at Sydney in the second Test when, opening the bowling against Sid Barnes, I discovered by sheer accident that I could cut the ball from leg to the off side – the leg cutter. As I realized only too well that Barnes knew all about my inswinger I tried to deceive him by stopping the movement of the ball. The design was for the ball to hold its course and go straight through. Allan Peach, the former Surrey player, had taught me how to stop the inswinger with the new ball by holding the ball across the seam. I was able to do this, and instead of the ball moving in to Sid as he had expected, it went away from him off the pitch. His consternation matched my inner surprise and satisfaction.

After looking at the pitch with suspicious disbelief he stared at me and exploded: 'What the hell's going on?' I realized from that point I could add the leg cutter to my armoury. My aim was now to *spin* the ball at speed.

Getting The Don's wicket at Adelaide was the turning point of my career. It came with my ninth delivery to him, and he was good enough to say it was the finest ever bowled to him. He described it as starting on the off stump, swinging late to hit the pitch on the leg stump and finally coming back to take the middle and off. I cannot have ever bowled a deadlier ball. One surprise on that evening was that Bradman went in to bat only ten minutes before the close of play. Lady Jessie and John were leaving the ground to avoid the rush, when they heard a mighty roar from the crowd. Later Jessie told me that the noise had prompted John to say to her: 'I suppose that's Dad hitting another four.'

In the second innings I all but bowled The Don first ball. He played forward, failed to make contact, and his off stump was missed by a coat of paint. My compensation for what would have been the unique feat of getting him out for a 'pair' was that he possibly had some respect for my bowling. He also knew I could make the ball move from leg to off, as well as the inswinger.

Such was the background to our duel in English conditions in 1948. The plan was hatched and I was keen to put it to the test. With two forward short legs and Hutton at backward short it was imperative to bowl a full-length ball *either on or just outside the off stump* if it was to have a chance of success. A popular fallacy at the time was that I attacked the leg stump. Not so at all. The ball, directed at the off stump, made pad-play as a second line of defence far too dangerous. I knew that if I could be accurate with my direction and length Bradman would be forced to offer a stroke, and, what was most important, be induced to play forward. Forced forward into a half-cock position even Bradman would have no control over the direction of the ball if it swung late into him. Hopefully any snick would go to backward short leg which, in fact, it did on three successive occasions.

In passing I ought to stress that the ball does not always do the expected. If it does not swing or cut, the batsman is as much deceived as the bowler is gratefully surprised. There are times when the action alone induces movement. As a variation I sometimes tried to hold the course of the ball which was an extra hazard for the batsman looking

Film sequence of one of the most beautiful of fast-bowling actions — Lindwall

for movement. I firmly believe in the fundamentals of a full length and straightness. A full length causes the batsman to think whether he has to go forward or back, and allows the full development of swing and cut. The best ball ever bowled is less likely to take a wicket unless it is straight, and it is inviting disaster against Australians not to bowl a full length on the off stump. Too many bowlers pitch short because they are afraid of being hit in front of the wicket, and for a reason not clear to me there are some who consider it a 'loss of face' if they have a mid-off.

Would Bradman have dealt with my methods in a different way a decade earlier? There is no way of finding out, but my respect for him is such that I cannot believe he had a weakness which he could not have overcome. Or that, had he set his mind to the problem, he could not have conquered wet pitches. The late Hedley Verity, the one spin bowler who should have known, would have none of the oft-repeated contention that Bradman was only a good-wicket batsman. Bad pitches in Australia are so bad that it is usually futile to try and devise a successful counter technique. There is a sound theory that in trying to do so, normal, natural timing is upset. Basically Bradman was a marvellous games player, and reached high standards at lawn tennis, squash and golf. Whatever the challenge in sport, business, writing or cricket administration The Don excelled if he put his amazing powers of concentration to the task at hand, and I cannot accept that there was anything in batting technique beyond him. Contrary to some opinion I believe he was primarily an orthodox batsman, at least in the sense that he had all the fundamental priorities exactly right.

As a bowler I knew I had a chance if I saw a slanting bat used in defence. Bradman's defensive bat was as straight as it could be – almost puritanically orthodox. He always made full and brilliant use of the crease, his movements with his small feet were quick, precise and ordered. Co-ordination of movement and his razor-sharp brain reached perfection. He attacked with all the recognized strokes on both sides of the wicket, and he improvised with all the confidence and skill of a virtuoso. His grip with both hands turned over the handle, which rested on the ball of his right thumb, meant he was unsurpassed with the hook and pull strokes. The bat turned over the ball with his famous roll, and the ball was kept religiously on the ground. It was claimed his grip reduced the power of his driving, but he had only to make a slight adjustment to drive profitably. Like all the finest batsmen he would not be tied to defence if he could possibly avoid it; his whole philosophy was based on domination from start to finish; he had all the strokes – which almost goes without saying – and the will and nerve to crush a bowler's heart. If, as it is often claimed, cricket is a game of mental attitudes then The Don had a league start, and I wonder how many bowlers failed to do themselves justice merely because he was at the other end? Ruthless? Well, if so, the same can be said of all heavy scorers. Bradman's job was to score as many as he could for his side and to play to win. He played hard and fairly, but I suppose the very nature of his successes inevitably aroused jealousies.

While I can understand the tardy acceptance of Bradman by the late Sir Neville Cardus, whose aesthetic eye searched for elegance, I am surprised Maurice Tate and others in Australia in 1928–9 forecast difficulties for Australia's young champion in English conditions. Unless he straightened his bat later in his career Bradman, as I have already stressed, was technically perfect in defence. Also, what could not have perceptibly changed was his amazingly quick footwork and eye and masterful back play. Bowlers were left with no possible margin of error, for anything short was murderously cut or pulled. Given the chance he would readily use that lethal pull the first ball he received, as Surrey discovered at The Oval in 1948. Stuart Surridge, Surrey's enthusiastic skipper, was the bowler, and that admirable all-rounder Jack Parker was at short leg. Surridge pitched short and before Jack had time to move the ball had hit the fence. Bradman mostly struck his pull square of the wicket, the power was incredible, and the ball hardly ever left the turf. One sign of his control was the absence of uppish shots, and one of his dictums was: 'If you hit the ball on the ground there's less chance of getting out.' How disarmingly simple it sounds.

If genius is the art of doing the simple things properly Bradman was a classic example. While lesser players tend to create complications, or theorise themselves towards a state of mental exhaustion, Bradman knew precisely what he intended to do, and went his way with the minimum of fuss. He always kept his score moving. I would glance at the scoreboard thinking he had been tolerably contained, and be surprised to see how quickly he had progressed. He always ran the first run as fast as he could, and expected to get two to third man. While the average batsman would look for no more than a single The Don aimed to get two. Pressure was at once put on the fielder, and looking up he might fumble or throw wildly and end by conceding an extra run. Pressure was put on the field as well as the bowler. As expected The Don's placing was superb and produced a non-stop flow of singles and twos. When I first played against him I was taken aback by his speed between the wickets even at the end of a long and arduous innings. Even the fittest tend to wilt in their running after a tiring day, but Bradman was every bit as quick and active at the end as the begining of an innings. No matter where the field was set Bradman refused to be tied down, and he still found gaps with consummate ease. I was astonished to see that with a slight and subtle change of grip he would alter the angle from which the ball left the bat. His placements amounted to an exact science, and were a constant source of concern to me, particularly before I had learned where to set my field. A bowler can easily be rattled by the steady seepage of singles, and I think Bradman enjoyed his battle of wits with the field. Once he and I were discussing David Sheppard (long before he became the Anglican Bishop of Liverpool) and Bradman made this perceptive comment: 'It's easy to set a field for him as he hits the half-volley on the off stump to mid-off. He should try and miss sometimes.'

Once The Don was set he manipulated the field like a master

puppeteer. He was so quickly into position with those tiny feet (at least by my standard!) of his that he could change his stroke with impunity. When going down the wicket to slow bowling he always got close enough to make sure the ball was between his legs at the moment of contact with the bat. Thus he remained perfectly balanced and co-ordinated, and avoided that dreaded unbalanced stretch which lands even good batsmen in trouble against spin. To watch Bradman handle the leg-breaks and googlies of the late Peter Smith was an education. Though he was inclined to be a bundle of nerves on the big occasion Smith was a very able spinner with a deceptive late dip in flight. If Bradman found the ball dipping as he was making an attacking shot he would still go through with his shot but, unlike so many other batsmen, would be content with a single or two instead of his intended boundary. His adjustment was made calmly and with complete control.

When making his famous pull shot he sometimes had two distinct movements with his left leg which would finish behind the leg stump. The crease was his territory to be used to maximum advantage much in the same way as Mohammed Ali used the ropes in the ring. I commend every batsman, young or old, to study old films of Bradman in action. They would marvel at his use of the crease, the speed and certainty of his footwork, and perhaps absorb the truth that intelligent attack is the best form of defence.

Before I went to Australia I heard many contradictory stories about him. I was determined to take him as I found him. I can truthfully say I have never found him anything but a thoughtful, kind and considerate friend and a hard but fair opponent.

From *Cricket Choice* (1981)

Dudley Nourse — a punchy stroke to leg by a big man light on his feet

Godfrey Evans –
Max Miller of the Cricket Scene

TREVOR BAILEY

Godfrey Evans was, quite simply, the finest wicket-keeper I have seen. At his very best he was capable of making catches and stumpings which no other man would have considered chances. An instance of this occurred in the Test trial at Bradford when Jim Laker ran riot to the tune of eight wickets for two runs. Don Kenyon moved back to a ball that turned and lifted unpleasantly. He played it down and Godfrey managed to catch it one-handed, a full length *in front* of the batsman and equally astonished short legs. I was one of these and had not even moved! On another occasion during a Scarborough Festival match, Billy Sutcliffe glanced a delivery from Alec Bedser wide, off the full face of the bat. Godfrey, as usual standing up to Alec, anticipated, took off and caught the ball one-handed while literally horizontal.

Like so many great players, Godfrey thrived on the big occasion, and it is fair to say that he was normally a better keeper for England than for Kent. For it is not possible to turn in superlative performances every day of the week as a wicket-keeper.

The central figure in the field must always be the man behind the stumps. Not only does he have the opportunity to make more catches than anyone else, but he delivers the *coup de grâce* in the majority of run outs, and he is also responsible for the stumpings. He can transform the whole appearance of the fielding side, camouflaging the poorer returns and adding colour to the proceedings. He is the hub around which the remainder of the team revolves and Godfrey revelled in all this. His bubbling enthusiasm also did much to keep his team going, especially towards the end of a long, hot, unsuccessful day in the field. He was a tonic with his 'We only need two more wickets tonight and we're through them', even though the score at that particular juncture was 330 for 2!

I have played over fifty Test matches with Godfrey Evans and consider the 1950–1 series in Australia his most outstanding. I cannot remember him putting down a catch, or missing a single stumping in five Test matches, while in addition he made a number of 'impossible' catches, especially off Alec Bedser. Godfrey's keeping helped Alec Bedser enormously, and one catch full length down the leg side which dismissed a plainly hypnotized Neil Harvey from a glance off the face of the bat, will always be with me. . . .

What was the secret of his success? Apart from sheer ability and a superb eye, it was very largely a matter of vitality. Many people can be brilliant for a short period of time, but it takes a very exceptional person to be just as full of life and just as spectacular an hour before the close of play on a really hot day at Adelaide after five successive sessions in the field. The fact that Godfrey Evans was a born entertainer who welcomed the limelight, and possessed a flair for the spectacular and the audacious, not only made him a universal favourite with spectators; it acted also as a spur to the fielders to maintain the standard he set himself.

In two respects Godfrey was fortunate. He was able to take a swift nap and awake refreshed under the most difficult circumstances. On numerous occasions I have seen him come in at lunchtime, have a drink and then curl up and go to sleep, completely oblivious to the noise of a dressing-room. The other reason underlying his success was his ability to dismiss instantly from his mind any mistake he might make. Many wicket-keepers spend five minutes apologizing for a dropped catch and the rest of the day bemoaning that particular blunder. This may be understandable, but it does not help when the next chance comes along.

Very occasionally he did have a bad day. His worst was at Leeds in 1948 against the Australians, when they turned defeat into victory with a large second innings score on a worn wicket as chance after chance went down. From a purely personal angle I shall remember him dropping Neil Harvey at Manchester. Neil had just come to the crease and managed to get an outside edge. It travelled sweetly to Godfrey, standing back, who was throwing it and appealing when down it went. Throughout Neil's hundred I was haunted by that moment, but not Godfrey. . . .

[As a batsman] Godfrey was at his best in a swashbuckling attacking role, for his defence was never sound. He liked to hit hard and often – in addition to the normal strokes he became particularly adept at a shovel shot with which he used to scoop the ball out towards mid-wicket, using plenty of right hand – and to scamper enthusiastically between the wickets. His running was a tonic to the spectators, the fieldsmen, and certainly not least to his partner. He introduced a note of genuine comedy, but never forgot the importance of the stolen single or the advantage to be gained by backing up.

The most significant partnership I had with Godfrey was against the West Indies in 1950 at Old Trafford. The pitch was one of the worst I have ever encountered, a broken beach on which Eric Hollies made the odd delivery rear shoulder high, as well as turn, and the English batting collapsed against the spin combination of Ramadhin and Valentine. When the 'Cheeky Chappie' joined me we were in serious trouble with all the accredited players back in the pavilion and less than 100 runs on the board. Godfrey was completely undeterred. He cut and carved with such impunity that he not only scored a remarkable century, but together we managed to make the record stand for that particular wicket. Before the end the West Indians were not sure where to bowl. England consequently regained command and went on to record our one victory of the series.

The most satisfying boundary Godfrey Evans ever struck was against the Australians at Adelaide. With only four runs required to win the game and the Ashes I foolishly lost my wicket. In he went, smote the ball to the mid-wicket pickets, and the champagne was waiting for him by the time he returned to the pavilion.

From *The Greatest of My Time* (1968)

Roy Ullyett's cartoon of Godfrey Evans, a wicket-keeper of such unquenchable enthusiasm that he could hold a flagging team together

Victory Calypso, Lord's 1950

EGBERT MOORE

('Lord Beginner')

Cricket, lovely cricket,
At Lord's where I saw it;
Cricket lovely cricket,
At Lord's where I saw it;
Yardley tried his best
But Goddard won the test.
They gave the crowd plenty fun;
Second Test and West Indies won.

Chorus   With those two little pals of mine
Ramadhin and Valentine.

The King was there well attired,
So they started with Rae and Stollmeyer;
Stolly was hitting balls around the boundary,
But Wardle stopped him at twenty.
Rae had confidence,
So he put up a strong defence;
He saw the King was waiting to see,
So he gave him a century.

Chorus: With those two little pals of mine
Ramadhin and Valentine.

West Indies first innings total was three-twenty-six.
Just as usual,
When Bedser bowled Christiani
The whole thing collapsed quite easily,
England then went on,
And made one-hundred-fifty-one;
West Indies then had two-twenty lead,
And Goddard said, 'That's nice indeed.'

Chorus: With those two little pals of mine
Ramadhin and Valentine.

Yardley wasn't broken-hearted
When the second innings started;
Jenkins was like a target
Getting the first five into his basket.
But Gomez broke him down,
While Walcott licked them around:
He was not out for one-hundred and sixty-eight,
Leaving Yardley to contemplate.

Chorus: The bowling was super-fine
Ramadhin and Valentine.

West Indies was feeling homely,
Their audience had them happy.
When Washbrook's century had ended,
West Indies' voices all blended.
Hats went in the air.
They jumped and shouted without fear;
So at Lord's was the scenery
Bound to go down in history.

Chorus: After all was said and done,
Second Test and West Indies won!

Port-of-Spain, Trinidad. In the centre, the Savannah, where thirty games of cricket could take place simultaneously

Barbadian Heroes

E. W. SWANTON

Barbados is a small island, pear-like in shape, the most easterly of that long straggling chain of islands which together form the West Indies. It is far from the largest of them, nor has it the most inhabitants, though it is, I think, the most densely populated. Still, a quarter of a million is not a lot. In English terms it has roughly the population of Coventry, just as in size it compares with the Isle of Wight. Yet in terms of cricket it looms like a giant, its players giving both the backbone and the inspiration to one generation of the West Indies teams after another. . . .

Not least important in the evolution of Barbadian cricket has been the personality as well as the skill of the chief performers. Sir Harold Austin brought early West Indian teams to England, a man of great substance on the island, an excellent cricketer and indeed by all repute for the first quarter of the century its uncrowned king. Of him I cannot write first-hand, but of the other Barbadian hero of his generation I just can, for it happens that the visit of the first West Indian team to play Test matches in England, that of 1928, coincided with my modest emergence as a cricket writer. George Challenor then, at forty, was past his best, and could not quite match his batting five years earlier when with 1,556 runs in the summer he emerged third in the English averages. But even to this youthful, untutored eye, he was a player of pedigree, an off-side stroke-maker in the classical tradition.

As C. L. R. James has pointed out, the development of West Indian cricket is unintelligible unless it begins with the batting of Challenor. Coming to England as a boy of eighteen in Austin's side of 1906 he absorbed the methods of the golden age of batsmanship: of Ranji and Fry in their heyday, of MacLaren, Johnny Tyldesley, Spooner and Jackson. Back home Challenor developed his own play on the lines of the masters, founded indeed a school of his own. To quote James once more, George Headley recalls Challenor's play against MCC on a wet wicket at Bridgetown as late as 1930, when at the other end to Derek Sealy he showed that young man how to play Rhodes and Voce. As a schoolmaster at Combermere he taught and influenced Frank Worrell, upon whose style, more than any other, modern West Indian batsmanship is based. Thus the influence of Challenor persists today.

But it is time to move on, and we must take a big leap through the thirties, which was not a specially rich period in Barbadian cricket even if one recalls several good players who toured England at that time, and notably, besides Sealy, the fast bowlers, Herman Griffith and 'Manny' Martindale.

When G. O. Allen's team sailed for the West Indies at the turn of the year in the third post-war winter of 1947–8 their landfall, as it should be for all touring teams, was Barbados. In due course we had our first sight of the excellent Kensington field with its modest pavilion, the thick palm grove at one end, the solid new Challenor Stand at the other, the long, white concrete walls forming the sight-screens which, with the hard, true pitches and the clearest light from pale blue skies, help to make a batting paradise. John Goddard, the Barbados captain, called up a strong, stocky young fellow just going out to have a net, and said, 'This is Everton Weekes. We hope he'll make a few runs against you.' Thus I met my first member of the trinity of Ws destined so soon to burst upon the world of cricket. Frank Worrell was twenty-three when this first post-war West Indian series took place, Weekes was twenty-two, Clyde Walcott twenty-one. There was in fact a little less than eighteen months between the oldest and the youngest, and all three were born within very short range of the Kensington ground. They are hard to separate in point of skill and achievement, different though their physiques and methods have been. Here, for instance, are their respective batting figures in Test cricket:

	Innings	T.NO	Runs	Highest	Average	Hundreds
Walcott	74	7	3,978	220	56·68	15
Weekes	81	5	4,455	207	58·61	15
Worrell	87	9	3,860	261	49·48	9

If Worrell's batting has been just a little less prolific it is no doubt because he played less frequently against the weaker countries. Six of his nine hundreds were made against England, another against Australia. He was also a left-arm swing bowler good enough to take 69 wickets in Test cricket, while Walcott apart from his batting had

65 victims as a wicket-keeper. In performance they cannot decently be divided though Frank's triumphs as a captain set him apart....

The trio are associated so inevitably as household names today one had almost forgotten that but for that little bit of luck which even great sportsmen need the three might just possibly have been two with Everton trailing quite a long way in the rear. His captain's hope that he might make 'a few runs' against us in 1947–8 was literally accurate until, having played in the first three Tests, he squeezed into the last of the four because someone fell out through injury and therein made his first hundred for the West Indies. Later the same year he went to India, getting hundreds in his first four Test innings, so making a world record with five in a row. But for a run-out when he had scored 90 it would in all likelihood have been six. From that point he never looked back, but if chance had not given him his last opportunity against England on 'Gubby' Allen's tour he might not have been chosen for India.

Everton's only other set-back, if such it could be called, was his eclipse in the Tests in Australia of 1951–2, but in that he went on playing with a damaged thigh that only rest could cure it is an episode that redounds to his credit rather than otherwise. Fortitude was always a great element in his play and I have little doubt that of all his innings he is proudest of the 90 against England on the fiery Lord's wicket of 1957 when he finally emerged bruised and battered from head to toe. It was this same groggy limb that led to his retiring first of the three. Whereas Clyde played last for the West Indies in 1960, Frank in 1963, Everton did not offer himself for Test selection after 1957–8. He did all his great deeds, in fact, in eleven seasons though he continued to play for and captain his native island, of which he now is the official coach.

If Worrell's batting was the epitome of grace and Weekes was the stocky executioner, Bradman-like in the clean efficiency of his cutting and hooking, Walcott in form was the most exciting player of the three, and, I think, in West Indian conditions the most devastating. Whereas Weekes' physique encouraged him to practise the back-foot strokes, so Walcott's height and weight of frame proclaimed him as a driver. He made twelve of his fifteen Test hundreds on home pitches, and five of these at Kingston where the straight boundaries seemed so short when he was in full cry that mid-off and mid-on, fielding to the fast bowlers, were usually right back on either side of the sight-screen. One stroke there sticks in the mind as an illustration both of his power and of the psychological effect that can be produced by a single blow. In the first Test of 1953–4 Len Hutton overloaded his attack with fast bowling (as he was apt to do) giving Alan Moss of Middlesex his first game for England to the exclusion of Laker. Moss duly appeared second change with instructions to keep them quiet if he could. In his first over he bowled something a little over a good length to Walcott. As Moss was still following through the ball came whistling past his head like a bullet, hit the concrete wall that forms the screen and flew back more or less at the bowler's feet!

Walcott's greatest triumphs came on the first Australian visit to the West Indies wherein he averaged 82 in the series without a not-out, including five hundreds. Twice he got two in a match. If a testimonial were ever required as to Walcott's stature as a batsman it would be given with enthusiasm by Lindwall and Miller, who on that tour were on the receiving end. The West Indian performance in that rubber was a disappointment but Walcott's magnificent play, and especially his driving, made up for much.

Worrell, as I say, won the palm as a stylist. He was the most complete batsman of the three, and the most adaptable. With him timing and execution made up so thoroughly for a relative lack of power that several of his best innings were scored faster than anything achieved by the other two. On the other hand his concentration was such that when a long rearguard seemed to be called for he did the job magnificently. One thinks particularly of when, in answer to a vast English score, at Trent Bridge in 1957, he played through the West Indies innings for 191 not out and so saved them from defeat. He was better suited temperamentally for this sort of effort than either of his great contemporaries.

But it is Frank's leadership of the West Indies on the two tours in Australia and England of 1960–1 and 1963 which gave him a place in cricket that can never be challenged. He went to Australia at the age of thirty-six, the sole survivor of the triumvirate, ripe in experience and in the philosophy of the game and the response he evoked from his side helped to make the tour a triumph, alike for cricket and for himself. There must have been the strongest possible temptation after so brilliant a climax to retire rather than undertake the rigours of a six-day-a-week tour of England more than two years later. But he shouldered the job and achieved another success scarcely less spectacular than that in Australia.

Such was the legacy that Frank Worrell handed on.

From *The Cricketer's Bedside Book* (1966)

A Laker Over

JOHN ARLOTT

No cricketer would dispute the proposition that Jim Laker was the finest off-break bowler of his time; and he probably was the best of any age. There have been many in this kind; especially in England where the wet and drying pitches that serve as their killing ground occur more often than in other countries. Until recent years virtually every English county side included one of the species. Men such as Tom Goddard, John Clay, George Macaulay, Jack Newman, Raymond Illingworth, Vallance Jupp, Fred Titmus, David Allen,

'Bomber' Wells, John Mortimore and Brian Langford all had their days when they were all but unplayable. None of them, though, was so complete an off-spinner as Jim Laker. His captain could call on him for any type of operation to be asked of an off-break bowler, on good wicket or bad, and he would do it as well as anyone has ever done.

Six feet tall, powerfully but not heavily built, well balanced and strong-legged, he had all the physical advantages for his craft bar one. He lacked the extremely long fingers which enabled, for instance, Tom Goddard, Athol Rowan, Lance Gibbs, Jack Newman, Peter Jackson or John Clay to spin the ball with relative ease. Laker turned it as much as any of them but, to do so, he had to stretch his first and second fingers so widely that eventually the top of his index finger was bowed into an arthritic condition so painful that at times he simply could not bowl; and finally it ended his playing career. . . .

Memory recalls him, fresh-complexioned, strong-shouldered, fair-haired, hitching his flannels as, at a constabular roll, he walked six strides back to his mark; tongue in cheek, casual, relaxed. Then came his run – of four, five, perhaps six, paces; he deliberately varied his approach to defeat the batsman's timing. Always, though, he came up, wrist sharply cocked, profiled, sideways on to the batsman, his left arm high, the hand cupped as if in a votive act. His delivery swing was classically full, the bowling arm driving on down. He changed pace subtly; and even varied his degree of spin by changing his grip – which was based on the tip of the index finger placed across, and not beside, the seam. So, especially on a responsive pitch, he could alter the width of turn from ball to ball. Like all the masters of flight, he could impart a considerable amount of overspin and, consequently, such steep dip as to produce the illusion of a half-volley in a good-length ball. He bowled one that went with the arm, which constantly deceived good batsmen, a faster ball, a yorker, and sometimes generated an unexpected amount of bounce. He was always, and essentially, a thinking bowler; and the spectator on the boundary edge, who could not detect his variations at such range, could appreciate them when he saw a batsman play an over of apparently similar deliveries with six different strokes. After he had bowled a ball he used to walk back and, in the moment before he turned, look up into the sky, often with half a smile which he never explained. An over finished, he would take his cap and perch it on his head at a Beattyish angle, peak pointing high, and saunter off, generally to the gully, where he held some good catches.

He took punishment phlegmatically. Hit for six, or when a catch was dropped off him, he would roll his eyes long-sufferingly upwards, give that finger a gentle rub, and stand tapping his toe on the ground, hand outstretched for the return of the ball. If he took a wicket he turned quietly away; no sign of excitement; at most, some dry, side-of-the-mouth remark. The completeness of his technique was apparent in the difference between his method on a turning wicket, where he went round the wicket and was a parsimonious killer; and on a plumb, easy pitch, where, bowling over the wicket, his control and variations

Two studies of Laker bowling, in 1952 and 1956

imposed care on even the best of batsmen. It would be accurate to say that he was at his best from about 1950 to 1958; though his career might well have continued longer but for that cruelly damaged and deformed finger. Sometimes, while he was waiting to bat, he would sit for hours on end rubbing Friar's Balsam into its tortured rawness. If it was soft, it would bleed; if a callus formed, it would tear away; it was a Catch 22, that finger. It was apparent, though, when he returned to play the occasional matches that handicap allowed, for Essex between 1962 and 1964, that his mastery of his craft was as complete as ever. Indeed, until relatively recently, he turned out in charity matches where he could still engage first-class batsmen, and quite outclass those of lesser quality.

From *John Arlott's Book of Cricketers* (1979)

The Greatest Eighty in Test Cricket

RAY ROBINSON

Neil Adcock and Bert Sutcliffe were the central figures in the most sensational drama since bodyline rocked the cricket world twenty-one years earlier. The chief difference was that the batsmen under fire

[153]

from Adcock's bouncers were not tied to the stake by Jardine's ring of leg fieldsmen.

The scene of the drama is Ellis Park, where half-mast flags mourn the deaths of 151 people in the Christmas Eve train disaster between Wellington and Auckland. At this Johannesburg ground a few years earlier Arthur Morris made his first 0 in big cricket and Australians facing the Springbok fast bowler Cuan McCarthy on a greentop were within an ace of losing their first three wickets without a run.

The pitch's hard surface has a thicker topcoat of grass on Boxing Day, 1953. It is the kind of wicket that adds yards to a bowler's speed, feet to his bounce and inches to his smile of exultation. The South African estimate it to be faster – though not by much – than the Sydney wicket on which Lindwall and Miller shot them out for 173. Meeting such a bowler on such turf for the first time in their lives throws New Zealanders into confusion. Quick-flying balls from Adcock bruise several batsmen. One is bowled off his ribs, two collapse beside the wicket and another, Miller, goes to hospital coughing up blood after a blow on the chest.

When Sutcliffe comes in after New Zealand's first two wickets have gone for nine, as usual his fair, curly head is capless. Immediately a ball from Adcock rears towards him he tries to flick it away. It strikes the side of his ducking head with a crack heard all around Ellis Park like a gunshot. Sutcliffe sinks to the turf, one hand pressed to his burst left ear. The other still clings to his bat.

In horrified silence the crowd of 22,000 watch first-aid attendants bring out a stretcher to remove him. Many fear that the blow has killed him. After five minutes Sutcliffe rises on staggering feet, waves aside the stretcher-bearers and is helped from the field by his captain. The ambulance takes him to hospital where he faints while the injury is being treated. An X-ray is taken and by the time he returns to Ellis Park in the afternoon six NZ wickets have gone for 82. Wicket-keeper Mooney hangs on, doggedly keeping the ball out for more than two hours and rubbing his bruises between overs. Though Adcock is resting after his deadly effort the New Zealanders hardly look like reaching the 122 needed to avoid having to follow-on their innings.

The crowd shouts a hero's welcome as Sutcliffe reappears through the tunnel from the players' rooms deep in the stand. A pad of cotton-wool is strapped over his ear. To the fieldsman he looks dazed. The first thing he does is clout a medium-paced ball for six. The ball's fall over the leg boundary sets the tempo for the most thrilling onslaught on Test bowling since McCabe took his hook and cover-drive into retirement. Sutcliffe survives one high chance at 17. When Adcock comes back into the attack the left-hander pushes him to off amid a sympathetic murmur. It swells to applause as a cover-hit races for four.

Movement loosens Sutcliffe's ear-pad, so at 25 first-aid attendants go out to bandage his head. Looking like a warrior in a battle scene in the gallery of the Palace of Versailles, he saves the follow-on with three wickets to go.

New Zealand's need for runs becomes so urgent that Sutcliffe cannot be content to try for fours. The field's thick carpet of kikuyu takes the pace out of ground-strokes. So, if he can measure the ball quickly enough for a full-blooded stroke Sutcliffe goes the limit and smacks it over the wire fence. No slogging at everything, though. Sutcliffe the six-hitter remains Sutcliffe the batsman, his bandaged brow over the ball and a straight bat ready for anything demanding it.

That morning the team had left pace bowler R. W. Blair, twenty-two, in his hotel room overcome by the tragic news that his fiancée, Nerissa Ann Love, nineteen, was killed in the railway disaster. They were to have married a few weeks after Blair, a linotype operator, returned to Wellington in March 1954. So when the ninth wicket falls at 154 it looks like the end of the innings and the players begin to move towards the tunnel. But, with his team in a desperate plight, grief-stricken Bob Blair has come to Ellis Park to help if he can.

Amid a hush, he unexpectedly appears on the field. Walking to meet him, Sutcliffe puts a comforting arm around his bereaved mate's shoulders. As they go to the pitch together the crowd breaks the silence with prolonged applause.

The innings rushes to an end packed with excitement. Sutcliffe lifts his fourth, fifth and sixth sixes off Tayfield in one over. Thousands stand to roar appreciation of each stroke. Blair swings the off-spinner for another six to bring the cost of the over to 25. It is his only scoring stroke. The score leaps by 33 in ten minutes before Waite stumps Blair off Tayfield at 187.

Sutcliffe remains unconquered. Of New Zealand's 105 runs since his reappearance he has made 80, snatched from the torrent of disaster, with seven sixes and four fours. Johannesburg writer Vivian Granger's tribute: 'The greatest 80 ever made in Test cricket.'

Nobody doubts that. Until Sutcliffe played it, such an innings did not exist outside schoolboys' dreams.

From *The Glad Season* (1955)

The Faces of Fred Trueman

JOHN ARLOTT

The life of Fred Truman is not a single story nor a simple pattern. There is not one Fred Trueman but four – the basic Fred Trueman, Fred Trueman the fast bowler, Fred Trueman the man, and Fred Trueman the public image. He is no one of these four: he is all four of them; and it is difficult to set any order or priority among them. The original Fred Trueman – the miner and son of a miner who, in 1949, set off from Maltby with wonder and hope to play cricket for Yorkshire – still exists, though he is more deeply buried than the usual youthful self that is contained within every man.

Fred Trueman the mature fast bowler was a sharply pointed and astutely directed weapon; Fred Trueman the man has often been tactless, haphazard, crude, a creature of impulse. In Fred Trueman the public image, so many accretions of rumour and fiction have been deposited round the human core that the resultant figure is recognizable only to those who do not know him. The four are not easily reconciled; but they exist within one body – or at least under the roof of one name – and to untwine them is to destroy the essential unity of a composite – but real – character. Of course many of the stories about Fred Trueman are apocryphal; many are not; but even those referring to situations that never existed are ingredients of him, for he is partly a myth – indeed, he accepted a place in mythology with some eagerness. His life is recorded in gossip as well as in *Wisden*.

The lad of eighteen who, after Ron Aspinall was injured, played in four Championship matches of 1949 for Yorkshire would not arouse particular interest now; certainly he would not have done so in the middle nineteen-fifties: but 1949 was different. He was not remarkable but he was the uncomplicated, original Fred Trueman. He could not dream that he had come upon his historic cue. All cricketing England was as desperate for a fast bowler to fling back the humiliation imposed by Lindwall and Miller as ever America was for a white hope to humble Jack Johnson. By 1952 that hope had settled upon Fred Trueman and, if the primary Yorkshire character was not destroyed, it was soon encased in a new outer shell of what people wanted to see. He himself was to add fresh layers of behaviour which completed the Trueman of the public image. Even the final picture is not to be defined. A reigning Prime Minister – Harold Wilson, himself a Huddersfield man – described him as 'the greatest living Yorkshire-man': while Roy Ullyett made him the subject of his most violently funny caricature.

He played cricket for twenty years at first-class level – until the late nineteen-sixties, when he was thirty-seven, far past the fast-bowler's normal allotted span, which ends at thirty – and he took more wickets in Test cricket than anyone else has ever done. In that time the bounding energy and fierce pace of youth matured to a semi-instinctive, but also extremely shrewd, technique in handling the fast bowling machine that was a body perfectly constructed for precisely that purpose. For a decade – again much longer than the peak period of even the best of the kind – he was, when the fire burnt, as fine a fast bowler as any.

All this time he was travelling the world, acquiring experience, but still capable of quite boyish brashness; a creature of impulse and emotion who, almost beyond his own control, acquired a reputation – often, but not always, deserved – for violence and four-letter words.

'Fiery Fred' Trueman — the subject of Roy Ullyett's perhaps most famous cartoon

At length that reputation slopped over. There is a histrionic streak in him and, if the men of his own county insisted on seeing him as the archetypal Yorkshireman they themselves wanted to be – blunt, honest, strong, destroying bowler of high speed, smiter of sixes, taker of acrobatic catches, striker of wisecracks, cocker of snooks at authority – he was only too happy – in fact compulsively eager – to play the part. A newspaper column in which, freed from the former control of the Yorkshire cricket authorities, he can state strong opinions; a year round the North country clubs with a vaudeville act which the modest – and some not so modest – found 'blue', have deepened the artificial layers about the original Fred Trueman. Yet, peel it away and, at every level, you have Fred Trueman in varying degrees of his four personalities.

Those four identities, too, are often completely contradictory. He can be uproarious but also – though not often – silent, moody; he can be generous – and mean; he could bowl his heart out – or turn it in; he can be harsh – or gentle; he can be genuinely witty – and horribly crude; almost hysterically funny – and a complete bore; he can be intuitively understanding – and chillingly embarrassing: he can be arrogant – and as uncertain of himself as a schoolboy; he is pulled this way and that by his doubts and his emotions; he wants desperately to be liked and he is, at bottom, lonely. Least of all is it generally understood that, in the urge to succeed at the craft in which he excelled, he lived constantly on the sharpest edge of his nerves.

No one can be sure of holding a true balance between all the constituents of this man of conflicting characters. Indeed, no man can accurately describe another; he cannot even know him because he cannot discover all, while the other, however willing he might be, is not capable of letting anyone else know all about him. No one knows Fred Trueman completely; and none of those who know him at all would agree about him – if only for the fact that no two of them have seen the same Fred Trueman.

The unifying thread running through all the apparent contradictions is that of the fast bowler; not simply a man who bowled fast, nor a man who became a fast bowler, but one who knew from the first moment he considered such matters that he was going to be a great fast bowler. Others of expert knowledge might doubt it: he never did. He realized that there had to be a period – while he grew up – before the rest of the world realized it: but that was the only qualification he allowed. He was not merely a fast bowler in achievement, he was a fast bowler in the mind and in the heart. There is no characteristic fast bowler. Although Trueman and Statham, Statham and Tyson were so effectively complementary, they were, and are, even more different in personality than in bowling method. Fred Trueman was the kind of fast bowler he had created for himself; a larger-than-life-sized figure compounded in the imagination of a boy from the fancies, facts, loyalties, cricket, reading, traditions and all the other influences of a semi-rural, semi-industrial area of South Yorkshire in the nineteen-thirties. Whenever he acted in a considered fashion – and he did not always do so at the most important junctures of his career – he acted as that ideal fast bowler who lived in his mind would have done.

From *Fred: Portrait of a Fast Bowler* (1971)

An Incredible Finish

RON ROBERTS

The most remarkable Test match climax of all time produced a tie to the first Test match between Australia and West Indies here. There could not have been a more fitting result to a wonderful game of cricket with accent on good aggressive play from first to last. As Australia's captain, Benaud, said afterwards, 'Even after it seemed Australia must have been beaten, and then rallied to a point from which it seemed we should win, I felt it was a pity that either side should lose this match; and the result is good for cricket.'

It has certainly provided a tremendous lift to the series, but more than that, it has ignited a torch of hope for Test cricket the world over. England can feel proud to have given the game of cricket to the world. But if this is the way two of the Commonwealth countries can play an international match we should, with no loss of that pride, heed the bountiful lessons that were provided at Brisbane. Even without its astonishing climax, which would have defied the wit of the most imaginative Hollywood film director it was a fine game throughout, played in a spirit of challenge and of goodwill with no display of rancour at any stage by either side at the strange ebb and flow of events. I felt privileged as an onlooker to have been present.

As for that palpitating finish, Australia, needing 233 to win in 310 minutes, lost six men for 92. Then their great all-rounders Davidson and Benaud added 134 for the seventh wicket in even time. With only seven runs needed for victory and about as many minutes left Benaud called Davidson for a sharp single to mid-wicket. Solomon threw down the wicket with Davidson scrambling unsuccessfully to make his ground.

Hall began what was obviously the last over with Australia needing six to win. Grout swung at and missed the first ball and it dropped off the pad at his feet. The batsmen scrambled through for a leg-bye. Benaud went to hook the next and was caught at the wicket. Six balls left and five to win with two wickets to fall. Meckiff played his first ball firmly and ran a dramatic bye off the next. Four balls left and four to win. Grout swung and the ball went high on the on-side. Hall himself claimed the chance and dropped it, whereas others in the

One of the most famous of cricket pictures — that from the *Melbourne Age* showing the extraordinary climax, a tie, in the Test match between Australia and the West Indies, 1960–61. At the left-hand side of the picture stands Solomon who has just thrown down the wicket to prevent Kline scoring the single that would have given Australia victory. The batsman run out is Meckiff as Sobers and Kanhai appeal. The bowler is Hall, who is standing 'between' Solomon and the wicket

[159]

vicinity could have made the catch a simple matter. But who could blame the Herculean Hall for wanting to complete the dismissal for himself and who could blame West Indies for erratic fielding in the light of subsequent events? Meckiff pulled the sixth ball high towards the square-leg boundary with Hunte hot in pursuit. The batsmen ran two and went through for a third that would have given the match to Australia. Hunte's return, however, came fast and true to Alexander and Grout's headlong dive could not finish the match.

So the scores were level with two balls left. Kline, who had been unable to field in the morning because of throat trouble, now came to the wicket. Time had already been exceeded, but, of course, the final over had to be completed. Kline, a left-hander, turned his first ball to mid-wicket. Meckiff came charging down the pitch again on the frantic winning errand and, glory be, little Solomon again fielded cleanly and threw down the stumps direct. He had to hit them as Alexander had no time to get up to them himself, and hit them he did. Australia had lost their last two wickets going for the winning run. The West Indians pranced to a joyful calypso beat as they left the field, still not knowing whether they had won or tied, but conscious only of an epic match saved.

Their often criticized fielding saved them in the end, and for that Alexander generously praised the man who had deposed him as captain, Frank Worrell. 'It was Frank who pulled us through, constantly steadying us and urging us to keep cool.' Yet in the press box strong men, heroes themselves of countless Tests, had been unable to do that, instead jumping to their feet and shouting themselves hoarse as the game surged towards its 'believe it or not' conclusion. In the pavilion afterwards the players deliriously embraced each other while Sir Donald Bradman said, 'This was the greatest Test of all time.'

The fun had returned to big cricket with the teams too excited to nurse regrets on so narrowly missing the winning chance. While Worrell joked with the umpires, mockingly telling them they should have signalled 'one short' for Meckiff's two in the final over, Mackay congratulated the special hero in a match of heroes, little unassuming Joe Solomon. 'Well thrown, Joe,' said Mackay, adding with a twinkle in the eye, 'but I thought your action a bit suspect.' That was the sort of spirit that prevailed right through.

The one unhappy aspect on this historic occasion was the smallness of the crowd, but those there made their voices felt far and wide – as indeed one hopes the sequence of events had done – and they will have something to tell their grandchildren about – if they are prepared to believe it.

From *Playfair Cricket Monthly* (1961)

Peter May straight-drives Davidson for four (1961). The Australian fielders are, from left to right, McKenzie, Mackay, Benaud, Simpson and Grout

Tom Cartwright

The Medium-Pace Bowler as the Meanest Man in Cricket

PETER WALKER

Every so often cricket throws up a performer whose talent arouses a sense of awe amongst his fellow-players. Such a man is Tommy Cartwright, capped a mere five times for England in the 1960s, but a bowler of such enormous skill and application that his name is used throughout the cricketing world whenever the subject of conversation turns to the definition of the word 'professional'.

The medium-pacer is the linchpin of English county cricket, a fact which mystifies people overseas, where such kind are regarded as cannon fodder for batsmen and in terms of importance about as useful as cold water at a banquet. Abroad it is either sheer pace or artful spin that count, but on the more yielding English pitches, where the ball gains enough purchase to alter direction if pitched on the seam and will also swing in the heavier, water-charged atmosphere, bowlers like Cartwright, Lever, Hendrick and Botham are guests of honour. Yet medium-pace bowling, with its lack of visual aggression or artful flight, finds few sympathizers either in the press box or from supporters on the boundary edge. But, as the Americans neatly put it, on the receiving end it's a different ball game!

For one thing, when bowling on a helpful pitch, a class performer like Tommy Cartwright not only makes the ball deviate in the air with late swing either way but also causes it to alter direction after landing. When all this happens inside the space of half a second from the time the ball leaves his hand until it arrives at the other end, the problems of combatting it are colossal. Genuine fast bowlers are usually pretty straight from hand to bat. Spin bowlers, because of the parabola of the ball, do give you a split second in which to change either your stroke or your mind ... or both. But the medium-pacer literally gives you nothing. He's the meanest man in cricket. Because of his reduced speed compared to opening bowlers, his control over length and direction must be far more accurate, particularly if the pitch is unhelpful and the atmospheric conditions not conducive to swinging the ball in the air.

It is in this way that Cartwright in his prime was unique in contemporary English cricket. An assassin on a wicket which gives him the slightest encouragement, he is capable, even at the age of forty-two, of sending down over after over of minutely directed just-short-of-a-length bowling which eventually makes even a batting Job commit hara-kiri! No one else in the game combines skill and application to such a degree. . . .

When I come to picture him in the twilight of my life, it is the run-up and delivery action I shall remember as much as anything that subsequently happened down at the receiving end. The seven-pace run-up begins with a small dip of the slicked-down, centre-parted black hair. The jaunty, slightly bucking stride brings him easily to the crease and the swing into the delivery position is a coaching manual's illustrated dream. Up goes the left arm high, leading shoulder well round, front leg braced, the head rock still and the eyes looking over the shoulder down the wicket at the blade of grass the ball is intended for – at least, one could swear that he has a solitary piece in his sights! The delivery itself is high and loose, but well controlled, with the right arm classically brushing the ear as it sends the grenade on its way.

Between his ears is the bowling 'Brain of Britain'. Cartwright has an encyclopedic memory of batsmen and their habits. The grunt of effort that accompanies each release of the ball has a variable pitch depending on what type of delivery he has bowled; and the range of that is considerable too! Originally he only bowled inswingers to a heavily packed legside field, relying on the slant of the ball to a right-handed batsman to hit the inside edge or catch him LBW. But he soon altered the groove of his action and broadened his horizons to include not only the ball which went the other way in the air towards the slips but also variations of movement either way off the pitch. In his next season it was possible to read from his action which way the ball was going to swing in the air (no one, not even the bowler, can nominate with certainty what is going to happen after it has pitched). But inside another twelve months, Cartwright had so honed and refined his new-found skill that the subtle changes in his body and wrist position at release were almost undetectable. From now on no one was safe, and

for the next fifteen years Cartwright, together with Derek Shackleton of Hampshire, who operated in similar style, was consistently amongst the heaviest wicket-takers in the game, Tommy's biggest crop being in 1967, when he took 147 first-class wickets in all.

Cricket has unquestionably been the dominating force in his life, yet unlike so many other accomplished sportsmen, Tom is both intelligent and objective enough to analyse not only his opponents' strengths and weaknesses but also his own. It was with this in mind that we sat in a basement corner in the Swansea pavilion and talked:

Walker: Batting as often as I did against you, Tommy, I recall how impressed I always was by what I believe are your two main qualities – your obvious control over where the ball is going and the unrelenting strain you place upon a batsman by bowling at a particular weakness of his. How much of this do you work out beforehand?

Cartwright: Oh, I can remember back years and years how I got such and such a player out. Especially if he is a big-name batter. Before each season I look down our fixture list, which grounds we are playing at, and even at this early stage I begin to think about how to bowl at the key batsmen in each county. I don't believe any bowler worth his salt would give you any different answer.

Knowing your opponent in cricket is just as important as in boxing, and rather like boxing there is a softening-up process which a bowler like myself, who lacks real pace, has to inflict on a batsman before attempting to drive home the knockout blow. I always bowl with a pattern in mind. By that I mean I size up batsman 'A' and

Left: the joy of driving fast bowlers — Ted Dexter at Lord's, 1963

Right: Wesley Hall, as quick and true a fast bowler as ever performed, in action in the same Test match.

[163]

decide on a certain combination of deliveries which will set him up for the wicket-taking ball.

I never run up expecting every ball to get a wicket. I think in two or three-over permutations – like a series of outswingers delivered from wide of the crease getting the batsman accustomed to moving his feet into one position. Then I'll try another outswinger, this time from close to the stumps fired across the batsman. Unless he is a very fine player, there's a good chance that his feet will go into the position from which he played the earlier deliveries but that the wider angle of the ball swinging away towards the slips will drag him after it. It could hit the edge, or if the ball comes back from off the seam, 'go through the gate' between bat and pad and bowl him. And if it hits him on the pad, I might get an LBW decision. This is how I always bowl. I really concentrate on putting a planned series of deliveries together rather than bowling each ball with everything in it. . . .

The art of bowling is the developed ability to read batsmen, to propel the ball with accuracy into the target area over long periods, to be as mean as Scrooge about giving away runs and never to release the pressure on a batsman, however well set.

From *Cricket Conversations* (1978)

The Brilliance of Left-Handers

JACK FINGLETON

Is it an advantage to be a left-handed batsman? Apart from Barry Richards, of South Africa, it is impossible to refute the argument that the most brilliant batting in recent years has come from the left-handed Sobers, Pollock, and the West Indian, Lloyd. Considering their smallness in numbers, it is remarkable that left-handers have been so prominent down the years. In other days, there was the great Frank Woolley, of Kent and England, and Ransford and Hill of Australia. Bardsley, also of Australia, and Mead, of England, were heavy-scorers but they weren't in the same brilliant class as the three named above. Percy Chapman and Jack Gregory were exciting, swashbuckling left-handers and in recent years these have been the exuberant Donnelly, New Zealand, and Harvey and Morris of Australia. Left-handers, all of them!

When Sir Donald Bradman saw Graeme Pollock for the first time in Perth, in October 1963, he said Pollock could well make in all ways the success of the Springbok tour. Pollock had just hit a century (eighteen fours) in eighty-eight minutes. Sir Donald doesn't lightly enthuse. His patronage, like that of royalty, is not widely distributed

Russell Drysdale used to make sketches from life of cricket crowds. Here is one of his most characteristic studies, of a vocal denizen of The Hill at Sydney

and he proved prophetic about Pollock. He hit at Sydney and Adelaide two of the most scintillating Test centuries seen in Australia.

Those with memories mellowed in cricket said Pollock was Frank Woolley all over again when they saw Pollock hit 122 in Sydney. Many recalled how the tall man of Kent – Pollock is also over six feet – flowed forward to the kangaroo-bounding fast bowling of Jack Gregory and clobbered the ball through the off against the picket fence. Old men are apt to say, in deference to their own generation, that they will never see the like of so-and-so again; but before Pollock in Australia we had seen Sobers, who scaled even higher heights than Woolley.

Nobody in cricket has given me more sheer delight than Sobers. His brilliance has been breathtaking. For the West Indies and South Australia, for which state he played for a number of Australian summers, he has played many of his greatest innings in Australia and the classical ease of his strokemaking recur readily to memory. One day in Sydney, on his first tour of Australia, he moved forward to play Meckiff off the front foot. Of a sudden, he went into reverse and off the back foot, with a cross bat, he hit Meckiff wide of mid-on for a huge six. This stroke was unsurpassed in its brilliancy of conception and execution. Meckiff was no slouch in pace and only a genius could so quickly and completely change the whole nature of his stroke.

In his last innings in Sydney, for an MCC side, I saw Woolley hit a double century, but he never hit with more power on the off than Pollock did in his Sydney Test century. One cover-drive off O'Neill was unforgettable. It travelled, one thought, almost with the speed of light to the boundary. In this innings of 122 – and Pollock was then only nineteen years of age – he hit one mighty six to leg, square, and with thirty yards to spare over the fence. He scorched nineteen fours, most of them on the off. He interspersed his off boundaries with some hefty sweeps to leg yet one thought the leg-side was not his strength. Benaud fished for him often in this innings, with several near nibbles, but there wasn't a chance to hand until he reached 104. His 122 was exactly half his side's total when he was dismissed and he retired to an acclaim seldom heard on a cricket field.

Pollock's second 50 was hit in fifty-seven minutes and this rich glut of strokes was shown on a pitch which, only some seven months before, was denounced by both English and Australian Test batsmen as an impossible one on which to play strokes!

Several weeks later in Adelaide, Pollock sent 22,000 spectators into rhapsodies as he played an even more brilliant innings. The Australians had struggled over 450 minutes for 345 runs. It wasn't thrilling to watch, and Pollock's first 50 in eighty-six minutes was like a sea-breeze in a heat-wave. His second 50 almost took the breath away. It took him only forty minutes! Sitting in the pavilion, Gary Sobers was one of the spectators who rose to their feet to applaud Pollock back.

Once again, as in Sydney, Pollock specialized in off-driving, in a lazy, languorous manner that sent the ball whizzing away. But he also pulverized Benaud and Simpson with his smiting to leg. Pollock differed from Sobers significantly in his footwork. Sobers rarely danced down the pitch, as I remember him, but this day Pollock went yards down the pitch to both Simpson and Benaud. He hit Benaud far and wide over mid-wicket for six; he went even better against Simpson, hitting him for two sixes off successive balls.

All Pollock's sixes were hit towards Adelaide's Cathedral, just outside the ground. 'Murder in the Cathedral,' murmured Bill O'Reilly. Pollock also hit two successive balls from Simpson for four so that he hit 22 runs off four successive balls. No wonder the crowd roared! I saw old-timers in Nip Pellew, Stan McCabe and Clarrie Grimmett stand with the thousands to acclaim Pollock that day. His century was chanceless, carving the Australian attack into small

pieces. It is given to few to inject such enthusiasm and enjoyment into a crowd.

In writing at the time that Pollock was Frank Woolley all over again, I had an analytical look at Pollock and wrote this: 'As soon as one looks at Graeme Pollock at the crease, one begins to think of how he could be improved. His stance is an ugly one. He holds his short-handle bat at the bottom of the handle. As he stands well over six feet, he has to pop his posterior in the air to fit in everything and he forms an ugly, elongated, upside-down figure of S as he stands awaiting the ball. In such a stance his head is far away from his feet. He cramps himself, one feels, on the leg side and, indeed, he is cramped on that side and, if he has a weakness, it is just behind square-leg. But suddenly his stance is immaterial as he blazes forth with ferocious, fiery off-drives that surge across the turf.'

Pollock was only nineteen when I wrote this. He proved in Adelaide that he was almost as strong on the leg as on the off, and in subsequent innings against Australia in South Africa Pollock has shown that it is merely a toss-up which is the better batsman when Sobers and Pollock are both at their top.

I have never tired of singing the praise of Gary Sobers. So many times to me he has been absolute batting perfection. Nor is that all. He

The brilliance of left-handers — Gary Sobers (left) and Graeme Pollock has been an amazing fieldsman, taking wonderful catches in the slips and throwing the stumps down from the field, and he is the best all-round bowler the game has known. I once described his bowling as being like a packet of mixed vegetables – something of everything – and, indeed, there has not been a type of left-hand bowl that Sobers has not used. In 1968, in Australia, he was worried by a piece of floating bone in his right shoulder. It hurt him, oddly, to bowl his over-the-wrist spinners. After three overs of fast bowling in the Brisbane Test, Sobers turned to slow, orthodox spin, breaking from the right-hander's legs, and took 6–73 off 37 overs.

Sobers said this was his best bowling in a Test and he thought it interesting that he should have gained such figures by reverting to the type of bowling he first used in cricket. . . .

I have seen Sobers play immortal innings and strokes not reminiscent of any other batsman. So, too, with Bradman, McCabe, Compton and Hammond. They displayed an individual flair in playing strokes that one could recognize immediately in one peep after rounding a pavilion corner. I have watched Sobers many times and thought he had only one chink in his armour – he doesn't always pick the bosie, which is strange for a man who bowls a perfect one himself. . . . Strangely Sobers was not extravagant in his foot-work. When Barry Richards faced up to Gleeson in South Africa, he waltzed down the pitch before Gleeson had bowled and hit him for four fours in one over. This showed a blatant disdain for Gleeson's ability to turn the ball, but Sobers always played Gleeson from the crease in Australia, and with suspicion. His footwork, then, was confined; but it was impeccable in the crease and his batting was helped by a long reach. . . .

There is an abiding memory of the centuries I have seen Sobers hit. In retrospect, there never seemed a period in them when he didn't look like hitting a century. Some centurions struggle, go slow and fast in patches, have their lucky streaks, possibly bog down in the nineties and emerge, at last, gasping at the three-figure mark. There was nothing like this about Sobers. He just flowed on and on, his technique and stroke-play on a pedestal.

His best shots were the two most spectacular and most productive – the drive and the pull. In the drive he had a full flow of the bat and, like Pollock, he possessed an intuitive genius that enabled him to cleave the fieldsmen on the off side. There was no stroke he could not play. He could cut – Martin Donnelly says later that few left-handers cut – and square-cut and force majestically, off his toes. This requires the very epitome of timing. I have written in another place of his very own inspirational stroke when he stood tip-toe, as if in defence, only at the very last fraction of time to swivel his body and send the ball screaming past square-leg. This stroke was pure genius.

Sobers was a complex study when he came to Australia in 1968, coming from a heavy county season with Nottinghamshire. His cricket appetite was clearly jaded. He made touring history by not playing for his own country in the opening game at Kalgoorlie. I met him, during that match, at the Australia Open golf in Perth and there was no mistaking where his sporting interests had been diverted. .... I often saw Sobers on the cricket field going through the motions of a little wedge golf shot. Obviously, he found on the golf course the mental relaxation denied him on a cricket field. He continually wore a frown on the field (one saw it through binoculars) and when taxed with not bowling himself enough in Adelaide, replied wearily: 'I am not a cricket machine.'

For all his frowns, for all his worries, for all his apparent cricket staleness, Sobers still managed to hit two peerless Test centuries in Australia in 1968. One was in Adelaide, 110 in 132 minutes with two sixes and fifteen fours; the other in Sydney, 113 in just over two hours, with twenty fours. In Adelaide he batted in his now-customary position of number six and ran out of partners. He fell in trying to keep the strike. It took a lot to budge him from that number six position.

Sobers cast a spell over the Australian attack in each innings but in each case his century was too late to give full value to his side. He came to bat at Adelaide at 4–107; at 3–30 in Sydney. A century innings from him in either city at number three or four would have had much more effect upon his side's innings.

Sobers has now hit twenty-five centuries in eighty-six Tests (I can't accept those matches in England in 1970, hastily arranged when the South African tour fell through, as Test matches, which, surely, are between one country and another). Bradman leads with twenty-nine Test centuries. Hammond has twenty-two, Harvey and Sobers each twenty-five, Sobers passing Barrington in Sydney. Sobers again hit his peerless form in England in 1970 but retention of keenness will be a big factor if he is to pass Bradman's twenty-nine. The cricket yoke is beginning to tell on Sobers.

I like to recall Sobers in that thrilling over at Swansea in 1968 when he hit Malcolm Nash for 6, 6, 6, 6, 6, 6 – over long-on, long-on, long-off, mid-wicket to the on, long-on, mid-wicket to the on. Two hits went right out of the ground. This was a world's record for an over in a first-class match. Nash was philosophical about it. 'I suppose I can gain some satisfaction from the fact that my name will be permanently in the records book,' he said. He wanted to have the ball mounted – but it never came back the last time Sobers hit it out of the ground.

And so I return to the original theme of this chapter – is it an advantage to be a left-handed batsman? Is driving easier for them than a right-hander? Or, and this is a point which gave me much thought, are some left-hand batsmen really stronger in the right hand and does this give them an advantage in driving in that their top hand, the main driving one, is the right hand? Golfers, right-handed ones, know how important is the left arm and hand in the drive and how abortive the stroke becomes if there is too much right hand, and too soon, in the shot.

Pondering on this, I wrote to Graeme Pollock, Gary Sobers and Frank Woolley in England, asking them pertinent questions. Pollock and Woolley were good enough to answer immediately and with most interesting information. I spoke at length with Arthur Morris and

Neil Harvey in Sydney and, after speaking with Martin Donnelly, he was good enough to put his magnificent thoughts on paper. Gary, not surprisingly, didn't get around to answering!

Pollock agreed with me that left-handers excel in the drive and, in his own case, says he has an advantage in that his top (right) hand is the stronger one. He plays every single-handed game right-handed. He writes right, throws right, plays tennis right but as soon as the two hands are required, such as in cricket and golf, he goes left-handed. But Sobers, Pollock writes:

is left-handed in everything he does. This is probably the reason for his strong on-side play off the back foot, where his left hand dominates.

Left-handers are probably fortunate because most bowlers tend to move the ball away from us. This gives you lots of room in which to play your shot, whereas with the ball coming into the body you are inclined to become cramped. It is said that left-handers are weak outside the off-stump, but this is only natural because of the terrific concentration of bowling directed at this side of the wicket.

The same can be said for right-hand batsmen when facing a left-arm quick bowler from over the wicket. How many right-handers are suspect outside their off-stump to this type of bowler? Left-hand batsmen have to contend with this angle of attack for 90% of their batting time. The biggest bugbear for left-handers is the rough outside the off-stump from the third day onwards of a Test. Off-driving then has to be treated very carefully. Only when the ball is right up can the shot be played with any confidence. This is the reason why all left-handers like to bat first because this eliminates for a while the problem of rough outside their off-stump.

Neil Harvey writes right-handed, bowled right, kicks with his right foot and plays tennis right-handed. This suggests he is a more natural right-hander than a left one. When it comes to two-handed action (including wood-chopping, he said with a wide grin), he goes left. His right did the work in the drive but his left in the cut, square-cut and the pull and he was most proficient in all these strokes.

I asked him which eye was stronger. Martin Donnelly had put to me the interesting and intricate theory that the left hand side of the brain dominated the right eye, which seemed to give the left-hander another advantage, but Harvey, now bespectacled, staggered me by saying he was weak in both eyes. 'Ever since I was fourteen,' he said, 'I have seen strange shapes. I could never read the scores on the board. Our Australian team in South Africa once had their eyes tested and only Drennan had worse sight than mine. The specialist said to me, "Who leads you out to bat?"'....

Frank Woolley wrote me as follows:

I don't think left-handers are fortunate in being left-handers. My experience was that more right-hand bowlers can make the ball move in the air into a right-hander and away from a left-hander, which is the most difficult ball to play. Also, a left-hand batsman

has to cope with the bowler's rough and particularly in my time on a 'sticky' wicket. These, with covers being used, are no longer known in the game.

Because of the bowler's rough, a cover-drive was always difficult for a left-hander, or so I found it. My left hand was always the main force in my batting. My right hand, for me, was only a steadying hand, just with my thumb and first finger, which allowed the bat to go straight through. But I am not left-handed in all things. I write right-handed, eat right-handed, play billiards right-handed and pick up most things with my right hand.

At eighty-three, Frank apologized for what he described as his scribble. He said his right hand was full of arthritis. I thought his writing magnificent!

Martin Donnelly, as rich a character as he was an all-round

Left: the young Garfield Sobers, who took an English wicket in his second over in Test cricket, and four in that innings

Right: Gary Sobers: the fast bowler he later became, his springy, athletic action perfectly caught by Patrick Eagar

[171]

sportsman, wrote me an enthralling letter on the subject. He is a left-hander in all things – writing, eating, playing tennis, throwing, shooting and kicking:

You ask which was my 'motive or power hand'. I am not certain that these are the same. I would regard my left hand as the power hand because this is the one that puts most power into shots, whether off or on-driving, slashing behind point (I almost said 'cutting', but few left-handers I saw really played the cut shot properly) or in hooking or pulling. However, the top hand, in my view, must always be the control hand and the guiding hand. You might even call it the motivating hand – in all shots. It must be primarily responsible for the arc through which the bat moves up and down and in so doing must harness and direct the power hand (i.e. the bottom hand), which is the hand that dictates speed and power. This is the hand with which the bat is moved in executing any stroke.

To my mind, the golden rule in batting is that the top hand should have at *all times* not only a firm but a tight grip on the bat and this grip should never be changed or relaxed in the playing of any stroke (either defensive or offensive). Clearly, the hands work together, but basically, as I see it, the top hand must be the control hand, the bottom one the power hand.

On the eye question, I checked with an eminent ophthalmic surgeon who said there was no basic rule about eye dominance and certainly gave no support whatever to my hopeful, but embryonic theory about the right eye being dominant in left-handers and the left eye dominant in right-handers. However, we did establish that M.P.D. is left-eye dominant. Incidentally, the simple test on this one is to point your index finger at a focused object on a wall and then to close each eye in turn. The eye that sees the finger in line with the object is the dominant eye as opposed to the one which throws the finger off to the left or right.

I hope not too many right-handers find, as I did when I tried this test, that their right eye is the stronger one. If a right-hand batsman's shoulders are not allowed to come round too far to the bowler, thus giving him what is known as a two-eyed stance, the left eye does much more work in batting for the right-hander than the right one! . . .

Arthur Morris is left-handed in everything, and left-footed also. He says his left hand was definitely stronger – and his left eye also stronger. 'I don't use my top hand very much in batting,' Morris told me. 'I think I drove mostly with my shoulders and wrists, but I didn't drive in any pronounced fashion, neither to the off nor on. I think I was more a square-player and forcing them off my toes.' And, I might add, an exceptionally good player, too.

There is the case for left-handers, as I see it, although it is to be noted that some of the famous left-handers do not agree on all points. What can be agreed upon, however, and especially when remembering their meagre numbers, is that left-handers have been far more outstanding in brilliancy in recent years than their right-handed fellows.

Pondering that, I wondered whether left-handers might not profit from having the right hand the top one on the bat when I reflected that many golfers consider the top left hand to be the dominant one in a right-hand golfer. Golf can teach batsmen a great deal in driving. So many batsmen are bottom-hand conscious and I can think of no better illustration than Bobby Simpson. Simpson played golf off scratch and he possesses a glorious golf swing, fluid and full. Yet, when he came to batting, his bottom hand was the dominant one and he never drove as freely as nature equipped him to do. I think, in the main, this was brought about by the period in which Simpson played. He, with others, saw a vacancy in the Australian Test team for an opener and, in making himself into an opening batsman, Simpson concentrated upon defence and so used his bottom hand more than the top one. . . .

Yet, in the drive and the use of the top hand, golf, I repeat, has an important message for all batsmen because the drive is the very foundation of good batsmanship. It is the safest of all shots because the bat comes to the ball full face, minimizing risks; it pays the richest dividends in runs scored and, finally and most importantly, it has a demoralizing effect upon bowler. No bowler, and particularly a fast bowler, likes to be driven. A bowler is encouraged when he sees a batsman cutting or deflecting, taking risks, but no bowler likes to be consistently driven. It is then that he tends to drop the ball short so that the drive, as I see it, is the dominant stroke in batting. It paves the way for the other strokes.

It is their ability to drive that makes Sobers and Pollock two such brilliant batsmen. Whether nature has given them an advantage over right-handers is something to be pondered. All that remains for me is to express my thanks to so many brilliant left-handers for telling me so much about themselves.

From *Fingleton on Cricket* (1972)

Colin Bland – The Art of Fielding

LOUIS DUFFUS

In the Lord's Test of 1965 England were in a flourishing position. They had confined South Africa to 280 in their first innings and had reached 240 for four.

Ken Barrington was at the height of an innings of mounting mastery. He had scored 91 and hit a six and eleven fours. None of the bowling caused him any difficulty.

Batting at the Pavilion end, he played a ball towards mid-on where there was no fielder. Spontaneously he and his partner Mike Smith set off for what appeared to be a comfortable run. He had played the same stroke twice previously and Colin Bland, standing a couple of yards to the mid-on side of the square-leg umpire, had not been able to prevent a run. To a degree he seemed to encourage it.

This time he anticipated the stroke. With a clear start he raced less than ten yards, picked up the ball with his left hand, transferred it to the right and sent it crashing into the stumps at the Nursery End. Barrington was run out.

Later in the innings while fielding more towards mid-wicket, he ran to his right, twisted his body and, as Jim Parks scampered to regain his crease from a reversed call, threw the ball, which remarkably passed between the legs of Parks, and hit the middle stump. He too, was out while scoring with increasing freedom and forcefulness.

From being in a winning position in a match which roused excitement throughout its entire course. England were hard pressed to avoid defeat. At the end of play they needed 46 to win and had two wickets to fall.

Bland, who had made 39 in the first innings, followed it with a top-score of 70 in the second.

For a fielder to hit the stumps and, perhaps, achieve a couple of run-outs is not exceptional but in Bland's case the odds were so heavily against him that his feats were well nigh miraculous.

All through that tour and previous tours both in South Africa and Australasia, his accurate throwing and skill in fielding captivated onlookers. Many were drawn to watch the South Africans play, very largely because of the prospect of watching the speed, grace, precision and power which compounded his genius. To me, fortunate to witness all twenty-two of his Test matches, his fielding was a source of recurring exhilaration.

At Lord's he touched a pinnacle of proficiency that has distinguished his whole span of cricket. Through long, lonely hours of dedicated practice, he raised the art of fielding to a new dimension, and his own performances into the realm of legend. It is an academic argument whether, as some maintained, Bland was the greatest fielder of all time but there was no question that his talent far outshone the gifts of all his contemporaries.

It so happened that on the British tour, apart from his first Test, his fielding was not the best he had produced. One reason was because he was seldom placed on the boundary, a position which allowed him to demonstrate his wonderful 'arm' and almost uncanny judgement of distance. He made a realistic assessment of his skill when he said, 'all this publicity has been embarrassing. Apart from Lord's, I haven't equalled my standard at home.' . . .

The New Zealand tour of 1961–62 had been a triumph for John Reid. His powerful batting, combined with a superior number of innings, brought him more runs in the season than more distinguished predecessors in Denis Compton, Neil Harvey, Jack Hobbs and Len Hutton.

He played several devastating innings and with his score at 60 in the fourth Test in Johannesburg he was well set for another such assault. He hit two successive fours off Godfrey Lawrence, then slammed him with all his might deep into the covers.

With a low trajectory the ball travelled too fast for normal human anticipation but, having picked up its flight, Bland flung himself forward at full stretch, caught the ball in his finger-tips and lay for several moments as though some sculptor had immortalized for generations to come one of the most remarkable catches seen at the Wanderers.

From *Cricket: Stars of Today* (1970)

'1969. Australian pattern short white coats adopted by umpires in England'

Bernard Hollowood captures a point of change in cricket custom for Rowland Bowen's 'Dates in cricket history' in his book *Cricket: A History of its Growth and Development throughout the World*

Majid Khan

PETER WALKER

Great is a word bandied around in sport like a shuttlecock, but in reality there are very few cricketers who deserve the label. One I would suggest is Majid Jehangir Khan, former Glamorgan, Cambridge and now the leading Pakistan Test batsman. If in sporting terms greatness can be defined as the ability to outplay all around you, then cricket must surely provide one of the most searching tests. Yet recognition of an individual's brilliance need not necessarily always shine in the spotlight of open competition.

At the windswept, icy county ground in Derby in 1969, Majid put on the most memorable exhibition of batting skill it has been my good fortune personally to witness. It took place in the Derbyshire nets during one of those seemingly endless breaks waiting for heavy overnight rain to drain through a waterlogged outfield. Huddled around the medieval dressing-room brazier thoughtfully provided by the Derby committee to combat the spine-chilling draughts that used to waft through the racecourse ground pavilion, the former headquarters of the county, the Glamorgan team's conversation turned to the art of batting. We had just come from a game against Sussex where Jim Parks Jnr had made a hundred against us on an unpredictable wicket. We agreed that it was the speed and precision of his footwork that had kept us, and Don Shepherd in particular, at bay. At that time, Shepherd was one of the country's most feared bowlers, a man of immaculate length and direction who bowled off-breaks at a brisk medium pace. On a turning wicket he was virtually unplayable, and touring teams in this country had gone away from games against Glamorgan at Swansea with a sigh of relief that the myopic England selectors did not include him in any of the Test sides.

While the discussion continued to and fro across the brazier, Majid, never at any stage of his career a talkative man, sat silent, orientally impassive. It was only when we had appeared to have exhausted all lines of debate that he spoke: 'You don't need any footwork in batting, just hands and eye'. In terms of length, this amounted to a major speech from Majid, then in his second season with Glamorgan, having joined on a special registration in 1968, the year after he had toured the UK with Pakistan. The Welsh county committee had no doubt been influenced in their signing of him, by his innings of 147 in eighty-nine minutes against Glamorgan at Swansea and the fact that his father, the distinguished Indian cricketer Dr Jehangir Khan, had been a pre-war Cambridge contemporary of Wilfred Wooller, the Glamorgan secretary. These factors quickly helped to forge a bond which was to last until 1976.

At Derby on that bleak day in June 1969, Glamorgan were on the crest of a winning streak which lasted throughout the season, culminating in them taking the Championship for the second time in their first-class history with an unbeaten record to boot, the first time this had been achieved since Lancashire in 1934. Success is a heady brew and there were many challengers to Majid's claim that footwork counted for nothing.

Within fifteen minutes, three of our front-line bowlers, including Don Shepherd, lined up in a net outside with Majid padded up at the other end about to have his theory demolished. For twenty minutes, on a rough, unprepared, and quite-impossible-to-bat-on wicket where the ball flew, shot, seamed and turned, Majid Khan stood absolutely motionless, parrying the ball as it lifted, cutting or hooking unerringly if it were wide, driving with frightening power if overpitched and swaying out of harm's way when if lifted unexpectedly. Unless he allowed it, not a single ball passed his bat, not a chance was given, not a false stroke made. The bowlers were at full throttle, yet by our own reckoning afterwards that twenty-minute session must have yielded the young Pakistani around 75 runs! He had defied every known textbook instruction, improvised strokes that just did not exist and, without uttering a word, had emphatically made his point. In the presence of genius, no rules apply.

From Cricket Conversations (1978)

Boycott Scores Noisy 200

ALAN GIBSON

COLCHESTER : Yorkshire have scored 347 for one wicket in their first innings against Essex.

An opening partnership of 240 and a double century by Boycott, put Yorkshire in a strong position on a sunny day at the attractive, if not exactly pastoral Garrison ground at Colchester. Boycott, who scored 200 here last year, must be considering joining the Army.

Yorkshire took only two points for batting and at times were barracked for scoring slowly, but there were mitigating circumstances. The pitch was slow – Essex showed their opinion of it by resting Lever. It was hard to score runs quickly, especially in front of the wicket. East and Acfield were steady in length and direction – indeed there were few loose balls from anybody for most of the day – and the Essex fielding, so swift and accurate, must have knocked ten runs an hour off Yorkshire's rate – helped, to be sure, by a slow outfield.

Boycott, until the latter part of his innings, scored mostly off the back foot. He cut and forced the ball to the offside, and sometimes hooked. After he had reached his hundred he began to let his drives go, and very handsome they were. Sharpe moved efficiently along, accepting a supporting part, never missing the chance of a nudge or two, occasionally cutting delicately and late.

The last time I saw a Yorkshire opening pair put on over 200 against Essex was in 1932, when Holmes and Sutcliffe scored the famous 555 at Leyton. The difference between that partnership and this that strikes me most concerns the noise. Holmes and Sutcliffe were not only quick between the wickets, they were quiet. They ran with only an occasional crisp call, often with a nod, a lifting of the finger, often with no mortal sign that could be detected, yet how rarely with a shade of misunderstanding.

The present Yorkshire system is for both bastmen to shout simultaneously, pause and then shout again. If, as happens about once an over, this has not cleared the situation up, it is considered wise to keep shouting. This is especially the policy of Boycott, whose progress down the pitch is often one long ululation.

It was to this sound of revelry that Sharpe departed, eight short of his hundred. Boycott thereafter gave his voice rather less work, and

[177]

One of Geoffrey Boycott's most productive strokes — the square drive

his bat rather more, surging in noble waves towards his second hundred, which he reached at ten past six.

On only forty-five occasions, I estimate, did Boycott give Essex the slightest hope. Just before lunch he played and missed at Boyce; at 84 he popped a ball which had checked just short of cover; there was one appeal for leg before which may not have been too far away, and on forty-two occasions he might have been run out. He has reached his thousand runs for the season in eleven innings.

YORKSHIRE: First Innings

*G. Boycott, not out	..	..	..	..	.. 221
P. J. Sharpe, run out	..	..	..	..	.. 92
D. E. V. Padgett not out	..	..	..	.. 18
Extras (lb 9, nb 7)	..	..	..	.. 16
Total (1 wkt) ..	..	..	..	.. 347

J. H. Hampshire, B. Leadbeater, R. A. Hutton, *D. L. Bairstow, C. M. Old, G. A. Cope, D. Wilson, M. K. Bore to bat.

FALL OF WICKET: 1–240.

Bonus points: Yorkshire: 2

ESSEX: R. Ward, B. C. Francis, G. J. Saville, K. W. R. Fletcher, G. Barker, K. D. Boyce, **B. Taylor, S. Turner, R. N. S. Hobbs, R. E. East, D. L. Acfield.

Umpires: S. Cook and D. Evans.

From *The Times* (24 June 1971)

The Thousand

NORMAN HARRIS

From the county ground at Northampton the cricket-writer for a national newspaper, on the phone to his office, was getting a little irritated with his editor's queries. A cricketer stood on the brink of one of the game's most coveted achievements, a thousand runs before the end of May, and the sports editor's cross-examination seemed almost to suggest doubts that the circumstances were real or valid. 'Well,' said the writer, 'he's been around for several seasons, he's matured and steadily improved . . .' In a sense, however, the editor's puzzlement was understandable.

Glenn Turner, a young opening batsman from New Zealand, had made regular hundreds for Worcestershire (including a county record of ten in a season) and played some very long innings in Test matches, twice carrying his bat: but to a distant observer his name did not seem to have resounded around the land like that of Bradman or Hammond. Men who offer great deeds are expected to possess names which ring in the mind, they are supposed to dominate the stage like great actors, and certainly they must *look* like men and not boys. Glenn Turner, even at twenty-five and with fashionably long hair protruding from under his cap, still looked extraordinarily youthful with his boyish face, slender arms, and thin wrists. Indeed, at a distance he looked not unlike a schoolboy. This was the batsman who, as May 1973 ended, was threatening to do what no one had done since the War, to join the six men (Grace, Hayward, Hammond, Hallows, Bradman, and Bill Edrich) who had scored the Thousand before the end of May.

On closer inspection, the youthful-looking batsman was not so improbable a claimant. His initials, G.M.T., rightly suggested exactitude and constancy of performance. His style was the complete antithesis of the solid-set, massively *effective* Bradman. His back-lift had a pristine straightness, he played his front-foot shots *en point*, with a classically high follow-through of the elbows. He seemed to sharpen his shots, so that somehow they looked long and pointed. The meticulous care of his strokeplay was mirrored when, fielding at slip, he fastidiously flicked and patted the turf with the toe of his boot. An intelligent mind sought to remove emotion and tension and to leave room only for calm analysis; he *always* seemed to know how and why he was out and to, so to speak, 'rationalize' it away. But the over-riding factor, especially so far as the Thousand runs was concerned, was the ability to concentrate when it really mattered. That concentration could be fierce. There was already impressive evidence of it.

During his record-breaking season for Worcestershire in 1970, he achieved his highest Championship innings of 137 on the last day of one county game and then on the very next day, in another game, improved it with an unbeaten 154. This capacity to re-summon and maintain concentration was seen again in the West Indies, this time on a formidable scale. Early in New Zealand's tour, he made the first double-century of his career, 202 in nine hours. In his next innings, in the first Test, he superseded that by carrying his bat for 223, in nine and a half hours. Later on that tour, against Guyana at Georgetown, he made 259 in ten hours – then followed up again on the same pitch, in the Test match, by exactly repeating this 259, this time in eleven and three-quarter hours. On each of the four times he reached 100 on that tour he went on to pass 200.

So, the application was clearly there, if he wanted to seek the Thousand. Whether the target was in his mind very early in New Zealand's 1973 tour is doubtful. But it certainly arose in the public mind after he started with 41 and 151 not out in the opening match against Derrick Robins' XI and followed with 143 against Worcester – 335 runs even before April was finished. With the press continuing to record these totals, and his team selecting him for every game, there was no ignoring the target even if he wanted to. Wet weather meant fewer batting opportunities in the next three county matches and also a couple of failures. Good weather and wicket at Cardiff provided around 50 in each innings against Glamorgan, as well as reinforcing his good form. When he came to Lord's for the MCC match, starting on 19 May, the aggregate stood at 630 and needed another long innings to bring the Thousand within striking distance.

Now, like it or not, the pressure got to Turner. Batting first at Lord's, he went some twenty minutes without scoring. In that time he felt physically sick with anxiety, and wished he could quit the field. The feeling passed when the first run was scored and, in a long partnership with Parker, he proceeded to play his best innings of the summer, one which was chanceless and in which his confidence ultimately led him to hit sixes off both Birkenshaw and Underwood. At the declaration, he had 153. In another opportunity at the end of the game, he was bowled with a stunning delivery from Cottam for three. Still, the target was now just 201 runs away, and he had three matches.

The following Saturday he went to the wicket at Leicester (with this match and one to follow) needing 133. The goal was large, but within reach. Such statistical goals are perhaps unnatural to cricket, and on this day Turner seemed to freeze. Against the opening bowlers he gathered runs carefully, but when the slow men appeared he came to a halt. On the Leicester wicket the ball was not coming on to the bat as he would have liked, and Birkenshaw and Balderstone did not bowl a loose ball. Had they done so, even just one, it may well have freed Turner and opened the way to the hundred. In fifty minutes after the fall of the first wicket Turner had scored only five to Congdon's 17. Then, most untypically, he played the shot of frustration, got a top edge to his sweep and was easily caught. He had taken most

Glenn Turner's thousandth run
by the end of May, 1973

of the morning to make 30. 'It's funny,' he confessed at lunchtime. 'It's the first time I can ever remember that, as the bowler was running up, I was thinking, "This ball could get me out".' Subsequently, Congdon went on to get such a score as Turner needed, 134. In the second innings, Turner was 10 overnight, only to see the final day rained out.

He had, it seemed, left it too late. The next game, against Northamptonshire, would be played on 30, 31 May and 1 June. With two days of the match before May ended, New Zealand would have to bat first if Turner was to have any chance of two innings; more likely he would have just one. The pressure was too great now, to have to go out and make the 93 necessary runs in one innings. Additionally, it looked as if the pitch would be wet. But if any batsman could bat on such a knife-edge as this, and make the prescribed runs, here was one with the mental capacity.

The rain which had rained the last day at Leicester continued into the night and made the following morning damp, though clear enough. The wicket that had been prepared looked as if it would be especially slow to improve, and another was cut on the other side of the square. While cosmetic work was done on the rest of the square, and a mid-afternoon start anticipated, Turner marshalled the autograph hunters who threatened to besiege him. Sitting on a seat by the pavilion railings he patiently signed his way through a queue of boys which stretched some fifty yards out into the field. Northants won the toss and put New Zealand in. Turner was afterwards to describe the wicket as 'dangerous', a forthright description for a rational mind not usually given to dramatization.

Play began at half-past three under cloudy skies. Against Dye, the left-armer, and Hodgson, a tall young bowler, the batsmen began quietly. Turner was soon withdrawing his bottom hand quickly, and standing on tip-toe to play the lifting ball. He was given a bonus by a full toss from Hodgson, which he put through mid-off for four; but straightaway he edged just short of the slips, and twice cut without making contact. Dye was worrying him, and the slip fieldsmen remained in a state of anticipation. With 12 on the board, his partner Parker was LBW to Dye. Congdon came in and was soon taking the ball on the body. On 16, Turner went for the off-drive against Dye and the ball nicked down into the slips. Low on his left hand, Virgin at first slip could not hold it.

Play to tea had been little more than survival for the batsmen. But afterwards Turner began to make rapid progress. Against Dye he twice played handsome square-cuts to the boundary. He seemed to relish these shots, and now he had the confidence to steer the ball down to third man for singles – risky, perhaps, but his judgement was sure. Soon enough the attack was joined by the turbaned Bedi, the best slow left-arm bowler in the world. An unnerving prospect, except that Turner normally enjoys playing slow bowlers. He soon square-cut Bedi for four, and then square-drove him for another. They were both speciality strokes, the first clipped away from very close to the body, the second more of a 'flat-bat' to a ball of more width and fuller length, both of them potentially hazardous strokes but played with emphatic confidence. The second took him to his 50 – with the rush after tea, scored in only 90 minutes. It was now 10 minutes past five. He had another 80 minutes to go on to 93.

Then, with a bold and less typical stroke, he swept Bedi for four – and then tried it again, and missed. Perhaps this worried him. A few months before, in a Test series in New Zealand against Pakistan, he was out three times in five dismissals to the leg-spin of Intikhab, each time to the sweep. It had also got him out at Leicester. And now when he also played and missed at Willey, he reined in his strokes. At the other end Congdon took up the shot-making, and the larger part of the strike. Sheltering Turner he may have been; more likely he was just playing, as always, as well as he possibly could whatever the circumstances. Contrivance so often leads astray the best laid plans. Near the end of the day Congdon even took a sharp single to cover, which had Turner scampering. So Turner added just 15 in the last hour, and ended the day on 70. Was his conservatism in the last hour a loss of nerve? Or was it a sign of strong nerve that he was prepared to wait, and give himself 23 more runs to make in the morning? Certainly it was now quite obvious that there would be no second innings for him before the end of the second day.

At least, the weather had held when the play resumed the next morning – but only just, for the cool grey skies threatened light rain. Twenty-three runs, it seemed, could be knocked off in a few overs. But they were not. The bowling was taken up again by Dye and Hodgson. Turner now would not be beaten by either, but the only runs he could score were singles down to third man: he gained just three in the half hour. Twenty runs seemed a long way off, the tension great.

Photographers and television cameramen waited – prepared to have nothing, after all, to report. With the clock just past mid-day, Hodgson dropped one short and Turner seized on it, square-cutting for four to take him to 79.

Now Bedi came on. In this situation his bowling could be expected to be as un-erring as Turner's concentration; and it was. The period of play which followed, on this modest county ground, was of an excellence scarcely matched at any level of cricket. Turner as usual elected to play most deliveries, as indeed he had to. Once, Bedi got one to jump past the defensive stroke. Once, Turner moved down the wicket to him and cover-drove through Larkins at cover for four. The continuity of the drama was broken as, at the other end, Congdon mistimed a pull to short mid-wicket and walked out for 72, having added 17 this morning to Turner's 14, and contributed to a partnership worth 154. There was further distraction when Turner, backing-up, started for a run only to have to dive back to safety as Milburn made a good stop and return. Otherwise, all the play seemed to crystallize on Bedi curving the ball through the air, to be met by Turner's straight bat dropping the ball in front of him or pushing it calmly and firmly down to mid-off – while he waited, and waited, for the one that was dropped a fraction shorter . . .

Bedi had been bowling for half an hour, and Turner in all the first hour had gone from 70 to 85. Then the bat flashed at an off-stump ball, which went with a pistol crack to the boundary behind point. It was the speciality shot, played to a ball which is really much too close to the body (and off stump) and not short enough for square-cutting, a ball which other batsmen might start to play and then leave – or, if they did flash at it, would be likely to snick. But Turner, positioned with weight spread equally between front and back foot, watching it with an eagle eye, tucks in tight on it and, almost off his right hip bone, flashes it away. A 'slash' for want of a better term, but propelled with the speed and certainty of a bullet.

It is not a bad ball, a loose ball, from which Bedi has been hit for four. He will not be blaming himself. But does he bowl it again? Does he tempt the batsman to repeat the risk, or does he avoid the batsman's strength? He starts a new over, with Turner on 89, wanting one boundary. This time each of the six balls is played with the straight face of the bat, or left. The tension is acute, heightened by the cameras trained on every ball of the maiden over.

At a quarter to one, Bedi bowls again to Turner . . . Again the front foot goes forward, the weight suddenly shifts back again, the eagle eye follows the crack of the bat and the ball rifling away to the backward-point fence.

The clapping spectators, and the players who run forward to offer warm congratulations, seem more relieved and pleased than the batsman. Still, the innings certainly changes gear as he goes in carefree style to his hundred, reaching it with a four snicked past slip, and finally hits a towering off-drive to be caught for 111 – rightly enough, off Bedi.

Afterwards, he maintains that he tried to disallow himself feelings of satisfaction, and when television interviewers want to know his 'secret' he tells the BBC and a bemused audience of millions: 'Well, most batsmen tend to play either from the front foot or the back foot, and to play either the line or the length; and I suppose, basically, I am a front-foot, line player'.

From Great Moments in Cricket (1976)

West Indies v Pakistan

World Cup, 11 June 1975, Edgbaston

TONY LEWIS

The story began for Pakistan two days before. Their captain, Asif Iqbal, was admitted to hospital in Birmingham for a minor but painful haemorrhoid operation and withdrew from the side, handing over the captaincy to Majid Khan. This was an immeasurable loss. Asif is one of the finest exponents of one-day cricket. His batting can supply the surge of brilliant strokeplay; his medium-fast bowling was very much part of Pakistan's strategy, and as a fielder he was bound to set the sparkling example. One was mindful, too, that it was at Edgbaston in 1971 that Pakistan plundered England for 608 for 7. The benign wicket remains but their chances are slimmer without Asif.

A second absentee restricted them further. Imran Khan, Majid's cousin, was locked in a battle with the examiners at Oxford University. He would be missed as an all-rounder, more especially his lively seam bowling. It meant that Majid had two fast bowlers of experience, Asif Masood and Sarfraz Nawaz, and two others medium-paced, Naseer Malik and Pervez Mir. Presuming they all bowled their allocation of twelve overs each, it left another twelve to be shared between the leg-spinners Mushtaq, Javed Miandad and Wasim Raja. The captain would need a shade of luck to make it work. Compare the West Indies line-up – Roberts, arguably the fastest bowler in the world, Boyce and Vanburn Holder, both genuinely fast and experienced; Bernard Julien, an established Test player and a useful variation with his left-arm-over-the-wicket style.

Then Clive Lloyd had an option. If it was medium fast bowling required, he could put himself on, generally neat and tidy, short of a length. Then lurking in the background was off-spinner Vivian Richards, an occasional bowler, but useful. Lance Gibbs was selected in their fourteen, but omitted.

If Pakistan won, the West Indies would need to beat Australia in that sell-out match at the Oval on Saturday next to reach the semi-finals. Even then, Pakistan might just have nosed them out of place, on a superior scoring rate. So there was much to play for, as I gathered when I got to the ground just as the first over was being delivered.

At Edgbaston it is possible to walk around a path outside the stands where there is no sight of the game. It was along this that I hurried to the press-box. The noise was deafening and most certainly foreign. A crescendo of roars, from the bottom of the scale to the top, told me that Andy Roberts was racing in to the accompaniment of a vast West Indian chorus. It was followed by a brief split second of silent anticipation, a click of bat on ball, and then a gush of counter cheering and chattering from the Pakistanis. Spectators arriving a little late raced up steps to the stands, argued with gatemen, shouted at friends, jabbered away at anybody – a magnificent confusion of dialects. If I closed my eyes I could have been in the Kensington Oval, Barbados, or Karachi, a feeling confirmed when I took in my first view of the serried ranks. A coloured crowd indeed, two-thirds of them West Indian or Pakistani, and Edgbaston's terraces, so often grey and deserted, had disappeared beneath the stamping feet of 18,000 spectators all caught up in the joy or pain of following the fluctuating fortunes. As a privileged outsider one could find oneself literally trapped in one of the many large green and white flags waved about in a frenzy, or feel one's eardrums shattered by West Indians banging beer cans to the rhythms of war.

Pakistan had won the toss and batted, but lost Sadiq when the score was just 21. Then Majid and Zaheer eased their way out of a possible crisis, yet found it difficult to increase the tempo when they wanted to. Keith Boyce and Vanburn Holder restricted them both at this stage with skilful defensive bowling just short of a length on middle and leg stumps.

Flashing drives soon revealed the easy nature of the wicket. Majid sorted out his footwork which had looked stiff and imprecise to begin with and, ball by ball, he grew into a more formidable threat to West Indies. The game was truly alight.

Fredericks moved like a cat low to the ground to snatch up a couple of sizzling shots in his prehensile fingers and flipped the ball back over the stumps from cover point. Keith Boyce let his arm go from the outfield like a human sling; over seventy or eighty yards the ball travelled at a level a foot over stump high, almost defying even the safest second run. The Pakistan batsmen knew that, if put under pressure, Boyce is the sort of athlete who might next time pick-up on the run and add a leaping throw, all in one movement. Then, of course, there was the king of the jungle, Clive Lloyd. Zaheer drove Boyce powerfully wide of Lloyd at mid-on. The captain turned and raced over the bone-hard outfield like one of the great coloured sprinters burning up the hundred metre track. The ball was arrested on the boundary line, and winged back to where it belonged, straight into Deryck Murray's gloves, with one vicious revolution of a flaying arm. The intensity, the sheer quality of it all (and it was only half an hour after mid-day – seven and a half hours to go!) left one shaking one's head. It is easy to exaggerate sometimes, but even more unforgivable not to recognize moments of true excellence when you see them and savour them briefly before they die with the next ball, or, in this case, with the next day.

Clive Lloyd next made a decision which surprised many. He called upon Viv Richards, the part-time off spinner, to bowl to these two fine players whose eyes were well set. In his first over he got Zaheer LBW as he carelessly tried to pull a shortish ball which did not turn. Roberts returned to test Mushtaq, but to no avail. Majid lashed Lloyd high and wide of mid-on, then fell to a ball of higher bounce, caught behind for 60.

Mushtaq's steadiness settled the innings at a time when Wasim Raja was prepared to hurl his bat at almost anything. Had he mistaken the thirty-seventh over for the last?

It was at this moment that Lloyd and Julien settled to bowl well. Mushtaq's timing kept his score on the move, however. He even charged down the wicket to Boyce, who considered this such an insult to the fast bowling trade that, with the tiger in his eye, he let go a 'beamer' which narrowly by-passed Mushtaq's moustache and got the message home. Kallicharan dropped Wasim Raja just before Boyce produced the most perfect yorker to dismiss Mushtaq, all leading up to a last over chaos which included two run-outs. Vanburn Holder was the bowler and the central figure. Mir went at the striker's end and Miandad at the bowler's. Miandad, 17, had played with pleasing confidence and it is easy to understand why hopes have arisen in Pakistan for his successful future in the game.

The final total of 266 allowed Pakistan the satisfaction of knowing that the West Indies could not afford to be frivolous about it.

Yet the Caribbean cricketers are unpredictable souls. Fredericks, Greenidge, Kallicharran and Kanhai tried to launch themselves with extravagant strokeplay, a haste quite irrelevant to the target, to the bowling, to the wicket – the lot. To see it was to be reminded of words penned by the West Indian journalist Tony Cozier of his countrymen's temperament which mostly brings them strength and individuality, but occasionally destroys them:

The aim of every young West Indian cricketer is universal but pursued more zealously than elsewhere: to hit the ball harder and bowl it faster than anyone else.

No player feels the chafing against the grain of his nature more acutely than a West Indian, contained for over after over; no player feels less delight in stock bowling – steady, economical, medium-pace, tick-tock stuff. Other men can jog around sturdily and usefully like pit ponies; the West Indian craves the padding grace and the striking power of the panther.

Thus departed Greenidge, Fredericks and Kallicharran for 36 runs, though I would not wish to devalue the performance of Sarfraz who had taken three wickets for ten runs in 3.4 overs.

Clive Lloyd changed the mood, Kanhai too had just got the message when he hacked a wide full pitch on to his stumps. Richards and Boyce offered yet more feverish renderings, but Julien lined up with the sane and resolute, and joined his captain in an important stand.

It was the young leg-spinner, Javed Miandad, who beat Lloyd with a perfectly pitched googly. The umpire, John Langridge, responded positively to a loud shout for a catch by keeper Wasim Bari. Lloyd expressed his surprise and annoyance; Langridge was in no doubt at all.

Holder then batted with relish for the job but at 203 for 9 he was gone too and Pakistan had virtually won the match fair and square. So what followed was a near-miracle borne of the very equation of possibilities which can make the game of cricket the perfect drama . . .

Majid first took an understandable decision, one above criticism. He resolved to try to bowl out the last man by allowing Sarfraz to use up his overs. With five overs left, Sarfraz, Javed and Naseer had finished their quota. Roberts had defended in the main with the forward lunge, while Deryck Murray, a batsman of orthodoxy and correctness, selected his scoring shots with perfect nerve and judgement.

These two came together in the 46th over. With six overs to go, 29 were wanted, and the West Indian crowd, which had fallen silent, began the rumblings of what was to be a giant eruption. Sixteen runs were required from four overs. Pervez Mir bowled a maiden. Sixteen runs from three overs. Ten runs off two. So the last over arrived with five runs needed for victory – Andy Roberts taking strike.

But who was to bowl? Asif Masood had finished, Pervez Mir had three overs to go but had bowled the last over at the other end. Mushtaq might be the man; he had already turned his arm over for two overs conceding seven runs. Or there was one alternative, the lower trajectory leg spin of Wasim Raja. Wasim was chosen, though he attempted to bowl medium-paced seamers. Two leg-byes came behind the wicket on the on-side (one of them an overthrow) – poor Pakistan were suffering now, and were probably losing the game for the first time in seven hours' cricket. First two runs, then one – all over, and it was simply left to Tom Graveney to judge Sarfraz Nawaz the Man of the Match, a consolation deserved. Only two fine sides could make a match such as this had been.

It is possible that Majid could have catered for a stronger last over than that bowled by Wasim Raja but, in truth, it was the batting which won it, not the bowling which lost it.

Deryck Murray is one of the more orthodox sons of the Caribbean, a neat looking man, tidy in his play too. He hit the ball particularly well through the off-side field on this day, and hooked swiftly when the bouncer was sent down to blast him out. He was not to be moved. It was a demonstration of personal resolution. His mouth must have been dry with the million visions of success and failure which raced through his mind and, by the end, his very soul must have been stretched by the constant temptation to abandon restraint and rush for his shots. That innings said more about his character than a hundred visits to a psychiatrist's couch.

From *A Summer of Cricket* (1976)

Pukekura Park, New Plymouth, one of New Zealand's most picturesque cricket grounds surrounded by pohotukawa, the New Zealand 'Christmas tree'. Ten thousand people can be accommodated on the grassed terraces

Greg Chappell's Hip Shot

MIKE BREARLEY

Greg Chappell playing a characteristic shot off his hip. We often had a man at backward square-leg especially for this shot and occasionally had him close in case he hit in the air a little way. There is no name for this shot. Greg plays it with a straight bat off a ball from a fastish bowler from around leg-stump or middle-and-leg. Very few batsmen can play it – most people are just nudging it round the corner, but he plays it there with a free flow of the bat. Notice the upright balanced position, no tendency to fall over towards the off side. He is tall –about 6′ 2″ – and on his toes, so that even if the ball bounces a bit more than usual he can still play it down from, say, waist height. He is very much a 'sideways-on' player, that is, he generally keeps his left side facing down the wicket towards the bowler; in this shot, we can see that just after he has hit the ball his left side is facing behind square-leg, so that from his initial position he has swivelled through an angle of more

Above: Greg Chappell's hip shot

Standing ovation at Lord's for
Greg Chappell

than 90°. I remember him playing this shot at Lord's off balls from
Lever and Old that were good balls, moving in to him down the slope,
and he still had time to play this forcing shot when most of us would
have been glad to get a thick edge to fine leg for one. The man who
played this shot as well as Chappell, and similarly, was Sobers.
Amongst Englishmen, only Amiss has it as a stock stroke, and he is not
so tall, so he cannot play it as well when the ball bounces. I think this
shot of Chappell's impresses the players more than the public because
we know how hard it is to play. Anyone can play the odd off-drive or
late-cut that look good. To say, though, that it is a professional's
professional shot implies too little, it suggests a workaday, bread-and-
butter shot, and this is more than that. It is very central to my image
of Chappell.

From *The Return of the Ashes* (1978)   [189]

Procter – The Finest Import

PAUL FITZPATRICK

The presence of overseas players is frequently offered as a prime cause for the ills of English cricket. It seems often to be forgotten that overseas players were introduced into the sport in numbers in the late-1960s to attempt to revive a county game close to, in danger of, death . . .

Yorkshire have rightly earned respect for adhering to their stern principles of qualification. If you were born at the wrong end of Todmorden then you must find a county other than Yorkshire to play for. But that county, large and powerful and influential and with no overseas players to retard its development, has had little success in the era of the overseas player. What might they not have done if Mike Procter had been one of their number?

Here surely was the finest import of them all, a player whose loyalty, honesty, determination to give always of his best, and an enviable all-

round talent, enriched Gloucestershire cricket in three decades . . .
Now that he has gone, you wish, when you had the opportunity that
you had taken the trouble to watch him more often; and to have
studied him more closely. He was of the county of Grace, Jessop and
Hammond and there is no sense of irreverence in mentioning his name
in the same sentence.

One of the fascinating things about Procter was the startling
contrasts that he brought to his cricket. The unorthodox in cricket is
appealing, and Procter's bowling, in those days when he used to come
hurtling to the wicket from thirty-five yards, was all the more
compelling because of its singularity. The short urgent strides, the
appearance of bowling off the wrong foot . . . chest as square-on as if
he were breasting a tape . . . that whirring right arm, catapulting over
like some fiendish medieval weapon of destruction.

There are feats and figures to show that his batting was a similar
mixture of energy and force. At Taunton in 1980 he struck six
successive sixes off two overs by Dennis Breakwell reaching 93 in
forty-six minutes, 84 of those runs having come in boundaries – a
useful way of sparing creaking joints.

Much earlier, in 1970, for Western Province against the Australians,
he hit the last five balls of an over by Ashley Mallett for six and
advanced from 100 to 155 in twelve minutes.

Two shots of O'Keeffe caught by
Brearley off Underwood in the
Centenary Test, England v
Australia, 1977

Yet Procter the batsman was textbook orthodoxy compared with Procter the bowler . . . calm, unhurried, selective. Possibly Breakwell, Mallet and other bowlers might disagree, but Procter's batting assaults never possessed the raw violence of an attack by a Jessop or a Botham. Procter's assassinations were carried out with just the hint of compassion for his victims.

An innings which demonstrated his certainty and selectivity of stroke was a masterful unbeaten 134 at Cheltenham last year, when Middlesex went into the final day winning the match by a distance and ended it beaten and chastened by the brilliance and assurance of Procter's strokeplay. Time was not on Procter's side that day but there was never the hint of desperation, never the suggestion of the slog.

Twice since he joined Gloucestershire Procter has taken 100 wickets in a season, the last time after his knee operations of 1975. But although on occasions since 1975 he has produced many a really quick spell of bowling he no longer is in possession of that awesome sustained pace that was to startle so many unsuspecting batsmen back in 1968 when he first arrived here.

Alan Hill, the Derbyshire batsman, tells a story of his former captain, Brian Bolus, for whom crisis was a faithful traveller. Before Hill and his opening partner were due to go out to face Procter at the start of a match Bolus tried to give them some words of encouragement: 'Now lads, I don't want you to think that Procter is fast,' he intoned. But even before he had finished the sentence a note of panic had entered his voice and almost hysterically he blurted out next, '*He is fast . . . but I don't want you to think he is.*'

The Australians discovered just how fast when he and Peter Pollock repeatedly shot away the top of their batting in that crushing 4-0 win over them in South Africa in 1970. These four Tests were the last of Procter's seven appearances for South Africa, a brief enough international career which yet yielded forty-one wickets, a rate of striking to impress Ian Botham or Andy Roberts.

It is a source of deep personal regret, as it must be to so many talented South African cricketers, that he has been denied the Test stage for so long. But he is philosophic about it now and grateful for the few Tests that he did play. That sense of gratitude deepens when he thinks of a brilliant player such as Clive Rice who never has played, and quite possibly never will play, in a Test match.

From *Wisden Cricket Monthly* (November 1981)

Viv Richards

DAVID FOOT

Isaac Vivian Alexander Richards is the most attractive sort of hero.
He is a fallible genius. He flirts with the record book when, we

suspect, he could monopolize it. His cricket, always potent and often pure, is unwaveringly instinctive.

In four years or so he became arguably the best batsman in the world. This is not extravagant journalistic talk. It is the considered opinion of respected pundits, fellow-professionals – their judgements too easily influenced at times by cynicism, cautious praise and even envy – spectators and friends who sycophantically follow his fours and foibles.

Vivian Richards' lissom grace has been compared to Worrell and his pugnacious power to Weekes. At the County Ground in Bristol, where memories are long and loving, he has suddenly paraded a succession of poetic cover boundaries, wickedly reminding his rare detractors that he can score just as sweetly through the offside, and generating spontaneous simulations of how Wally Hammond did it the same way.

He is usually in a hurry. 'I occupy the crease to score runs,' he says with simple logic, at the same time implying criticism of others whose apparent self-perpetuating philosophy of batsmanship bores and baffles him. He never publicly indicts another cricketer – not even the occasional Australian who has been known to let fly an intimidating oath at him to complement a bouncer.

Vivian plays his cricket like a West Indian. There's a calypso rhythm in his swing. He boyishly enjoys hitting sixes best of all just as he did more than a decade ago when his friends from the grammar school back in Antigua ran joyfully to retrieve the ball.

Yet oddly, he plays like a Somerset man, too. It is unthinkable, one feels, that he could have joined any other county. He happily agrees as each April he returns to his Taunton friends and favourite fish-and-chip shop. The people are warm and visibly rural. He likes the cosy market-town pubs and the obsessional cricket banter.

'I owe so much to Somerset. They gave me my real chance,' he will say in a moment of confidence. When he says that he is being both loyal and honest; there's nothing remotely devious about him. If he thought Somerset CCC were run by a bunch of amateurs ready to cheat him over a contract, he'd quickly tell you. He doesn't and there is mutual affection – and so there should be. . . .

A stray word or two of praise from Colin Cowdrey began the process. 'I'd played against him twice in Antigua,' Cowdrey recalls. 'I particularly remember the second time. There was this delightful young fellow with a jaunty air and cheerful approach. He was wearing his cap in a special way that appealed to me. And he had a big smile to go with it.

'The crowd was obviously behind him. I got the impression that he was already something of a hero although I'd hardly heard of him myself. I noticed the same crowd feeling when Andy Roberts, also from Antigua, was running up to bowl that day. Vivian, I remember, was so natural – strong and quick.'

And Colin Cowdrey's passing lines of admiration, contained in a report carried by *The Cricketer*, sent Len Creed, a Bath bookmaker, hurrying out to Antigua, ostensibly on his holidays. Len's capture is now part of West Country folklore. . . .

What did Brian Close make of him? In fact, he took to him the moment they were introduced – more warmly, I fancy, than he took to one or two of the other pros at Taunton and before that at Headingley.

Close, nurtured in Yorkshire where wickets were never wantonly sacrificed, suddenly found himself handling an easy-going young West Indian, largely uncoached and with not much knowledge of the ritual of championship cricket in England.

'I took Vivian round in my car and we talked cricket all the time. Never once was he difficult to handle. I gave him a bit of stick once or twice because of a lack of concentration. But that shortcoming could be put down to a sort of naïvety on his part about first-class cricket and what was expected.

'He was from the start so unbelievably calm, with none of the natural West Indian exuberance, as far as I could see.'

Close remained captain of Somerset until 1977 and he continues to savour the memory of Richards' hooking and the shots he played off his toes.

Richards could, however, look languid, almost indolent, between the wickets. The skipper must at times have heard the collective gasps at Taunton, Bath and Weston as this great batsman squeezed in after a suicidally strolling single.

'Viv could be exceptionally fast when he wanted to,' he recalls with twinkling emphasis. 'There was this attitude of mind, I felt, as if he was saying he could hit so many fours that there was really no point in taking singles!'

Opinion on Brian Close as a county captain may vary sharply. Richards' admiration goes back to the days when the intrepid Yorkshireman was squaring up to Hall and Griffith. Richards missed hardly a ball of that tough confrontation as it was relayed over a crackling radio set.

Vivian gives a touching account of the occasion Close first acknowledged the newcomer's promise. Swansea seems an unlikely venue for a Yorkshireman and an Antiguan to discover an initial rapport which never lessened.

'This bloke,' Brian Close tells me with honest deliberation, 'is the most exciting player I have ever run up against – and remember I have seen many of the great players. If Vivian was batting, you didn't want to miss a shot.'

Close clearly knew how to keep a fatherly eye on him. But how coachable was he? A player of this exceptional talent could surely inhibit many a coach.

Peter Robinson, who took over from Tom Cartwright at Somerset as county coach, says frankly: 'You don't tell a player like this when he is doing something wrong – he comes to you. Viv had a little bit of trouble with his batting when he returned in the April of 1978. He'd go into the nets on a Sunday morning and David Gurr and myself

Vivian Richards, on the attack,
exciting as ever

would bowl to him.

'We talked about it. He has always been easy to talk to. His pick-up had got a bit wider than it was. Viv soon put that right.'

Like Greg Chappell before him at Somerset, Richards was quick to adapt and work out the different game in England. Privately he admitted how disconcerting it could be at the start of a county cricket season after several months on the hard, reliable strips of the West Indies or Australia.

Australia has always had good leg-side players. But opponents in England are still astonished by Richards' prodigious on-side strength – the way he strikes the ball, often, from middle and off.

One well-known umpire said to Peter Robinson: 'Christ, how does he do it? He's only got to miss it and he'll be LBW.'

He very rarely does miss if, of course. It's noticeable how sides have tried to counter him. In the one-day games they pack the leg-side with six fielders and hopefully wait for him to get himself out.

Yet he is quite capable of leaning on an exquisite cover drive, as perfectly executed as anything you will see in the contemporary game. Robinson highlights that magnificently muscular six over extra cover – as demonstrated to gasping and almost disbelieving television viewers during the Gillette Cup semi-final match with Essex in 1978 – which Richards can daringly reveal at a time when the bowler is determinedly aiming at leg stump. 'Somehow he makes the room for it. You don't coach that kind of thing. Vivian is a wonderful improviser.'. . .

On summer evenings at Taunton, after a day's cricket, Vivian occasionally wanders round to the Westgate Inn, kept now by Roy Marshall, the former Hampshire opening batsman who was born in Barbados. Roy, who also coaches at King's, Taunton, was as a batsman forceful and stylish. His cricketing discussions with Richards, at times long after the customers have gone home, are invariably intense. He confesses himself amazed, for instance, at the way medium-paced bowlers have to put a mid-wicket back on the boundary in an attempt to curb Richards.

Flawless timing . . . strong hands . . . powerful shoulders . . . comfortable stance . . . Marshall says the Antiguan has all of these. 'I have never seen anyone hit a ball so hard and with so little effort. Plenty of players can hit hard but not with Vivian's apparent lack of effort.'

Vivian Richards has ended games with a theatrical flourish, stage-managing his six into the car park. He has put the ball between the tombstones in St James churchyard at Taunton and into the gents' lavatories although not, curiously enough, into the River Tone, the one-time speciality of Arthur Wellard.

Just occasionally he has played an exclusively defensive role. Peter Robinson cites a match against Middlesex when Richards unselfishly kept one end going while Brian Rose approached what looked like being a century. 'Still beautiful to watch,' says Robinson.

The small county ground, with its scorebox threatening to slide off the roof and its scoreboard glistening in the sun like a polished dining-table, its two lines of trees, iron Jack White gates and peeling Edwardian decadence inside, is where Vivian Richards has grown from a weekend cricketer to the best – at his best – in the world. Somerset supporters have been privileged observers, witnessing the exasperating aberrations at the crease that punctuate lithe, peerless skills made for the poets. . . .

He is in no sense a complicated batsman with worries etched on his face as the ball cuts back wickedly off a green, capricious English wicket. He doesn't analyse every shot. His confidence is exceptional.

When he walks to the wicket at the county ground in Taunton, the farmers leave the market across the road just as they used to when Harold Gimblett was batting. His arrival at the crease in sporting

VIII *The Cricket Match:* Claude Muncaster

IX *Village Cricket:* Gerry Wright

X *Village Cricket Team:* Gerry Wright

XI *The Cricketers:* Sir Russell Drysdale

XII *Playing out time in an awkward light:* Frank Batson

XIII *The Cricket Game:* David Inshaw

XIV, **XV** Fast bowlers hunt in pairs. These studies of the Australians Dennis Lillee (left) and Jeff Thomson (1975) are by Rosemary Taylor, who has concentrated upon sport in her paintings because she is fascinated by the human body in disciplined movement. Unlike earlier painters of sport, who often used the subject as a pretext for doing landscapes, she keeps her attention sharply focused on the human figure; and no follower of cricket can mistake in these paintings the style — even from behind — of two of the fastest and most exciting of modern bowlers, perfectly captured.

XVI A maidan in central Bombay: photograph by Patrick Eagar

arenas around the world brings an audible rustle of collective excitement unique in the current game.

The public, for reasons that are chemical as well as technical, markedly like or dislike top sportsmen. They all like Richards. While they marvel at his almost casual skills, they are never quite sure whether he is going to crack another record or be out. That, as part of the human condition, is the appeal of the man.

From *Viv Richards* (1979)

Gavaskar and the 'Broad Bat'

TED DEXTER

Sunil Gavaskar stands five foot five inches high, about the same size as Napoleon. Although he never conquered Europe or invaded Russia, Gavaskar has persistently wrought havoc at the crease. And if there is a single part of his batting style which accounts for consistent success against the strongest attacks in the world, it is the 'straightness' of his bat.

Now that may seem the most elementary requirement for any good player, but it is surprising how few manage to show the full face of the blade hanging down in a perfect perpendicular. The ability to do so gives rise to the most coveted compliment amongst connoisseurs of batting, which can be applied unstintingly to 'Sonny' Gavaskar, i.e. he has the broadest bat in the game.

The broad bat phenomenon is hard to pin down. It does not necessarily belong exclusively to the stonewall, defensive brigade, nor is it necessarily the trademark of batsmen who seldom get the bat out of the vertical and into the horizontal plane. Geoff Boycott, for instance, would not be considered a 'broad bat' man, and neither would Neil Harvey nor Colin Milburn, for all their individual brilliance.

There may be a slight prejudice in favour of very small men whose full-size bats simply look bigger in contrast to their small stature. Hanif Mohammad, for instance, would qualify for this category, but even this piece of logic fails to explain the whole story. It is a simple fact that some batsmen make more of their bat than others.

Perhaps the broadest bat of my time, and I fancy that most of my generation would agree with me, belonged to Peter May. There were times when, for the bowler, it seemed as though he had the proverbial barn door in his hand. I don't know whether any suspicious blighter ever had the temerity to measure across the face of May's bat; hundreds must have been tempted, and when a man could make a maximum width of $4\frac{1}{4}$ inches (10·8 centimetres) look like double, then who could blame them. After May, a big broad man himself, I would be happy to nominate Gavaskar as next in line.

Gavaskar was born in Bombay, in 1949: his uncle M. K. Mantri had kept wicket for Bombay and India. Certainly there are some impressive facts and figures in Gavaskar's career. On India's tour of England in 1979, Gavaskar played all four Tests for an average of 77·42. In the last Test at The Oval, India, set to make 438 and so to win the game, failed to do so by only nine runs. It was Gavaskar again. He stayed put for eight hours for 221 runs.

The great shame about that magnificent innings was that it only earned India a draw, when the winning of a memorable Test match was there for the taking. The Indians can point to a sudden rush of umpiring decisions against them for their sudden loss of impetus, but they must know in their hearts that they lost the match by keeping back their next best batsman, Viswanath, when ten minutes of him in the middle with Gavaskar must surely have brought the prize they so richly deserved.

The 1980 *Wisden* records: 'When he sets his sights high, he builds his innings with meticulous craftsmanship, limiting himself to the strokes he knows best – drives through the covers, past the bowler, and between mid-on and mid-wicket. But when he lets his hair down, his range of shots and the power behind them are quite astonishing.'

Gavaskar was the first Indian to score over 700 runs in a Test series, and the first ever Test player to score over 700 runs in a debut Test series. But there were some problems. I can do no better than quote K. N. Prabhu on Gavaskar in *The Cricketer*, July 1971. After a successful transition through schools, colleges, and University cricket, 'he learnt that cricket would be a game of ups and downs, that it could be hard going at the highest levels.' So he got down to some homework, toured the West Indies, and, in the first and second Tests, made 65 and 116 – with Sobers of all people failing to gather easy catches early in both innings.

Prabhu goes on with some discerning and qualified comments: 'His tall scores are apt to give the impression that he is a lovely and venturesome batsman. This would not be a strictly accurate picture. Gavaskar is not the gay cavalier that Engineer is; he is also not one of the dull dogs... he is the sort of batsman who is likely to be appreciated in Yorkshire no less than in Kent... he has a thumping square drive and the ability and willingness to advance on quick feet to attack the spinners – factors which should please the discerning follower of cricket.'

The other problem which has affected Gavaskar's career is the same problem which seems to dog Indian Test cricket as a whole, i.e. problems over leadership. Whereas in England the hiring and firing of captains may be overinfluenced by the media, in India it seems to be unduly governed by internal political considerations amongst the administrators.

The Nawab of Pataudi (the younger) seemed a natural and effective leader, and yet the job soon passed to apparently lesser individuals.

Gavaskar defends against Willis, Lord's, 1982

The same has happened to Gavaskar. Here is a man with the drive to make things happen, and the character to engage the co-operation of his team-mates, but those terms of captaincy have been abruptly cut short for no apparent reason. The effect on Gavaskar the batsman has been noticeable when he returned to the ranks. A certain disinterested air creeps into his normally assertive attitude, and it is a tribute to his basic concern for Indian cricket, and to his own standards, that he has continued to get his head down when it matters.

Nowhere was this more conspicuous than on the 1979 tour in England. Following the team round in the early summer, I saw any amount of fancy strokes from Gavaskar, but it was not until the eve of the first Test that he took the trouble to take a hundred off Hampshire. Then in the Tests, he was not quite convincing for a while – when Gavaskar is not quite 'right' it is usually loose play outside off-stump that tells the tale – but as the series wore on and his services became of increasing importance to the team, so his resolve visibly hardened, leading up to that magnificent 221 runs at The Oval. Gavaskar sent a lot of people home happy on the two days of that memorable innings – his hundred, his double hundred. When you remember that he has barely had an easy series in his life, always playing against England, Australia and West Indies, it is a superb record.

From *From Bradman to Boycott* (1981)

Miracle at Leeds

DAVID FRITH

At twenty-past-two on Tuesday, 21 July 1981, at Headingley Cricket
Ground the greatest reversal ever seen in a Test match was completed.
Hours after Bob Willis had rocketed a yorker through Ray Bright's
defence to snatch an 18-run victory for England, the enormity of the
turnabout had still not soaked in fully.

The point at which the resident bookmakers were offering 500-1
against England in this third Cornhill test match was around three
o'clock on the fourth day, when England were 135 for 7 in the follow-
on and still 92 in arrears. Hotel bookings for that night were being
cancelled, and the English depression had deepened to somewhere
between the levels of Valium and alcoholism. Even when the laughing
Botham continued picking off fours with gorilla power and surveyor's
precision, the imminent prospect of being two-down with three to
play produced English exasperation in equal dollops to Australia's
incredulous satisfaction. If only we had all realized what lay in store.

The match had embodied numerous landmarks and frustrations in
its first $3\frac{1}{2}$ days. On the opening day John Dyson, the handsome
schoolteacher from Sydney, made his first Test century in his twenty-
second innings, but Gower and Botham both dropped Chappell, and
rain stole three-quarters of an hour nett. On Day 2, the same amount
of time was lost, but the extra hour was played through, and England's
wicket-keeper, Bob Taylor, marked his fortieth birthday with two
catches, while Botham claimed five wickets in an innings for the
fifteenth time – and the first time since the Test before he was made
captain. The dropped catch this day besmirched poor Gooch's name,
Hughes adding a further 24. The third day, Lillee's thirty-second
birthday, saw his pal Rod Marsh equal and then pass Alan Knott's
Test record of 263 wicket-keeping dismissals, Marsh playing in his
seventy-first Test against Knott's 93. Lillee took five wickets on his
birthday, one of them at the end when England followed on, Gooch
going for the second time that day in the space of four scoreless balls.
The frustration and disappointment felt this Saturday round the
ground – and up and down the country – was exacerbated by the
latest umpiring disaster: a minute or two after six o'clock the ground
was bathed in bright sunshine; yet Messrs. Evans (in his first Test)
and Meyer had decided that conditions were not suitable at 6 p.m.
and had ordered the covers on. A little discretion here would have
worked wonders. But it was played by the book, and some of the
spectators not only chucked cushions but vowed never to return.

Monday, the fourth day, saw English wickets tumble with
monotonous regularity, while criticism of the occasionally spiteful
pitch became widespread. (Even Australia's cricket manager, Peter

Philpott described it as a 'disgrace' for a Test match.) The milestone this day was Lillee's 142nd England wicket, taking him past Hugh Trumble's Ashes record. After 3 p.m., however, all the incident and memorabilia which had gone before slipped to the back of the mind as the astonishing England fightback came to pass.

Hughes successfully called 'heads' for the third time in the series, but for the first time chose to bat. Selection of spinner Bright may have committed him to do so with fine cracks already on the pitch; but England's omission of Emburey meant that Australia were committed to facing a four-prong pace attack. The ball moved around but 55 runs were made by the eighteenth over, when Wood fell to Botham's third ball just before rain interfered. The afternoon brought with it a grim struggle, Dyson battling like a Woodfull, Chappell, spared at 3 and 7, clinging on for all his pedigree was worth. He lasted until the sixty-third over, and at half-past-six Dyson ran Willis down to third man to reach his hard-fought century. Dilley returned to bowl Dyson first ball, and nightwatchman Bright joined his captain to see it through to 203 for 3 at the close.

The new ball was taken early on the second day, and Dilley, after hitting Bright resoundingly on the box, yorked him, gesturing to the crowd in the outer who had been shouting their opinion of his often wayward direction. Meanwhile, Willis was bowling some fiery but fruitless overs, once beating Hughes three times after jerking his cap off with a snorter of a short ball. This the crowd loved. Hughes, as ever, was looking for runs and striking with gusto. After the luncheon rain hold-up he reached his fifty with a vindictive-looking cover-drive and by tea he was 81, with Yallop a measured 34, and Australia well on the way to shutting England out.

Botham was now embarked on a long, productive spell. Leave it with me, he told the skipper, and I'll get you five wickets. Hughes was the first, spooning back an attempted leg-side shot. An in-curver trapped Border. The old Botham luck accounted for Yallop, who played at a widish ball and didn't miss. Taylor took the edge. Lawson was bounced back, and Marsh was bowled heaving ambitiously. The declaration came at 401 for 9 and England had a nasty eight minutes to see out.

If the follow-on could be avoided a draw seemed assured. But in 17 overs England slipped to 42 for 3, Alderman having Gooch LBW as he tried to play his first ball to leg. Brearley caught behind after some determined resistance, and Boycott being bowled by a ball from Lawson which defied analysis. It pitched on or just outside off stump, passed outside his left pad, and took the leg stump around halfway up. As the rangy fast bowler buzzed a ball past Gower's head, England's task seemed no easier than that of the policeman who had been trying to restore order to the riot-torn streets of Liverpool and London.

Sometimes Gower would stroke a boundary, standing stock still in the knowledge that the ball could never be intercepted. Gatting too pounced on the half-volley when it made one of its rare appearances. But when Lawson hit Gower in the ribs, it obviously hurt. Dyson

The joy of immaculate, solid defence: Ian Botham

dropped him at slip after lunch, but Lawson had him next ball, an impossible lifter which Marsh took high above his head. Soon Gatting was gone; then Willey, hopping as the yorker screamed through. Taylor saw 27 runs added before he got off the mark. Soon he too was out, and England were down to Dilley.

Botham's 50 came in 75 minutes, to noisy acclaim, before Marsh broke the record with a mobile catch. Then Old went; then Dilley; and England were back in again. Gooch edged low to Alderman, and Sunday prayers in many a village church must have turned towards the invocation of rain.

Even then, England, if not 500-1 against, must have been very long odds, only the weather seeming to be their champion. Brearley went the same way as Gooch, and Gower, nine overs finding his first run, touched a seamer heading for first slip. The demoralization when Gatting was LBW again to a low ball was increased just before lunch when a lifter from Lillee sent Boycott's head back and his helmet toppling to earth. Willey, with his woodchopper's forearms, and Boycott, a seething mass of concentration, held firm for 19 overs, picking up twos and the odd boundary. Willey punched the ball with awesome strength, and sometimes uppercut it to third man; but this stroke was his undoing. Hughes placed a man there, and the catch was held, giving Lillee his Ashes record.

Botham, with nothing to lose, hit hard. But soon Boycott, 46 in 215 minutes, was gone, LBW well forward, and Taylor could not cope with a lifter. Thus the bottom of the graph was reached.

In the next 18 overs, either side of tea, Botham and Dilley put a gloss on matters with a booming stand of 117 – seven short of the record – in eighty riotous minutes. Botham was missed at 32, a hard left-hand chance to Bright at gully, and there were two big shouts against Dilley for catches behind. There was no other interruption to the batting assault, and the tiring Alderman found himself taken for 16 off an over. The ignominy of an innings defeat was erased and now even mishits were going to the boundary, a sure sign that whoever manipulates the luck of this cruel game had decided it was England's turn.

Dilley reached his first Test half-century with a cover-drive off Lillee which could never have been bettered by Pollock, and excitement rose a further decibel as Dilley smacked the ball to leg and ran four with the help of a desperate overthrow.

When Dilley was bowled as he aimed violently at Alderman, there was still a chance the match would be wrapped up that evening. But Botham went down the track and hoisted Alderman for six, then drove him disdainfully for four. A Hammond-like cover-drive off Lawson took the deposed captain to 99, and then a thick edge brought up his seventh Test century, his second against Australia. As a prolonged standing ovation brought a dewiness to the eyes of the sentimental, the scorers calculated that Botham had sprinted from 39 to 103 with a six, 14 fours and just two singles. His second fifty had taken a mere forty minutes, and his century had come in 157 minutes off only 87 balls. If the captaincy had not affected his play, it was the mightiest of coincidences.

When Bright came on in place of the weary Alderman, it was the first bit of spin for Australia in the 129th over of the match. He set no real problems. A blind hook at Lawson almost cost Botham his wicket at 109, but Marsh, leaping, could not hold a most difficult chance. By the time Old was out in the eighty-first over, England were 319 for 9, 92 ahead, the precious stand having realized 67, the 184 runs added since the fall of the seventh wicket having come in thirty-one overs. The crowd was now in a frenzy, the Australians reduced to waiting for something favourable to happen.

Willis stayed with Botham through the remaining minutes, during which Lawson was still able to whistle down some nasty short deliveries – and two accidental beamers. Botham passed his highest Test score, and completed the astonishing sum of 106 out of 175 runs in the two-hour session, raising England to 351 for 9, a lead of 124.

Still the match was to be Australia's. Unless the British blitzrieg had disguised the fact, the pitch now offered less to bowlers, and it would take another 50 or more runs to stretch Australia on the last day.

Speculation was confused, nonetheless, as the final act began, the field sunlit. Botham drove the new ball to add four to his overnight 145, and Willis took a single. That was to be the extent of it. Alderman took his sixth wicket, ninth of the match, as at Trent Bridge, and Australia's target was set: 130. After two balls it was 122, Wood helping himself off Botham. Four quick singles off Dilley put Australia in good heart . . . until Botham had Wood caught behind. Even then, panic was a mile away. Dyson was cool, Chappell grim. Old came on, then Willis, uphill and into the breeze, no-balling with galling regularity. Willey was tried. Willis switched to the Kirkstall Lane end. This was the decisive move.

Like a man possessed – and a twenty-one-year-old at that – Willis cam belting down the hill, hair streaming, knees pumping. A horrible ball jumped at Chappell and lobbed from his bat through to Taylor. Four overs later Hughes, having just had his hand sprayed after a bruising by Willis, nicked to third slip, where Botham swooped to secure a fine two-handed catch. Yallop, with lunch seconds away, was welcomed by a fast bouncer, and could only jab at his third ball for Gatting, perfectly balanced at close short leg, to plunge and hold the catch. Suddenly Australia were 58 for 4 – 72 still needed – and Willis had plundered three wickets for none in eleven balls.

The interval comprised forty minutes of simian chatter. The game's turnabout had an unreality about it. It was as if the Englishmen had only been fooling for the past few days; the rampant Australians now seemed helpless.

Old struck a vital blow by bowling Border through the gap, and when Dyson surprisingly got out, hooking at Willis, Taylor had equalled John Murray's first-class record of 1,270 catches, something which would normally have had headlines of its own. Six down for 68. Now seven for 74 as Marsh hooked what looked to be a six until Dilley positioned himself four feet in from the rope and let the ball sink into his large hands, below his chin. Willis' speed was too much for Lawson, who could only flick to Taylor, who now moved ahead of Murray. Eight down for 75, and all over bar the shouting. Soon it would be all shouting over the bar.

Yet the next four overs saw 35 runs hit by the predatory Lillee and Bright – pulls, uppercuts, sweep/drives. Englishmen knew it was too good to be true after all. No heart attacks were reported, and it was too sunny for anyone to have had an umbrella, the handle to be chewed through. This, though, was exactly the excruciating tension our forefathers knew at The Oval ninety-nine years ago, when The Ashes were created out of a shock seven-run result.

Lillee popped Willis up towards mid-on. Gatting temporarily lost his footing, recovered, ran in, and threw himself forward for Queen and country. He held it at turf level. Australia were 110 for 9.

If all this was agony, it was nothing against Botham's next over. Twice Alderman edged to Old at third slip, low, awkward chances. Both went down. So *that* was it? The English escapees to be recaptured at the very outer limits of the prison camp? Such vain expectation of an impossible win.

In stormed Willis again. One journalist remarked that if this is what effect his writing Willis off had had, he would do it more often. The Australian end of the press-box was quiet, thoughtful.

The yorker with which Willis finished it all will be set apart in history, like Saunders' delivery which gained a three-run victory for Australia at Old Trafford in 1902, or Peel's which produced a caught-

England *v* Australia, Headingley, 1981. Botham attacks, Marsh watches

Fast bowler's joy: Bob Willis at
Headingley

The end of the Headingley Test. The crowd's enthusiasm unconfined

and-bowled from the injured Blackham at Sydney in 1894, when Stoddart's England team won the only previous Test after having had to follow on. Eight for 43, Willis' best Test figures, were the best for England in a Headingley Test, bettering 'Charlie' Blythe's 8 for 59 against South Africa in 1907: but the match award went to Ian Botham for a little matter of 199 runs, seven wickets and two catches. Only Jack Gregory had previously recorded a century and five or more wickets in an innings in an Ashes Test.

It was England's first victory since that at Bombay, thirteen Tests ago. It was the first ever tasted by Willey, Gatting and Dilley. It was the first Test to be reflected on Headingley's new electronic scoreboard. (India will not regret the passing of the old: it once showed them four down for none.) Only a few sour words directed indiscriminately at the Press by England's captain and bowling hero dampened the euphoria.

While everyone drew fresh breath, groundsman Keith Boyce dug up a piece of the pitch to send to the Soil Research Centre for analysis. A portion should have been consigned to the Department of Information as a symbol and reminder of the fighting spirit which not only won a famous Test match but can win much larger social and economic battles.

From *Wisden Cricket Monthly* (September 1981)

The return of the leg-spinner to
Test cricket. Tavaré caught by
Javed Miandad, bowled Abdul
Qadir 54, England *v* Pakistan,
Birmingham 1982

V

Close of Play
Heroes and Mortals

'But memory will play again.
Many and many a day again
The game that's down, the game that's never done.'
Herbert and Eleanor Farjeon

Hitting Sixes

BASIL D'OLIVEIRA

When I was younger hitting sixes used to be the delight of my life. My father held it against me. He was a good player and this madness for sixes offended him. He wasn't coached and he didn't know anything about the game in the way that I have come to learn about it. But he was close to it and he would work things out for himself, weigh up batsmen's weaknesses, work out what bowlers were trying to do. He played for thirty-eight years and he didn't stop playing until he was fifty-three. As a boy I scored for his side and later on I played for them, too.

My sixes, though, were his despair. I didn't play with hard balls until I was sixteen and from then on my sole ambition was to knock the stuffing out of them as fast as they were manufactured. The higher they went the more satisfied I was. In the end he offered me a new bat if I scored a century without hitting a six. This was an enormous bribe, but I never won a bat.

Now, when the bat is not important, I have lost interest in sixes. As I tightened up my play, there was no room for the old fervour. That kind of approach was just not practical. I think it is the only aspect of my cricket that I have thrown away.

Probably because I am still close to those days I can't get worked up about kids trying to hit sixes when I see them now. Some professionals do. It seems to offend their sense of discipline. They know that, in their own branch of the business, it is impossible to carry on in this way. 'That kid,' they will say, 'is hitting the ball in the air too much.'

There is one irrefutable answer. Look at the kid's face. He thinks it's Christmas every time he does it. He is enjoying cricket, so let him go on enjoying it. If he wants to play in a better class he will work it out for himself, if he is intelligent enough. And, if he's not intelligent, whatever he does will not matter.

You can get old too soon.

From *D'Oliveira: an autobiography* (1968)

Opposing my Hero

ARTHUR MAILEY

More unemployment – and still I carried a cricket ball as I trudged the streets.

I had drifted into a lower grade of cricket, though it was still of a fairly good standard, and I was told by some of my team-mates that I was capable of bowling a very dangerous ball. It didn't come up as often as it should, but it might lead to something. However, I would be well advised to lessen spin and concentrate on length.

I was flattered that my fellow-cricketers should think that even a few of the balls I delivered had devil in them. All the same, there was a rebellious imp sitting on my shoulder that whispered: 'Take no notice, cobber. They're crazy. Millions can bowl a good length but few can really spin the ball. Keep the spin and practise, practise, practise.'

Then came a commission for a house-painting job. It was a house near Botany Bay and it belonged to my brother-in-law. Wages? A bat that had been given to my brother-in-law by a distant relative who had taken part in the 1904 English tour. But what a relative! It was Victor Trumper himself – the fantastic, legendary Trumper, my particular hero. A hundred pounds could not have given me more pleasure.

Fancy getting a bat which my hero had actually used in a Test at Lord's; a flattish bat with a springy handle and a blade curved like the bowl of a spoon. This was another link closer to the great batsman and I was more than ever determined to improve my bowling.

The 'wrong 'un', that legacy from the great Bosanquet, like Bateman's 'one-note man' seemed to be getting me somewhere, for after several seasons in Sydney lower-grade teams I found myself in first grade, a class of cricket in which inter-state and Test players participate.

At the same time, and having done my house-painting, I got another regular job. I became an A Class labourer on the Water and Sewerage Board.

Things were certainly coming my way; I had never worn a collar and tie to work before. My mother had always hoped that I would get a 'white collar' job like Mr Rumble some day – and here it was.

It is difficult to realize that a relatively minor event in one's life can still remain the most important through the years. I was chosen to play for Redfern against Paddington – and Paddington was Victor Trumper's club.

This was unbelievable, fantastic. It could never happen – something was sure to go wrong. A war – an earthquake – Trumper might fall sick. A million things could crop up in the two or three days before the match.

I sat on my bed and looked at Trumper's picture still pinned on the canvas wall. It seemed to be breathing with the movement of the draught between the skirting. I glanced at his bat standing in a corner of the room, then back at the gently moving picture. I just couldn't believe that this, to me, ethereal and godlike figure could step off the wall, pick up the bat and say quietly, 'Two legs, please, umpire', in my presence.

My family, usually undemonstrative and self-possessed, found it difficult to maintain that reserve which, strange as it may seem, was characteristic of my father's Northern Irish heritage.

'H'm,' said Father, 'playing against Trumper on Saturday. By jove, you'll cop Old Harry if you're put on to bowl at him.'

'Why should he?' protested Mother. 'You never know what you can do till you try.'

I had nothing to say. I was little concerned with what should happen to me in the match. What worried me was that something would happen to Trumper which would prevent his playing.

Although at this time I had never seen Trumper play, on occasions I trudged from Waterloo across the Sandhills to the Sydney cricket ground and waited at the gate to watch the players coming out. Once I had climbed on a tram and actually sat opposite my hero for three stops. I would have gone further but having no money I did not want to take the chance of being kicked in the pants by the conductor. Even so I had been taken half a mile out of my way.

In my wildest dreams I never thought I would ever speak to Trumper let alone play against him. I am fairly phlegmatic by nature but between the period of my selection and the match I must have behaved like a half-wit.

Right up to my first Test match I always washed and pressed my own flannels, but before this match I pressed them not once but several times. On the Saturday I was up with the sparrows and looking anxiously at the sky. It was a lovely morning but it still might rain. Come to that, lots of things could happen in ten hours – there was still a chance that Vic could be taken ill or knocked down by a tram or twist his ankle or break his arm. . . .

My thoughts were interrupted by a vigorous thumping on the back gate. I looked out of the washhouse-bathroom-woodshed-workshop window and saw that it was the milkman who was kicking up the row.

'Hey!' he roared, '– yer didn't leave the can out. I can't wait around here all day. A man should pour it in the garbage tin – that'd make yer wake up a bit!'

On that morning I wouldn't have cared whether he poured the milk in the garbage tin or all over me. I didn't belong to this world. I was playing against the great Victor Trumper. Let the milk take care of itself.

I kept looking at the clock. It might be slow – or it might have stopped! I'd better whip down to the Zetland Hotel and check up. Anyhow, I mightn't bowl at Trumper after all. He might get out before I came on. Or I mightn't get a bowl at all – after all, I can't put myself on. Wonder what Trumper's doing this very minute . . . bet he's not ironing his flannels. Sends them to the laundry, I suppose. He's probably got two sets of flannels, anyway. Perhaps he's at breakfast, perhaps he's eating bacon and eggs. Wonder if he knows I'm playing against him? Don't suppose he's ever heard of me. Wouldn't worry him anyhow, I shouldn't think. Gosh, what a long morning! Think I'll dig the garden. No, I won't – I want to keep fresh. Think I'll lie down for a bit . . . better not, I might fall off to sleep and be late.

The morning did not pass in this way. Time just stopped. I couldn't bring myself to doing anything in particular and yet I couldn't settle to the thought of not doing anything. I was bowling to Trumper and I was not bowling to Trumper. I was early and I was late. In fact, I think I was slightly out of my mind.

I didn't get to the ground so very early after all, mainly because it would have been impossible for me to wait around so near the scene of Trumper's appearance – and yet for it to rain or news to come that something had prevented Vic from playing.

'Is he here?' I asked Harry Goddard, our captain, the moment I did arrive at the ground.

'Is who here?' he countered.

My answer was probably a scornful and disgusted look. I remember that it occurred to me to say, 'Julius Caesar, of course' but that I stopped myself being cheeky because this was one occasion when I couldn't afford to be.

Paddington won the toss and took first knock.

When Trumper walked out to bat, Harry Goddard said to me: 'I'd better keep you away from Vic. If he starts on you he'll probably knock you out of grade cricket.'

I was inclined to agree with him yet at the same time I didn't fear punishment from the master batsman. All I wanted to do was just to bowl at him. I suppose in their time other ambitious youngsters have wanted to play on the same stage with Henry Irving, or sing with Caruso or Melba, to fight with Napoleon or sail the seas with Columbus. It wasn't conquest I desired. I simply wanted to meet my hero on common ground.

Vic, beautifully clad in creamy, loose-fitting but well-tailored flannels, left the pavilion with his bat tucked under his left arm and in the act of donning his gloves. Although slightly pigeon-toed in the left foot he had a springy, athletic walk and a tendency to shrug his shoulders every few minutes, a habit I understand he developed through trying to loosen his shirt off his shoulders when it became soaked with sweat during his innings.

Arriving at the wicket, he bent his bat handle almost to a right angle, walked up the pitch, prodded about six yards of it, returned to the batting crease and asked the umpire for 'two legs', took a quick glance in the direction of fine leg, shrugged his shoulders again and took up his stance.

I was called to bowl sooner than I had expected. I suspect now that Harry Goddard changed his mind and decided to put me out of my misery early in the piece.

Did I ever bowl that first ball? I don't remember. My head was in a whirl, I really think I fainted and the secret of the mythical first ball has been kept over all these years to save me embarrassment. If the ball *was* sent down it must have been hit for six, or at least four, because I was awakened from my trance by the thunderous booming Yabba who roared: 'O for a strong arm and a walking stick!'

I do remember the next ball. It was, I imagined, a perfect leg-break. [213]

When it left my hand it was singing sweetly like a humming top. The trajectory couldn't have been more graceful if designed by a professor of ballistics. The tremendous leg-spin caused the ball to swing and curve from the off and move in line with the middle and leg stump. Had I bowled this particular ball at any other batsman I would have turned my back early in its flight and listened for the death rattle. However, consistent with my idolization of the champion, I watched his every movement.

He stood poised like a panther ready to spring. Down came his left foot to within a foot of the ball. The bat, swung from well over his shoulders, met the ball just as it fizzed off the pitch, and the next sound I heard was a rapping on the off-side fence.

It was the most beautiful shot I have ever seen.

The immortal Yabba made some attempt to say something but his voice faded away to the soft gurgle one hears at the end of a kookaburra's song. The only person on the ground who didn't watch the course of the ball was Victor Trumper. The moment he played it he turned his back, smacked down a few tufts of grass and prodded his way back to the batting crease. He knew where the ball was going.

What were my reactions?

Well, I never expected that ball or any other ball I could produce to get Trumper's wicket. But that being the best ball a bowler of my type could spin into being, I thought that at least Vic might have been forced to play a defensive shot, particularly as I was almost a stranger too and it might have been to his advantage to use discretion rather than valour.

After I had bowled one or two other reasonably good balls without success I found fresh hope in the thought that Trumper had found Bosanquet, creator of the 'wrong 'un' or 'bosie' (which I think a better name), rather puzzling. This left me with one shot in my locker, but if I didn't use it quickly I would be taken out of the firing line. I decided, therefore, to try this most undisciplined and cantankerous creation of the great B. J. T. Bosanquet – not, as many may think, as a compliment to the inventor but as the gallant farewell, so to speak, of a warrior who refused to surrender until all his ammunition was spent.

Again fortune was on my side in that I bowled the ball I had often dreamed of bowling. As with the leg-break, it had sufficient spin to curve in the air and break considerably after making contact with the pitch. If anything it might have had a little more top-spin, which would cause it to drop rather suddenly. The sensitivity of a spinning ball against a breeze is governed by the amount of spin imparted, and if a ball bowled at a certain pace drops on a certain spot, one bowled with identical pace but with more top-spin should drop eighteen inches or two feet shorter.

For this reason I thought the difference in trajectory and ultimate landing of the ball might provide a measure of uncertainty in Trumper's mind. Whilst the ball was in flight this reasoning appeared to be vindicated by Trumper's initial movement. As at the beginning of my over he sprang in to attack but did not realize that the ball, being an off-break, was floating away from him and dropping a little quicker. Instead of his left foot being close to the ball it was a foot out of line.

In a split second Vic grasped this and tried to make up the deficiency with a wider swing of the bat. It was then I could see a passage-way to the stumps with our 'keeper, Con Hayes, ready to claim his victim. Vic's bat came through like a flash but the ball passed between his bat and legs, missed the leg stump by a fraction, and the bails were whipped off with the great batsman at least two yards out of his ground.

Vic had made no attempt to scramble back. He knew the ball had beaten him and was prepared to pay the penalty, and although he had little chance of regaining his crease on this occasion I think he would have acted similarly if his back foot had been only an inch from safety.

As he walked past me he smiled, patted the back of his bat and said, 'It was too good for me.'

There was no triumph in me as I watched the receding figure. I felt like a boy who had killed a dove.

From *10 for 66 and All That* (1958)

Schoolboy's Hero

ALAN ROSS

Carlyle, in his famous series of lectures, allowed for six categories of hero – the hero as divinity, as prophet, as priest, as man of letters, as King. It is an exclusive list, making no mention of statesmen, explorers, scientists, soldiers – or, for that matter, sportsmen. Carlyle, however, was much concerned with the development of spiritual power, with the manner in which authority could achieve justice. He was an idolater, certainly, but his idols were generally beyond the normal hierarchies of men. The hero, for him, had to be a great man: the idea of hero worship involved the notion of objective, abstract greatness. It was not a private human adulation of one who existed within a human scale. Carlyle was not that kind of man.

Yet the idea of a hero today, a hundred years after Carlyle lectured, has become something much more intimate. A cricket hero in this case could legitimately, of course, still be one of the legendary names of cricket: Grace, Hobbs, Hammond, Larwood, S. F. Barnes, Fry – an Olympian figure, almost without mortal failings. Any such would be a reasonable choice. Myself, I never had the affection – admiration, respect, yes – but never that warm glowing regard, for the lordly great, which my conception of hero worship regards as necessary. I prefer local heroes to national ones, on the whole: once they progress from the county to the country arena, I feel they can do without my secret dispensations or passionate advocacy.

I believe that heroes are necessary to children and that as we grow up it becomes more difficult to establish them in the increasingly responsive soil of our individual mythology. Occasionally, the adult imagination is caught and sometimes it is held: but the image rarely takes root. I do not know that we become more fastidious, more cautious; I think it is simply that we become less whole-hearted.

If I accept then that a cricket hero must belong to adolescence, I find myself choosing from among those that haunted my mind during the 1930s. It would be unthinkable that he should not have been a Sussex cricketer, though I confess I was much enamoured once of C. F. Walters (as who, having seen him bat, could not have been?). I might well have settled for Tate, the true idol of my youth, or Duleepsinhji, or J. H. Parks, especially during the year of his 3,000 runs and 100 wickets, or Alan Melville or James Langridge. My hero-worshipping really was in the plural: my heroes were, without reservation, the Sussex cricket team. I could have chosen George Cox, who has given me greater qualitative pleasure than any living batsman, not least for his habit of driving successive pairs of Yorkshire fast bowlers through every inch of cover boundary in the country and of cutting fast or slow ones through every compass bearing between wicket-keeper and gully. I could watch him field all summer, as with the Sussex bowling of his day, he nearly did!

Then, again, there is John Langridge, of the ritualistic gestures, more hieratical in preparatory movement than any African witch-doctor, whom I have probably observed, with bird-watcher's patience, over a greater period of time than any other player. John Langridge was not quite in the heroic mould, but, because of his value to Sussex, I forgive him anything, while in the summer of 1949 he had more than a fair share of my adulation.

Any of these could have done as symbol for the pre-war Sussex of my youth. That I have, in fact, chosen as my figurehead H. T. Bartlett represents in some ways a perverse and contrary decision, for generally we seek heroes in our own image: idealized, but also to be emulated. Bartlett was a left-hander, I a right-hander; he was batsman *tout simple*, and, for all my sudden batting cravings and hallucinatory phases of success, I was indeed a bowler. I imitated Tate as a boy, I spent two formative summers coached by A. F. Wensley. By the time Bartlett, in 1938, descended like a comet on the fairly sleepy fields of Sussex cricket, I was already absorbed at Haileybury in devising plans to bowl out Cheltenham at Lord's. What could Bartlett have especially for me? There was nothing possibly I could hope to emulate in his play. Yet, if I am to be honest, I have to admit that for two whole summers I could think of practically nothing but of H. T. Bartlett. Subsequently, he provided a number of disappointments: but at that peak period, both of his career and of my fevered imagination, he was a sight to behold!

I have never cared for my heroes to be either solemn or straight-laced. I know very little about Hugh Bartlett, and then I knew absolutely nothing at all. But he always gave the impression of having a healthy detachment from the game, of having an existence outside cricket that made his excursions into it both more perilous and romantic. Perilous his first few overs at the wicket certainly were; romantic he became, because not only was he pleasing in appearance, but the very nature of his genius was transitory. He made of this ephemeral, dashing, apparent recklessness a lasting quality: to those who tend to be attracted by the elusive, he was all they could ever require. I cannot remember, even in 1938, that he at any time exuded an air of comfort.

As a cricketer, domesticity was just not in his line. He began his innings usually as one who, suffering from violent astigmatism, has not only mislaid his glasses, but has in addition a fearful headache. He made a pass or two after the ball had gone past him: he lunged fitfully and missed: he stabbed down just in time at the straight ones: he sliced the rising offside ball over second slip: he snicked hazily past his leg stump. So, for about a quarter of an hour, it went on: or, to such an agonized onlooker as I, it seemed to go on. Then, suddenly, he would catch a half-volley or a long hop such a crack that the bowler, fearful of his own safety, lost all aggressive intention, and, with it, any idea of length.

Phase two then began. One no longer felt that the bowler was remotely interested in the stumps, but, having scattered his fielders round the boundary, relied now, in the form of bait, on a species of poisoned chocolate. Bartlett paid scant heed to these exiled boundary creatures: at alarming rates he drove between, over, and if needs be, through them. He was a firm-footed hitter, possessed of a long reach, and the trajectory of his drives was low and of a fearful power.

Something of his particular magnetism came perhaps from this violent transformation of calm into hurricane, not only in his own person, but in Sussex cricket generally. Sussex had on paper a handsome batting side in those days, but the two Parks, J. H. and H. W., were effective rather than ebullient, and in any case rather past their best; John Langridge took his time, as did his brother James, and there was only George Cox to stave off periods of total becalming.

Bartlett began that summer of 1938 quietly enough; it was at Leeds on 21 May that he played his crucial innings. Going in at No. 7, with Sussex five for 106, he set about Bowes, Verity, Smailes, Robinson and Turner to such effect that he scored 94 out of 125 in 75 minutes. He was magnificently caught by Leyland off a hit that would otherwise have gone for six. Before that he had twice hit Verity for three sixes in an over!

Of course, Bartlett's hitting powers were not exactly unknown. He hit fantastically hard at Dulwich as a schoolboy, playing for Surrey before he went to Cambridge, and he had his moments over the next three years at Fenners. But in fact – he failed in each of his three University matches – there was not the same exhilarating, annihilating quality about his batting, and it had begun to look to many as if the best was behind, not before. In the winter of 1937–8, however, Bartlett spent many painstaking afternoons at an indoor cricket school, and the effect was immediate.

Curiously, after Leeds, Bartlett did not play again for Sussex for a whole month. It was a period of unbearable anticipation. Then at Worthing against Worcestershire he returned to make 76 and 64, and one knew that envious men of the West Riding had not spirited him away for good. He followed this with 91 not out against Essex, and Sussex began a wonderful winning run. Bartlett's next appearance was at Lord's when he scored his now legendary 175 not out for the Gentlemen. Nicholls was hit for two vast sixes, then five fours in an over, Smith (P.) for two fours and two sixes in the next.

It was evident now that there was no fluke about it, though since they had not been made for Sussex, I could not but feel at the time that these runs had been squandered unwisely. Who could have possibly predicted they would continue? When Bartlett came down to Hove to play against Lancashire the following weekend he was a celebrity. His scores in that match were 72 and 63. Next came the Bank Holiday game against Middlesex, the first county match of the season I was myself able to see. Bartlett scored only 27 and 16, Gray bowled him in the second innings, and I have loathed Gray ever since.

But then followed one of those magic weeks whose events even now, twenty years later, I can remember in detail. Daily I took the train from my home in Ardingly to Hastings, daily the fortunes of Sussex exceeded the wildest prayers of the night before. There was in fact a certain Mephistophelian contract undertaken in those prayers. In them I vowed willingness to surrender any potential 50 or 5 wickets if Bartlett could be empowered to make a hundred and Sussex to win. I was playing two weeks of cricket that month, one of them for a club called the Vandals. I made no score of over 10, nor took more than two wickets in that first week. Sussex in the relevant weeks at Hastings beat Northamptonshire by nine wickets and Kent by an innings and 15 runs. Bartlett scored 114 in each of his two innings. I made no spiritual compact the week after, when I scored the first hundred of my life against Tonbridge on the Angel ground, and then followed this with 75 and 77 against the Bluemantles. Bartlett during those innings managed 8, 9, 0 and 0. I did not dare to bat again that summer. Without question – such heights can adolescent fanaticism reach – Bartlett's centuries gave me more pleasure than my own.

There was even greater joy in store! On 27 August the Australians came to Hove and Bartlett, batting only two hours on the second day, hit 157. He went to his hundred in under an hour – the fastest hundred of the season – and then took 21 in an over off Ward. Altogether he hit six sixes and eighteen fours. That season Barlett finished fifth in the first-class averages; above him were Hammond, Hardstaff, Hutton and Paynter. His own average was 57·33. It could not, of course, ever be like it again. Not that it was all over, by any means. That winter Bartlett went to South Africa with MCC, and though he did not play in a Test, he averaged 51 in first-class matches. 1939, too, had its rewards. Indeed, it started rather better than the previous year for Bartlett. He opened up with scores of 49, 49, 48, 24, 33, 60, 31, 74; he made 114 (a heraldic figure for Bartlett) against Nottinghamshire, 81 against Northants, and then rather fell away. As in 1938 he played almost entirely in home matches.

He had disappointing weeks at Hove and Hastings, and then I saw him at Eastbourne later in August against Worcestershire. Sussex, facing a score of 372, were about five for 180 when Bartlett went in with Jim Parks as his partner. Bartlett raced to 89 in forty-four minutes. He was caught then by C. H. Palmer off Martin at deep extra cover, and, as at Leeds the year before, had not Palmer held the catch it would have been a six. I do not ever remember such unconstrained driving. It was not only the ball up to him that Bartlett hit: he hit as often as not on the rise, without prior reference to the length of the ball, and with little care for the correct placing of the feet. It was largely a question of perfect timing.

By now, this joyous performance apart, Bartlett was a more responsible – if that is the right word – kind of batsman. He hit less in the air; he built up an innings more in the approved style. He was a remarkably accomplished player, swift to hook, with a steely square cut, a solid, thoughtful air to his back play. There remained the usual left-hander's failings outside the off-stump. By the time cricket got properly going after the war, Bartlett was in his middle thirties. He captained Sussex, but with no great success, personal or otherwise. He was a memory, not a hero.

Heroes in fact die with one's own youth. They are pinned like butterflies to the setting board of early memories – the time when skies were always blue, the sun shone, and the air was filled with the sounds and scents of grass being cut. I find myself still as desperate to read the Sussex score in the stop-press as ever I was; but I no longer worship heroes, beings for whom the ordinary scales of human values are inadequate. One learns that, as one grows up, so do the gods grow down. It is in many ways a pity: for one had thought that heroes had no problems of their own. Now one knows different!

Hugh Bartlett was not the greatest of Sussex cricketers, and it might have been better if he had not played after the war. His parting from the county was not of the happiest. Yet, for two seasons, he made of every Sussex ground on which he played a place of enchantment. You do not often hear these days the buzz of anticipation that habitually preceded his emergence from the pavilion. Sometimes when Godfrey Evans goes out to bat in a Test match, or when Frank Tyson comes on to bowl, but not often otherwise. We hear a murmur at Hove on behalf of David Sheppard, and sometimes for Jim Parks, or Don Smith. But it is nothing to what we felt when Bartlett, tall, brown, bareheaded, a little Byronic around mouth and chin, but fairer, more casual, walked with toes turned a shade inwards towards the wicket.

Perhaps simply it is that one is older, less roused to excitement. I do not know. But I remember the sea glinting, the flags fluttering, the crowd settling itself, and those terrible first overs when Pope or Copson

or Smailes or whoever it was, fizzed the ball over Bartlett's waving
bat – the agony of it, the unbelievable survival, and finally that great
ecstasy.

From *Cricket Heroes* (1959)

At Lord's

FRANCIS THOMPSON

It is little I repair to the matches of the Southron folk,
   Though my own red roses there may blow;
It is little I repair to the matches of the Southron folk,
   Though the red roses crest the caps, I know.
For the field is full of shades as I near the shadowy coast,
And a ghostly batsman plays to the bowling of a ghost,
And I look through my tears on a soundless-clapping host
   As the run-stealers flicker to and fro,
   To and fro:
O my Hornby and my Barlow long ago!

It is Glo'ster come North, the irresistible,
   The Shire of the Graces, long ago!
It is Gloucestershire up North, the irresistible,
   And new-risen Lancashire the foe!
A Shire so young that it has scarce impressed its traces,
Ah, how shall it stand before all-resistless Graces?
O, little red rose, their bats are as maces
   To beat thee down, this summer long ago!

This day of seventy-eight they are come up North against thee
   This day of seventy-eight, long ago!
The champion of the centuries, he cometh up against thee,
   With his brethren, every one a famous foe!
The long-whiskered Doctor, that laugheth rules to scorn,
While the bowler, pitched against him, bans the day that he was
     born;
And G.F. with his science makes the fairest length forlorn;
   They are come from the West to work thee woe!

It is little I repair to the matches of the Southron folk,
   Though my own red roses there may blow;
It is little I repair to the matches of the Southron folk,
   Though the red roses crest the caps, I know.
For the field is full of shades as I near the shadowy coast,

And a ghostly batsman plays to the bowling of a ghost,
And I look through my tears on a soundless-clapping host,
    As the run-stealers flicker to and fro,
    To and fro:
O my Hornby and my Barlow long ago!

Eighty-Five to Win

England's Second Innings against The Australian Eleven at Kennington Oval on Tuesday, 29 August 1882

JOHN MASEFIELD

THE AUSTRALIAN ELEVEN	THE ENGLISH ELEVEN
A. C. Bannerman	R. G. Barlow
H. H. Massie	Dr W. G. Grace
W. L. Murdoch (*Captain*)	G. Ulyett
G. J. Bonnor	A. P. Lucas
T. Horan	Hon. A. Lyttelton
G. Giffen	C. T. Studd
J. McC. Blackham	J. M. Read
T. W. Garrett	W. Barnes
H. F. Boyle	A. G. Steel
S. P. Jones	A. N. Hornby (*Captain*)
F. R. Spofforth	E. Peate

Though wayward Time be changeful as Man's will,
We have the game, we have the Oval still,
And still the Gas-Works mark the Gas-Works End
And still our sun shines and the rains descend.

Speak to me, Muse, and tell me of the game
When Murdoch's great Eleven overcame.
Laurels were tensely lost and hardly won
In that wild afternoon at Kennington,
When more than twenty thousand watchers stared
And cheered, and hoped, and anguished, and despaired.

Tell of the Day, how heavy rain had cleared
To sunshine and mad wind as noon-time neared,
Then showers (sometimes hail) on strong blasts cold,
Making a wicket good for men who bowled.
Such was the Day, when England's side went in
Just before four, with eighty-five to win.

The Finish

Grace, and the Captain (Hornby), led the way,
(Grace to face Spofforth) in beginning play.
Spofforth was bowling from the Gas-Works End,
Garrett across.
            The opposites contend.

What was this Spofforth, called The Demon yet,
For men forget, but cannot all forget?
A tall, lean, wiry athlete inly lit
With mind, and saturnine control of it.
Is it not said, that he, with either hand,
Could fling a hen's egg, onto grass or sand,
Clear seventy yeards, yet never crack the shell?

Then, when he bowled, he seemed a thing of Hell,
Writhing; grimacing; batsmen, catching breath,
Thought him no mortal man but very Death;
For no man ever knew what ball would come
From that wild whirl, save one from devildom.
Now the sharp fears came tugging at the heart,
As Cunning strove with Care and Skill with Art.

Hornby and Grace, with eighty-five to win,
Watched for some balls, then made the runs begin.

Ten had gone up, when Hornby's wicket went
(His off-stump), from a ball that Spofforth sent.
One, for fifteen; and Barlow took his place.
Barlow, our safest bat, came in with Grace:
Barlow, the wonder, famed in song and story,
The Red Rose County's well-remembered glory.
The first ball Spofforth sent him bowled him clean.
Two gone, of England's surest, for fifteen.

But Grace alone was power manifest,
(Of all men there, he is remembered best)
The great, black-bearded Doctor, watchful-eyed,
Next to our Queen, that vanished England's pride;
Grace was still in; and Ulyett joined him there.

Slowly the scoring mounted from the pair.
To Twenty, Thirty, Forty, and anon
Garrett was taken off and Boyle put on
And Spofforth changed to the Pavilion End.

Thirty odd runs and seven bats to spend,
Surely a task so simple could be done?
Ulyett and Grace seemed settled and at one.

Fifty went up, and then a marvel came,
Still something told by lovers of the game.
Spofforth sent down a ball that Ulyett hit,
No barest chance (it seemed) to mortal wit.
Snicked, high and wide it went, yet with one hand,
Blackham just caught it and dissolved the stand.
Three gone, for fifty-one.

                     Lucas joined Grace,
Two partners famed in many a happy case,
But not, alas, for then, for two runs more,
Grace was caught out, at fifty-three for four,
Caught from a ball by Boyle, for Boyle had found
All he could wish in that uncertain ground.

Still thirty-two to win, with six to fall,
Lyttelton joined, and brought delight to all,
Enchanting promise came, for runs were scored,
Lucas and he put sixty on the board.
And then the conflict quieted to grim.

For master-spirits when hopes are dim;
Australia's best, all at their best, were there.
Light, wicket, and themselves, all bade beware.
The field were all lithe leopards on the pounce:
Each ball had a new break at every bounce.

Twelve deadly overs followed without score.
Then came a run, then deadly maidens more.
Then Spofforth shattered destiny's arrest
And Lyttelton's mid-stump was scattered west.

Five gone, for sixty-six, but Hope, still green,
Felt, the last five would make the last nineteen.
Had we not Steel, and Studd, and Maurice Read,
Three superb bats? how could we fail to speed?
Here, Hornby, saving a reserve to win,
Re-made the order of the going-in,
Putting in Steel, not Studd, at fifth man gone,
Thinking that Studd might save us later on,
If any later on might need a stay.

A strain and anguish settled on the day.
As Steel came in; but Lucas cut a four;
Not nineteen now but only fifteen more.

Steel hit his first ball back to Spofforth's hand.

Then Maurice Read gave centre and took stand . . .

Read, Surrey's pride, who ever made hope thrill
In doubtful games when things were going ill.
If Read could stay . . .
                    But Spofforth's second ball
Made the mid-stump of Surrey's pride to fall.
Seven men out, and fifteen still to get.

But William Barnes was never careless yet;
A watchful batsman he, though skilled to smite,
Barnes joined with Lucas in the doubtful fight.

Wild was the cheerless weather, wild the light,
Wild the contesting souls whom Hope had fired.

All the Australian team were men inspired,
Spofforth had said the matter 'could be done',
And all the live eleven were as one.
The Hope was theirs, the Hope that ever wins,
The Hope that sways the tossed coin as it spins,
The starry Hope that ever makes man learn
That to the man who Hopes the luck will turn.
The twenty-two at bay were face to face.

The watchers' hearts stood still about the place.

In risk so hateful, hoping so intense,
One English watcher died there, of suspense.

Barnes hit a two; three lucky byes were run;
Ten or more to win, what joy to everyone.
All cheered for every run and faces shone,
Then Lucas played a ball of Spofforth's on.
Eight, of ten, out, and seventy-five the score.
'Over' was called: the fieldsmen loitered o'er.

They paused in little groups to mutter low
The secret hints the bats were not to know.
Then, watching Studd, they tautened, each in place.
Studd, our reserve, acclaimed a second Grace.

Studd stood at watch by Boyle, the Gas-Works End;
On Boyle and Barnes the minute's issues pend.
The ball had come to Boyle, who paused awhile,
To give it hand-hold in the sawdust-pile,
Then walked, intent, as he turned to run,
Saw twenty thousand faces blurred to one,

And saw, ahead, a great bat tensely wait
The ball he held, the undelivered Fate.

He ran, he bowled, his length ball took its flight
Down the drear wickets in uncertain light,
It lifted, struck on Barne's glove, and leapt
To Murdoch, watching point, who caught, and kept.
Nine gone, for seventy-five, and last man in.
Just nine more runs to tie, and ten to win.

Peate, Yorkshire's bowler, came in Barnes's place.
The last man in, with three more balls to face.*
Could he but stand until Boyle's over ended,
Stand, keeping in, then all might be amended.
The other end would bat, and Studd was there;
Studd, Cambridge Studd, the bright bat debonair.
A prayer to Peate went up from England's sons:
'Keep steady, Yorkshire, Studd will get the runs.
You, who throughout the game have done so much . . .
Now, stand . . . keep in . . . put nothing to the touch.'

Peate took his stand: Boyle bowled his second ball.

A tumult of glad shouting broke from all,
Peate smote it lustily to leg, for two.

The ball returned and Boyle began anew.   * Four-ball overs.
Seven to tie, and eight to win the game.

Boyle launched another, subtly not the same;
And half the white-faced watchers, staring tense,
Bit their umbrella handles in suspense.

The third ball came, but like a deedless day
It passed unhit, and ceased to be in play.

An instant's respite: only one more ball
And Studd will play, unless Peate's wicket fall.

Boyle took the ball; he turned; he ran; he bowled,
All England's watching heart was stricken cold.

Peate's whirling bat met nothing in its sweep.
The ball put all his wickets in a heap;
All out, with Studd untried; our star had set,
All England out, with seven runs to get.

The crowd sat stunned an instant at the blow,
Then cheered (and none had heard men cheering so),
Cheered the great cricket that had won the game.

In flood onto pitch the watchers came,
Spofforth and Boyle were lifted shoulder high.

Brief, brief, the glow, even of Victory.
Man's memory is but a moment green.
Chronicle now the actors in the scene,
Unmentioned yet, as Massie, who had made
Life-giving runs, with Bannerman to aid;
Jones, Giffen, Bonnor, Horan, all who shared
Those deadly hours when disaster stared.

Quickly the crowd dispersed to life's routine
Of Life and Death and wonder what they mean.
A thunder muttered and a shower fell
As twilight came with star and Vesper-bell.
Over the Oval, stamped where Spofforth bowled,
Reviving grass-blades lifted from the mould.

From *The Bluebell and Other Verses* (1961)

The famous cartoon of 'the
Demon' Spofforth. 'A tall, lean,
wiry athlete inly lit/With mind,
and saturnine control of it.' See
John Masefield's poem
'Eighty-Five to Win'

Second Test, 1963, Fifth Day

COLIN MACINNES

'They won't be playing,' said the taxi driver, gazing at the windswept skies, and with that joy-in-gloom so characteristic of our island race. But at Lord's they were, and I arrived just at tea-break to witness the most exciting hours of cricket I have seen in forty years.

Fearing the elements, only 6,000 of the faithful were now scattered round the wet, cold, darkening ground. To the west, cosseted in mackintoshes, sat the members, like senators at some Roman spectacle. To the east, the Caribbean contingent were massed enthusiastically as if preparing for some Birmingham or Little Rock. The displaced clergy wandered purposefully, very gentlemanly chaps mingled with gnarled provincials and hearties from the Tavern, and dotted here and there were rare members of the sorority of female fans. 'If a woman was hard pressed for a man,' one of them said to me, 'this might not be a bad spot to look around in.'

The West Indians now reappeared, loping, elegant, casual and dynamic, and placed themselves strategically at spots where the balls rarely failed, later on, to come. The embattled Close, looking stocky, reassuring and prodigiously *English*, stepped calmly onto the ground, accompanied by his junior partner Titmus. England were 171 for 5, and had to make 63 to win before stumps were drawn at 6, or the rain fell, or the light vanished – both of which latter seemed all too probable.

With the exception of a few vicious overs from Lance Gibbs (who 'slow' bowls with a whiplash like a scorpion's tail), the bowling was by Hall and Griffith: each with a run of over forty yards and a jet delivery so electric that one half expects the bowler to hurl himself, in person, like a long jumper, at the distant wicket; and if Griffith seems deadly, what word can one use of Hall, who's like a hurricane force of nature? He had been bowling in all, from the pavilion end, for three hours and twenty minutes, and his last ball was as lethal as his first.

The four overs after the tea-break took twenty minutes to bowl, and the hearties in the Tavern manifested some impatience – beginning to barrack in that deliberately non-gentlemanly style which is the approved mode of audience participation at the super-gentlemanly game of cricket. For this they were rebuked by many a shocked 'shush' and, more specifically, by a party of elderly and dignified Caribbeans who, braving the native wrath or envy, had ensconced themselves among the patriotic Taverners. 'Fair is fair',' one of these elder statesmen from the Islands reproachfully repeated. 'Win, lose or draw, what matters is the *game*.'

Close was now lashing out, hitting impossible fours off balls that must have been invisible to any naked eye but his, and sometimes

carrying the war into the enemy camp by charging down the wicket before the ball had been delivered. This so disconcerted Hall that, on one occasion, he stopped, as if in acute physical and mental agony, before hurling his ball, and began his eighty-yard safari all over again – this provoking more shouts of sabotage from the audience, and shriller remonstrations from the Caribbean representatives. Close made his 50 amid wild applause from the British sector, and decorous clapping from his courteous rivals on the field; then Titmus fell (caught McMorris at the chest off Hall), then Trueman, no longer Ferocious Freddie, on the next ball off Hall again in the same over. Only Allen and Shackleton remained, and Colin Cowdrey encased in a plaster cast.

When Close fell to Griffith at 70 the game belonged to anybody – and more, it seemed, to the fierce West Indians than to England's tail and one-armed casualty. The light was growing dimmer; rain occasionally swept in horizontal showers across the pitch; there was

Second Test, 1963, Fifth Day: in the last over, bowled by Hall, Allen and Shackleton take a quick single. Hall follows through and collides with Allen; they try it again as the ball goes through to the wicket-keeper, Murray, but Shackleton, taken unawares by Allen's call, is out-run to the bowler's wicket by Worrell, who was taking no chances of overthrows through throwing in

[229]

Twelfth man: John Lever

also the matter of whether Worrell would, or not, use the new ball (he eventually didn't, largely because in the poor light it would be more visible). All eyes were on the clocks: confusing instruments, since one registered six minutes' advance upon the other. And time, which had seemed earlier to favour England, when Close was still on the attack, now seemed to favour the West Indies in their task of demolishing our weakest batsman.

Could the tail hold on and win at least a draw? Could they almost incredibly hit a few fours, or even a six, and win? Nerves became so strained that a vulgarian holding a transistor radio blaring a superflous commentary on the game was almost lynched.

When Shackleton joined Allen, 15 runs were needed in about as many minutes. Almost to the end, these bowler-batsmen bravely risked defeat in victory, and restored their faith in cricket as a thrilling spectacle to every one of the 6,000 present. (It has always seemed to me hard, incidentally, that the poor bowlers must all bat, and not vice versa: something should be done about this, I feel, and batsmen be made to bowl and suffer an identical embarrassment.) When the last over began (Hall bowling), England were but six runs short.

Two singles were made off the first four balls, and on the fourth Shackleton was sensationally run out. Allen had started bounding down the crease, Murray threw the ball to Worrell at forward short leg, and the sagacious captain, not trusting himself to throw, raced down the field, ball clutched in hand, and whipped the bails off at the bowler's end before Shackleton could make it.

Now one-armed Cowdrey appeared and if, in the two remaining balls of the over, England could score six, or the West Indies get a wicket, the game could still be won by either side. An even more fascinating possibility existed, which was that Allen might have hit a single and leave Cowdrey to take the final stroke. If this had happened, would Cowdrey (against Hall) have hit a one-handed six – like Harry Wharton at one of those crucial matches at Greyfriars School?

But this did not occur: for Allen, preferring the fair chance of avoiding defeat to the near-impossibility of snatching victory, decided to stay put at all costs during Hall's two final whirlwind deliveries – and who can blame him? Tension, at this point was, as they say, 'unbearable'. Twice Hall hurtled down the field, and two times Allen prudently stayed stuck. The Caribbean spectators immediately invaded the ground, their heroes raced for the safety of the pavilion, and soon a mass of dark and wildly gesticulating figures were confronting the equally excited members. For in this memorable contest, no one had won because both teams deserved to.

My last glimpse, as the emotional temperature subsided, was of an athletic policeman, helmet awry, snatching away a stump from an enthusiastic West Indian souvenir hunter (what did the copper *do* with that stump afterwards, I wonder? Hand it in to the Black Museum at Scotland Yard?) And as we tottered into St John's Wood Road, I reflected how silly I had once been to write on the tedium of cricket. What I had forgotten is that though it can be inexpressibly dull, it can sometimes be more nerve-wracking than any other sport that I have seen – including bull-fighting, racing motoring, and soccer with Pelé on the field.

What is the explanation? I think it is that, when grace descends upon a game, cricket is *mathematically* exciting as well as physically: it's like a game played by champion atheletes who are also Grand Masters at chess. Additionally, there is the battle against time, and the correct use of it, which is an allegory of the part time plays in all our lives. For few other sports last, as this one does, for several days, during which teams and specially captains, must calculate their time-and-effort strategy to a nicety.

A final appeal is that the game is both so polite and yet so ferocious. There is all that clapping of your opponents, all that tactful by-play between overs, all those flannels, those caps and sweaters, those oranges and cups of tea! But there is also the hazard, which is greater even than in boxing; so that if – which *heaven forbid* – I had ever to face Wesley Hall or Cassius Marcellus Clay, I would choose Cassius as the lesser peril. Cricketers are brave men and, at the same time, so casual, so apparently unexcited; and when they are locked, as in this match, in a really vital struggle, and yet behave so coolly, they restore one's faith in human dignity; for to be valiant and calm is a marvellous human combination.

From *New Society* (4 July 1963)

Trueman takes his
three-hundredth Test wicket at
The Oval, 1964, against
Australia: Hawke caught by
Cowdrey

Epitaph
GEORGE McWILLIAM

As in life so in death lies a bat of renown,
Slain by a lorry (three ton);
His innings is over, his bat is laid down:
To the end a poor judge of a run.

Monday Morning in Retirement

FRANK KEATING

Two summers before I was born, Jack Crapp kissed his beloved mother goodbye, put his cardboardy attaché case under one arm, his bat under another, and strode down the hill to Bristol Temple Meads to start a long life's journey in professional cricket. The final week of April 1979 was the first since 1936 that he was not setting off again. For twenty-one years he played cricket at the highest level, and then umpired at the highest level for twenty-two more. He knew it was going to be hard to stomach this first free, summer's Monday morning. He knew it would be when the dreaded 'Dear Jack' letter arrived from Lord's in February. He had heard on the grapevine that two younger men had applied in the autumn. Anyroad, he knew he was lucky to have been given the summer of 1978. His obvious pleasure when I knocked on the door of the tidy-trim council house where he lodges warmed my cockles more than I can describe. He had not been forgotten after all, on this bleakest Monday morning of all his sixty-seven summers. His fond and cheery widowed landlady had lent us her downstairs sitting-room. He had got in half a bottle of Scotch and took a nip to celebrate and to ease the cold he's been feeling lately since the old ticker started playing up. He was going to have a pacemaker fitted any day now and he was that nervous about it. Then he produced a bottle of stout (he learnt how to deal with the Press when he was Gloucester's captain) and we pored over the snapshot scrapbooks.

The muzzy photograph on page one was of a gawky-slim left-hander, with the sad face of Buster Keaton, turning to survey the broken wicket – bowled middle stump for a duck by Tich Freeman at Gravesend forty-three years ago in his first Championship innings for Gloucester. Jack was a late developer. He was already twenty-three then. A succession of good scores in local Bristol cricket had finally persuaded the sceptical county coach, Harry Smith, to take Wally Hammond to watch him. 'Sign him up,' said Wally at once, 'and don't ever coach him, he'll do all right without coaching.' Hammond said he had tonsillitis and would be unavailable to play the first match of that 1936 summer against Oxford University. 'Put Crapp in,' he demanded. He hit 66 and stayed in for the Kent game at Gravesend. Because he was subbing for Hammond, possibly the finest slip catcher in history, Jack was told to go to first slip. He had never fielded there before. At once Frank Woolley edged him a fizzer. Jack held on to it. 'Woolley didn't go. He just unconcernedly started patting down non-existent divots on the wicket. He didn't even look round. "How's that?" I murmured, sheepish and feeling a fool. "Don't worry," said

our wicket-keeper, "he'll go in his own good time, he always does."'
And he did. After that Jack always fielded in the slips and he, too,
became one of the world's finest snappers up of snicks and trifles.

At the end of his first season he had a thousand runs under his belt,
and Tom Goddard told him: 'You'll be with us for a lifetime now
Jack – so get yourself a real decent pair of boots and you won't be
sorry.' He paid five guineas for a handmade pair from Stubbs and
Burt, the Bristol shoemakers; he never bought another pair in his
career: for twenty-one years as a player round the world and for
twenty-two years as an umpire he wore those same boots. I couldn't
see them now – he had lent them to the local Boy Scouts on the housing
estate to put them on show at their jumble sale. 'See the Boots that Jack
Crapp wore – 5p.'

In any Gloucestershire innings of my boyhood we were always still
OK if Jack was still there. He usually was. We knew he wouldn't let
us down, so he never did. Always calm and watchful, he could
suddenly break out and hit the thing with a clean and awesome
ferocity, then lean placidly on his sword, the handle supporting his
left buttock, while the ball was retrieved from miles away. 'Good ol'
Jack! Give 'em another one, Jack!' we shouted. But he seldom did it
twice in succession. Just once or thrice a session. Neville Cardus called
him 'the most charming of all professionals'. He scored more centuries
for Gloucester than Jessop and was the most successful left-hander in
the County's history, scoring 23,000 runs in all. He became a first-class
umpire. Unobtrusive, rapt in concentration . . . all was well with the
world when Jack Crapp was on umpire's duty, check hat on his head,
ticking off the half dozen with the clink of the six Victorian 'Bun'
pennies in the left-hand pocket of his long white coat. Which teams, I
asked him, were the best, 'the nicest' to umpire? 'Well, I can't have
Glorse, can I? But though I say it myself it's usually been a pleasure
doing their games. So, yes, my ideal match would be Lancashire v.
Essex. Both sporting teams those, always have been.' And the worst
fixture? 'Well, of late, although it hurts me to say so, Leicester and
Somerset always gave me most trouble.'

Had there been nationwide television coverage for that legendary
series in 1948 when Crapp was called up to stand resolute against
Australia's venemous attack it might have made him as much a
national hero as when, in roughly similar circumstances, David Steele
was beckoned from obscurity over a quarter of a century later. Not
once did Jack flinch from Lindwall and Miller. He scored a famous
century against them at Bristol and, with George Emmett, was
summoned to save Britannia's sinking ship at Old Trafford. (That was
the day I cried myself to sleep after George had failed.) I should have
had faith in Jack. He batted with doughty courage for the remainder
of the series. In the Oval Test Miller almost knocked his block off.
'Surprisingly, it didn't hurt too much. I had my cap on, see.' It was all
there in the scrapbooks. In glorious sepia: the push to mid-on off
Johnson to bring up his century; the dogged straight bat to Lindwall
at Old Trafford; the defiant stare down the track at Miller at the

Oval. In that match he was at first slip for Bradman's last innings. Was it true, I asked, that the great man failed to spot the Hollies googly because his eyes were full of tears? 'That bugger never had a tear in his eye in all his life,' said Jack.

He was born in St Columb, near Padstow, and proudly remains the only Cornishman ever to have played for England. His father was killed in France in 1917 when the boy was five. 'My mother was the finest woman you could imagine,' he said. 'She brought me and my sister to Bristol and did everything to keep us a family.' She died in the last war when Jack was serving in the R.A.F. He has been more sad-faced ever since. He has never married. 'Never got round to it. Not that I wasn't a bit of a Jack-the-Lad in my time, mind.' He went up to his bed-sitting-room and from a box under the bed he brought down the stump from his first Test match, and another from Port Elizabeth and the last Test of 1949 when England made 174 in ninety-five minutes to win by two wickets, with Jack hitting ten off Mann's last three balls to secure the famous victory.

Jack Crapp beckoned me outside to his little car. There was a cassette already in the tape machine. We sat in the front. When I was comfy and the doors were shut he switched on the thirty-year-old recording of John Arlott's crackly wireless commentary on that finish far away in the Empire . . .

'. . . and Crapp drives mightily again. And it's another four over Nourse's head. It's all over! Crapp has done it! England have done it!'

Through the driving mirror, I caught a glance of my old friend's face. His eyes had come over all misty. So had mine. We sat in silence till the spell was broken. We sat going nowhere for a long time.

From *Bowled Over* (1980)

Test Match at Lord's

ALAN ROSS

Bailey bowling, McLean cuts him late for one.
I walk from the Long Room into slanting sun.
Two ancients halt as Statham starts his run.
Then, elbows linked, but straight as sailors
On a tilting deck, they move. One square-shouldered as a tailor's
Model, leans over, whispering in the other's ear:
'Go easy. Steps here. This end bowling.'
Turning, I watch Barnes guide Rhodes into fresher air,
As if to continue an innings, though Rhodes may only play by ear.

Lord's on a Summer's Evening

NEVILLE CARDUS

Wherever a lover of the game may be he should turn his thoughts towards Lord's at the end of a summer day – at half-past six possibly, when the deep velvet shadow has been thrown by the pavilion across the grass, and the last ball has been bowled, and the players are coming from the field, and the ground boys are putting the ropes round the pitch, while a few of the crowd group themselves in silent wonder as they look at the bruised earth where until a moment ago their heroes thundered away with fast off-breaks and square cuts. The long day's end . . . yet there is never any one moment at Lord's at close of play when you can say that the crowd has gone home; for long after a general vacancy has come over the scene, and long after the seats and the enclosures and the Mound stand have become depopulated, and long after the last flash of white flannels has vanished, and even after the solitary writer high up in the Press box, more dilatory than his colleagues, has departed, one or two intimate figures will be seen

sitting in the westering sunshine, reluctant to return to the world. And in the stately Long Room, the old historical pictures hang on the walls like mirrors that have not only reflected but captured and fixed into eternal attitudes all the cricketers and cricket matches that have ever been looked at through the pavilion's great windows; and even already the game that we have watched this very afternoon is mingling with the accumulated store of all the cricket Lord's has ever seen.

From *English Cricket* (1945)

Two 'Cathedral' cricket grounds: (left) Worcester; (right) Adelaide

Cricket played by the Gentlemens' Club, White Conduit House, Islington, 1788

VI

More than a Game?

'A famous Liberal historian (G. M. Trevelyan) can write the social history of England in the nineteenth century, and two famous socialists (Raymond Postgate and G. D. H. Cole) can write what they declared to be the history of the common people of England, and between them never once mention the man who was the best-known Englishman of his time. I can no longer accept the system of values which could not find in these books a place for W. G. Grace.'

C. L. R. James in *Beyond a Boundary*

The Game Lasts Long Enough . . .

BERNARD HOLLOWOOD

I am devoted to open rugger, modern soccer (a brand of animated chess), tennis, golf, squash, baseball, billiards, ping pong and almost every other ball game. But cricket seems to me to be richer in potential, deeper in its emotional and cerebral possibilities and wider in artistic scope than all games. It is played, at its best, on a beautiful carpet of summer turf, a trim lawn, in an environment of trees in leaf, bright-painted pavilions and boundary rails, marquees, easeful deck-chairs and colourfully garbed spectators. The players' uniform is utilitarian and so becoming that a distinguished writer can describe the appearance of a Test team from the shadows of the pavilion as 'an exciting waterfall, a cascade of tumbling white expectation'. In other summer sports long flannels have given way to shorts, but in cricket they remain the most functional of garments, serviceable throughout the inevitable climatic vagaries of a long day in which players move through a cycle of such diverse activities as lunching, resting, conversing, strolling and exercising violently.

The game lasts long enough to be affected by changes in cloud cover, light, humidity, temperature, the consistency of the pitch and the 'speed' of the outfield; long enough for ritual and pageantry to be welcomed; long enough for individual character to unfold, for boys to become men, for reporters to write worthy prose, for casual meetings to ripen into lasting friendships, for luck to dart in and out of the proceedings and raise hopes that seemed shattered – and shatter hopes on the wing. A cricket match is a campaign rather than an encounter.

From *Cricket on the Brain* (1970)

A Liberal Education

ANDREW LANG

Cricket ought to be to English boys what Habeas Corpus is to Englishmen, as Mr Hughes says in *Tom Brown* . . . for cricket is a liberal education in itself, and demands temper and justice and perseverance. There is more teaching in the playground than in schoolrooms, and a lesson better worth learning very often. For there can be no good or enjoyable cricket without enthusiasm – without sentiment, one may almost say: a quality that enriches life and refines it, what life more and more is apt to lose, zest.

Though he who writes was ever a cricketing failure, he must acknowledge that no art has added so much to his pleasures as this English one, and that he has had happier hours at Lord's, or even on a rough country wicket, than at the the Louvre or in the Uffizzi. If this be true of one, it is probably true of the many whose pleasures are scant, and can seldom come from what is called culture.

Cricket is simply the most catholic and diffused, the most innocent, kindly, and manly of popular pleasures, while it has been the delight of statesmen and the relaxation of learning. There was an old Covenanting minister of the straitest sect, who had so high an opinion of curling that he said if he were to die in the afternoon, he could imagine no better way than curling of passing the morning. Surely we may say as much for cricket. Heaven (as the bishop said of the strawberry) might doubtless have devised a better diversion, but as certainly no better has been invented than that which grew up on the village greens of England.

From the Introduction to Richard Daft's *Kings of Cricket* (1893)

A Black Spofforth?

A. E. KNIGHT

When in imperialist vein, and tempted to dwell upon the political and social value of the game, its humanizing influence, and its charming *camaraderie*, one often wishes we were more imperial in our sweep, and included the black races as fellow-players, as is done in the West Indies. Some of these blacks have manifested wonderful skill and genius. A winter or two ago, I had a long chat with Chatterton, the well-known Derbyshire professional, who had such a brilliant record with Walter Reed's team out in South Africa. He had played at home against Richardson, Lockwood, and Mold, and against the greatest of Australian genius, Spofforth and Turner. He shook his head as the great name of Spofforth passed his lips, and agreed that much might be urged on his behalf in a claim as the world's greatest bowler. Yet the very ablest bowler he had ever met he believed to be, not Spofforth, but a South African black, Hendricks. The memory of this man's pace from the pitch, his quick swing away, alternating with a fine break-back, stirred a cold and critical nature to enthusiasm. Chatterton was certain that if the colour line had been less sharply drawn, and Hendricks been selected to visit England, his bowling would have been a revelation to us.

From *The Complete Cricketer* (1906)

Swan Green, Lyndhurst, in the New Forest, lovingly photographed by Patrick Eagar during play

The Game of the People

G. M. TREVELYAN

In Stuart times cricket had grown up obscurely and locally, in Hampshire and Kent, as a game of the common people. The original method of scoring, by 'notches' on a stick, argues illiteracy. But in the early eighteenth century cricket enlarged both its geographic and its social boundaries. In 1743 it was observed that 'noblemen, gentlemen and clergy' were 'making butchers, cobblers or tinkers their companions' in the game. Three years later, when Kent scored 111 notches against All-England's 110, Lord John Sackville was a member of the winning team of which the gardener at Knole was captain. Village cricket spread fast through the land. In those days, before it became scientific, cricket was the best game in the world to watch, with its rapid sequence of amusing incidents, each ball a potential crisis! Squire, farmer, blacksmith and labourer, with their women and children come to see the fun, were at ease together and happy all the summer afternoon. If the French *noblesse* had been capable of playing cricket with their peasants, their châteaux would never have been burnt.

From *English Social History* (1944)

[242]

Style in cricket — Hon. F.S. Jackson, photographed by G.W. Beldam, seems to epitomise the golden age of batting

Cricket in West Indian Culture

C. L. R. JAMES

All the inhabitants of the British West Indian territories are expatriates: the islands are so small that it was not difficult for the early invaders to exterminate the native Amerindian populations. Thus language, labour and economic processes, arts and sciences are moulded on the European pattern. Cricket has proved itself one of the most easily assimilated, most penetrating and most enduring. By now everybody plays, even women's clubs flourish.

West Indian immigrants are today probably the most active cricketers in the United States and they often invite teams of the most famous West Indian players to play games in New York. Cricket clubs are proving one of the most fertile means of integrating the West Indians into British society. The West Indian of all types takes his cricket seriously and plays it that way. That is not primarily a question of temperament. Cricket has been a permanent source of serious matters, social growth and differentiation, national unity, and social awareness.

L. N. Constantine, the famous West Indian player and now High Commissioner for Trinidad in London, has recently told us that though his father and an uncle were international cricketers and coached him, he and his brothers as children often played with bats made of coconut branches and balls of adaptable fruit. Things are not nearly so rural now. But it is evidence of the deep roots which cricket has sunk in the West Indies that it has never been seriously challenged by a game so relatively inexpensive and simple to organize as soccer.

Cricket in the West Indies seems to owe its origin to the garrisons there. In *The Pickwick Papers* (1836) Dickens refers easily to a cricket match played in the West Indies by two British officers. Trinidad became British only in 1797, yet in 1842, not ten years after the abolition of slavery, there was a well established Trinidad CC. By 1891 there was an intercolonial tournament between Barbados, Jamaica and what has now become British Guiana. In 1894–95 the first English team visited the West Indies.

From its beginning to this day cricket in the West Indies has expressed with astonishing fidelity the social relations of the islands. The early island teams consisted for the most part of Englishmen in the colonies associated with local whites; and black plebeians who were dignified by the title of professional bowlers. These bowlers were more ground attendants than professionals in the accepted modern sense. Some of them had come to the nets where their betters practised, picked up the ball and bowled, sometimes without shoes.

The brown-skin or black middle class produced a few good players but there was a sharp social gap between Englishmen and white or light skinned members of the upper classes and the black plebeians who bowled so well that they were sometimes given an opportunity to make a precarious living by their skill. (In Dickens' match a black bowler, Quanko Samba, had played a Homeric role). The black population of those days seemed to accept the conditions. They welcomed the Englishmen uproariously and even seemed to support them more than the local side.

Between 1900 and 1939 the development of West Indian society improved the status and conditions of the coloured middle classes with effective results in the organization of cricket as a national expression. In addition to clubs exclusively white, with perhaps a few coloured men of wealth or distinction, the brown-skinned middle class also formed their own clubs. So did the black-skinned middle class. In time the black plebeians also formed their own. These divisions (not always in every island iron clad) were not only understood but accepted by players and populations alike. All these clubs played every Saturday in club competitions and not infrequently a white member of the Legislative Council or President of the Chamber of Commerce would be playing amicably for his club against another most of whose members were black porters, messengers or other members of the lowest social classes. Cricket was therefore a means of national consolidation. In a society very conscious of class and social differentiation, a heritage of slavery, it provided a common meeting ground of all classes without coercion or exhortation from above.

English expatriates and their local associates retained their dominance in cricket not merely by social prestige and money but by their services. The wealthier clubs of the upper classes usually assumed the responsibility of inviting MCC teams and arranged for West Indian teams to visit England in 1900 and 1906. The black professional players were included and by 1928 the West Indies were granted Test matches. The outstanding personality in this steady advancement of the game was a Barbados white man – H. B. G. Austin, a fine player and very successful business man whose father had been Bishop of the West Indies.

Yet the expatriate Englishmen and the local white aristocracy, with some few coloured men who had won acceptance in these circles, were not the decisive forces in the inculcation of the cricket ethic which has so shaped and permeated West Indian social life. This was done by English university men, chiefly from Oxford and Cambridge. During the last third of the nineteenth and the first third of the twentieth centuries many of these were masters at the secondary schools in the larger territories and their social influence went far beyond their actual numbers.

At these schools for many years there were some two hundred boys, children of Englishmen and local whites, many sons of the brown-skinned middle class, Chinese, Indians; and black boys, often poor who had won some of the very few scholarships to these schools, and others, not too many, whose parents could afford it. These Oxford and Cambridge men taught us Latin and Greek, mathematics and English literature. But they also taught, rather diffused, what I can only call the British public school code.

The success of this code inside the classrooms was uncertain. In the playing fields, especially the cricket field, it triumphed. Very rapidly we learned to 'play with the team', which meant subordinating your personal inclinations and even interests to the good of the whole. We kept a 'stiff upper lip' in that we did not complain about ill fortune. We did not denounce failures but 'well tried' or 'hard luck' came easily to our lips. We were generous to opponents and congratulated them on victories, even when we knew they did not deserve them. We absorbed the same discipline through innumerable boys' books; books by G. A. Henty, the 'Mike' stories by P. G. Wodehouse, school magazines like *The Captain*. Generation after generation of boys of the middle class went through this training and experience and took it out into the West Indian world with them, the world of the games they continued to play and the world outside. The masses of the people paid little attention to this code but they knew it and one condition of rising to a higher status in life was obedience or at least obeisance to it.

To the degree that cricket embodied a national consolidation so much needed by the islands, it could not fail to express the growing consciousness of social differentiation. Though for a long time in the

West Indies the value of the services and the authority in cricket of men like H. B. G. Austin was unquestioned, cricket was a field where the social passions of the colonials, suppressed politically, found vigorous if diluted expression. On the cricket field all men whatever their colour or status were theoretically equal. Clubs of the lower middle class or black men who achieved international status were passionately supported by the mass of the population, and in return this section seemed to play with an energy and fire which indicated that they were moved by the sense of being representative which circumstances had thrust upon them. Members of various classes gave a moral support to teams and players of their own class, though my personal experience is that this sharp racial competitiveness very rarely caused any departure from the high principles of cricket sportsmanship, and sharpened up the game.

Individual players of the lower class, most often black men, became popular national heroes in whom the masses of the people took great pride. Yet it is doubtful if any player was more nationally admired and more of a popular idol than the late George Challenor, a white Barbadian and a member of the most exclusive of white Barbados clubs.

In one particular respect the growth of nationalist sentiment has invaded the cricket field and coloured public response to it. From the beginning the captaincy of the separate island teams was looked upon as an almost impenetrable preserve of the local whites. After World War II, however, public opinion and the number of fine players emerging from the middle classes and the plebeians made this preserve difficult to maintain and before long it broke down. But the captaincy of the West Indies team remained *the* patent source of social division. The explosions during the MCC tours in 1953 and 1960 were not in any way directed against British players or as representatives of the imperial power. In fact although the 1960 explosion in Trinidad, when the crowd threw bottles on the field and brought a day's play in a Test match to a premature close, took place at the height of a great agitation for national independence, no anti-British sentiments were either felt or manifested and the British players were very popular. The social antagonists which the outburst undoubtedly expressed were completely internal. They were directed against what was widely considered to be the persistent manipulation by the traditional authorities aimed at maintaining the privileges which, natural in the earlier days, were now held to be out of place. It was widely felt that for years conscious and indefensible efforts had been made to maintain the exclusion from the West Indies captaincy of men black in skin. It needed a vigorous campaign and a massive exhibition of popular feeling before Frank Worrell, a black man, was appointed captain of the West Indies team to Australia. Now organized cricket (and soccer) are both democratic and popular national institutions in the West Indian territories, which badly need such institutions.

More important still, Frank Worrell has shown that a black man can be an exceptional leader. One incident on the 1957 tour illustrates this well. One of the black fast bowlers was Gilchrist, whose career is a perfect symbol of the stresses and strains of West Indian social and political life. The twenty-first child of a rural family of twenty-one children, he was brought from the rural districts of Jamaica by a local businessman, given a job and forthwith showed his unusual energies and ability for big cricket. He went to India with the West Indies team, but had to be sent home for conduct unsatisfactory to the West Indian management. In Trinidad in 1960 posters appeared asking the public to boycott the game unless Gilchrist was selected. Regardless of charges made or charges proved, a great mass of the population feels that Gilchrist represents them and any action taken against him is an action against them, and he has become known as a stormy petrel of the game. Yet I witnessed a most revealing incident at Hastings in 1957. Gilchrist, a member of the touring team, was told by his captain that in festival cricket one did not bowl bumpers. Determined to oblige, Gilchrist allowed himself to be driven for five fours in one over: a notably tempestuous member of a tempestuous breed, fast bowlers, Gilchrist was determined not to offend his captain for that day – a middle-class black West Indian, Frank Worrell. He alone seemed able to exercise influence over the ebullient plebeian.

In one of his novels George Lamming, the Barbados novelist, has declared in the most unequivocal terms that the educated black middle classes must accept responsibility for whatever attitude to accepted standards may be shown by the black masses: 'Nor can I allow my own moral infirmity to be transferred to a foreign conscience labelled imperialist.' The relationship between Worrell, the Jamaican Senator with an economics degree from Manchester, and the plebeian Gilchrist indicates the tensions demanding resolution in the developing future of the islands, but also what cricket can do to restore them.

The West Indian's very consciousness of his own history is a product of his cricket in a very definite sense. In Britain, Drake and Mighty Nelson, Shakespeare, the Charge of the Light Brigade, the success of parliamentary democracy, the few who did so much for so many, these constitute a continuous national tradition. Underdeveloped, newly independent countries have to go back many decades, sometimes centuries, to find one. The West Indian people have none, at least none that they know anything about. To such people, Ramadhin and Valentine wrecking English batting, the three Barbados batsmen whose names begin with W, the front page scoring of cricketers like Garfield Sobers and Rohan Kanhai fill gnawing gaps in their consciousness and in their needs. Hence the popular passions which have on occasion overstepped the bounds. Yet when over a quarter of a million people in an Australian city came into the streets to tell Worrell's team goodbye, a spontaneous gesture of affection and respect, the West Indies, clearing their way with bat and ball, had made a public entry into the comity of nations. It has been done under the aegis of the men who more than all others created the British public school tradition, Thomas Arnold, Thomas Hughes and W. G. Grace. They would recognize Frank Worrell as a representative of all they were and stood for. But juniors grow up and have to make their own independent way. In cricket, the West Indies have evolved a style of their own, even if in independence as a whole they have yet to do so.

From *New Society* (6 June 1963)

Mad dogs and Englishmen go out to play cricket in the Boxing Day snow. But where are the dogs?

Cricket on Ocean Island

ARTHUR GRIMBLE

The Old Man was anxious to spread the gospel of the game more widely among the Gilbertese. He told me one Saturday to give the first lesson to twenty-two of the Company's labourers whom the police had inveigled up to the field. At the end of the practice, which had not proved very enthusiastic, I asked them if they would like another trial some time. 'Sir,' replied their spokesman with courtesy, 'we shall be happy to come, if that is your wish.'

I explained that there was no enforcement, but put it to him that the game was a good game: didn't he think so too? 'Sir,' he said again, 'we do not wish to decieve you. It seems to us a very exhausting game. It makes our hearts die inside us.'

I naturally asked why, in that case, he had said they were willing to have another go. He whispered seriously for a while with his companions. 'We will come back,' he answered at last, 'on account of the overtime pay which the Government, being just, will give us for ꞌplaying on its ground.'

Those early teaching days provided some pretty problems of umpiring. In one case at least, no decision was ever reached. Ari, a little quick man, and Bobo, a vast and sluggish giant, were in together when Ari hit what he judged to be an easy two. He proceeded to run two, paying, as usual, not the slightest heed to his partner's movements. The gigantic Bobo ran only one, with the result that both players were at Ari's original crease when the ball was thrown in. But it was overthrown; seeing which, Ari hurled himself upon Bobo, started his great mass on a second run, and then himself careered away on his third. Bobo finished his second, but by that time Ari was back at his original crease again, having finished his fourth. He started on his fifth, but collided with Bobo, who was making heavy work of his third, in mid-pitch. Both collapsed there, Ari on top of Bobo, and Ari's original wicket was thrown down. Which of the two was out? In point of fact, it was Bobo whom we sent back to the pavilion, but that was not an umpire's decision. It was because Ari's head had butted with great force into his diaphragm and left him gasping for medical aid.

Another case was much discussed. One Abakuka (Habakkuk) so played a rising ball that it span up his arm and, by some fluke, lodged inside the yellow and purple shirt with which he was honouring our game. Swiftly the wicket-keeper darted forward and grappled with him, intending to seize the ball and so catch him out. After a severe struggle, Abakuka escaped and fled. The whole field gave chase. The fugitive, hampered by pads donned upside down (to protect his insteps from full pitchers), was overtaken on the boundary. Even handicapped as he was, he would hardly have been caught had he not tried there, by standing on his head, to decant the ball from his shirt-front; and though held feet in air, he resisted the interference with such fury that it took all that eleven masses of brown brawn could do to persuade the leather from his bosom. After so gallant a fight, it would have been sad to judge him out. Fortunately, we were saved the pain, as he was carried from the field on a stretcher.

Ten years later, cricket was popular everywhere, and a better grasp of its finer points was abroad, but odd things still happened now and then to keep us alert. When I became, in my turn, the Old Man on Ocean Island, there was a game between two police teams in which the umpire of the fielding side, for no obvious reason (since nobody had appealed), suddenly bawled 'Ouchi', which is to say, Out. We were interested to hear what he meant, especially the batsman, but all the answer he gave was 'Sirs, you know not how bad that man is. *O, beere!*' The expletive usually denotes disgust at a nasty smell. We decided that a man's personal odour had little to do with the laws of cricket, and the batsman continued his innings. But, an over or two later, there was a legitimate appeal against him. In attempting a leg hit, he had flicked a strap of his pad and it looked from point's angle as if he had been caught at wicket.

'Ouchi!' yelled the umpire with splendid gusto.

'Ouchi?' queried his victim, 'and for what reason, O eater of unclean things, am I ouchi?'

'Rek piffor wikkut!' The decision was rendered to the sky, resonant with triumphant conviction.

We decided again that the batsman had better continue, but he was so shaken by that time that his stumps were pushed back by the very next ball, a deplorable long-hop.

'Ouchi!' gloated the umpire, 'ouchi-ouchi!' and followed his retreat prancing with glad hoots to the very pavilion.

We learned later that the complex behaviour of a light-hearted village girl was at the bottom of this regrettable business. But the sequel to the story has a nice flavour for cricketers. Both men gave up playing for a while; a few weeks later, however, they came to the Residency hand in hand, with garlands on their heads, to say they wanted to be taken into practice games again. By that time, I knew the background of their quarrel, and said something severe about umpires who imported private feuds into their cricket. 'Yes, Old Man, of a truth,' the offender answered, 'our sin was to play this game while we were contending over that female person. It is not expedient for men at variance about women to be making kirikiti against each other, for behold! it is a game of brothers. But now we are brothers again, for we have turned away from that female.' As a matter of cold, hard fact, it was *she* who had turned away from *them*. But that aspect of the matter was, after all, beyond the cognizance of the MCC, whereas finding that cricket is a game of brothers was sound beyond all argument.

But I like best of all the dictum of an old man of the Sun clan, who once said to me, 'We old men take joy in watching the kirikiti of our grandsons, because it is a fighting between factions which makes the fighters love each other.' We had not been talking of cricket up to that moment, but of the savage land-feuds in which he had taken a sanguinary part himself before the hoisting of the British flag in 1892. The talk had run mainly on the family loyalties which had held his faction together. His remark, dropping out of a reflective silence at the end, meant that cricket stood, in his esteem, for all the fun of fighting, and all the discipline needed for unity in battle, *plus* broad fellowship in the field more valuable than anything the old faction wars had ever given his people. I doubt if anyone of more sophisticated culture has ever summed up the spiritual value of cricket in more telling words than his. 'Spiritual' may sound over-sentimental to a modern generation, but I stand by it, as everyone else will who has witnessed the moral teaching-force of the game in malarial jungle, or sandy desolation, or the uttermost islands of the sea.

From *A Pattern of Islands* (1952)

'But whyever not? The soccer season's half gone at Christmas!' (*A Christmas card designed for The Cricket Society*)

Two cricketing Christmas cards, by Bernard Hollowood and D.J. Willis

Vitae Lampada

HENRY NEWBOLT

There's a breathless hush in the Close tonight –
Ten to make and the match to win –
A bumping pitch and a blinding light,
An hour to play and the last man in.
And it's not for the sake of a ribboned coat,
Or the selfish hope of a season's fame,
But his Captain's hand on his shoulder smote –
'Play up! play up! and play the game!'

The sand of the desert is sodden red, –
Red with the wreck of a square that broke; –
The Gatling's jammed and the Colonel dead,
And the regiment blind with dust and smoke.
The river of death has brimmed his banks,
And England's far, and Honour a name,
But the voice of a schoolboy rallies the ranks:
'Play up! play up! and play the game!'

This is the word that year by year,
While in her place the School is set,

Every one of her sons must hear,
And none that hears it dare forget.
This they all with a joyful mind
Bear through life like a torch in flame,
And falling fling to the host behind –
'Play up! play up! and play the game!'

A senior craftsman tests
the accuracy of a hand-carved
splice as he fits it into the bat

The Best Known Cricket Poems

GODFREY SMITH

It is curious but true that the worst cricket poem is also the most celebrated. Still, to describe it as poetry at all is to give it an accolade it may not have earned. The one piece of verse (handier term) that everyone knows is by Sir Henry Newbolt. The first four lines (*see above*): so far, so good. 'Breathless hush' is hackneyed, and 'the match to win' is tautologous. On the other hand, it must be allowed that 'a bumping pitch and a blinding light' does convey a lively impression of the sort of conditions we all remember if we have played any sort of cricket. True, bumping is imprecise – every ball bumps if it pitches at all – but we know what he means. So the scene is vigorously set for the *dénouement* of the game. Then, though, comes the ludicrous bathos that has nevertheless ended up in the *Oxford Dictionary of Quotations*: 'But his

Two more than life-size sculptures of a batsman and a bowler, by Henri Rossi; first quarter of the nineteenth century

Captain's hand on shoulder smote – "Play up! Play up! and play the game!"'

No captain worth his salt would now issue orders as daft and imprecise. 'Drop your bat on everything and leave it all to Blenkinsop' would be a sight more sensible; or even 'For heaven's sake, don't get run out or you're for the high jump, mate.' But: 'Play up and play the game' – what sort of a captain would say that?'

Well, just conceivably, a captain at Clifton (Newbolt's school) around the year 1880. I wasn't there so I wouldn't know. What renders the poem totally absurd is the second stanza.

The scene now shifts to some distant output of the Imperial Raj. The British Army is evidently up against it. The sand of the desert is sodden red, the Gatling machine-gun has jammed and the Colonel is dead. Things look pretty bleak. The regiment is blind with dust and smoke, the river of death has brimmed his banks, England's far and Honour a Name. Nevertheless:

> . . . the voice of a schoolboy rallies the ranks:
> 'Play up! Play up! and play the game!'

This is intolerable. Newbolt never saw a shot fired in anger or he would hardly have perpetrated such patent balderdash. Nevertheless, the absurdity, set in the aspic of the age it was written, was to bring him instant fame. In his book *Play Up and Play the Game*, published in 1973, Patrick Howarth traces the honours that fell thick upon Newbolt: Companion of Honour; honorary degrees from Bristol, Glasgow, St Andrews, Sheffield, Toronto, Oxford and Cambridge; the esteem of such eminent contemporaries as Robert Bridges, A. J. Balfour, H. G. Wells, Sir Edward Grey. 'Of all these distinctions and all this acclaim,' says Howarth, 'it can be said that they stemmed wholly from the publication of a relatively small number of poems, of

[253]

which the one whose stanzas end "Play up! Play up! and play the game!" was fairly representative.'

And yet, Nemesis was waiting just around the corner. 'Already in the 1930s, when I was a schoolboy,' Howarth continues, 'Newbolt's verses had become a subject of ridicule among the sophisticated young and even the not very young. Early in the 1970s I asked a group of intelligent and fairly well-read young people who had just graduated from Cambridge University . . . what the name of Sir Henry Newbolt meant to them. The answer was in effect nothing.'

The reverse might be said of Francis Thompson, who wrote the only poem to vie with 'Play Up' in popularity. This God-intoxicated, drug-dependent drifter seldom wrote a line that was not deeply poetic, and the haunting thrall of 'At Lord's' does not need the security of a cricket anthology: it would earn its place in any volume of Victorian poetry. The celebrated stonewaller Barlow and his big-hitting partner 'Monkey' Hornby, Lancashire openers in Thompson's young days, are eternally caught in the mind's eye; the sound has been lost but the effect is only to accentuate the dream-like quality of the nostalgic vision:

> For the field is full of shades as I near the shadowy coast,
> And a ghostly batsman plays to the bowling of a ghost,
> And I look through my tears on a soundless-clapping host
>> As the run-stealers flicker to and fro,
>>> To and fro:
> O my Hornby and my Barlow long ago!

Not much cricket poetry can approach that in its lyrical intensity.
From 'Cricket in Poetry' in *The Summer Game* (1981)

The Mathematician on Cricket

C. P. SNOW

Above all, G. H. Hardy was a man of genius. He was one of the great pure mathematicians of the world: in his own lifetime he altered the whole course of pure mathematics in this country. He was also a man whose intelligence was so brilliant, concentrated, and clear that by his side anyone else's seemed a little muddy, a little pedestrian and confused. No one ever spoke to him for five minutes without feeling that, whatever genius means, here was one born with it. And no one ever spoke to him for five minutes – not even serious-minded Central

European mathematicians – without hearing a remark about the game of cricket. Others have gained as much delight from cricket as he did; no one can possibly have gained more. His creative mathematics was, as he wrote himself in *A Mathematician's Apology*, the one great sustained happiness of his life; but cricket, from his childhood until he died in 1947 at the age of seventy, was his continual refreshment.

It was to that fact that I owed my friendship with him. I remember vividly the first time we met. He had just returned to Cambridge to occupy the Sadleirian chair, and was dining as a guest in Christ's. He was then in his early fifties, and his hair was already grey, above skin so deeply sunburned that it stayed a kind of Red Indian bronze. His face was beautiful – with high cheek bones, thin nose, spiritual and austere but capable of dissolving into convulsions of internal, gamin-like amusement. He had opaque brown eyes, bright as a bird's – a kind of eye not uncommon among those with a gift for conceptual thought. I thought that night that Cambridge was a town where the streets were full of unusual and distinguished faces, but even there Hardy's could not help but stand out.

As we sat round the combination-room table after dinner, someone said that Hardy wanted to talk to me about cricket. I had only been elected a year, but the pastimes of even the very young fellows were soon detected, in that intimate society. I was taken to sit by him – never introduced, for Hardy, shy and self-conscious in all formal actions, had a dread of introductions. He just put his head down, as it were in a butt of acknowledgment, and without any preamble whatever began:

You're supposed to know something about cricket, aren't you?'

Yes, I said, I knew something.

Immediately he proceeded to put me through a moderately stiff viva. Did I play? What did I do? I half-guessed that he had a horror of persons who devotedly learned their *Wisden*'s backwards but who, on the field, could not distinguish between an off-spinner and short-leg. I explained, in some technical detail, what I did with the ball. He appeared to find the reply partially reassuring, and went on to more tactical questions. Whom should I have chosen as captain for the last Test a year before (in 1930)? If the selectors had decided that Snow was the man to save us, what would have been my strategy and tactics? ('You are allowed to act, if you are sufficiently modest, as non-playing captain.') And so on, oblivious to the rest of the table. He was quite absorbed. The only way to measure someone's knowledge, in Hardy's view, was to examine him. If he had bluffed and then wilted under the questions, that was his look-out. First things came first, in that brilliant and concentrated mind. It was necessary to discover whether I should be tolerable as a cricket companion. Nothing else mattered. In the end he smiled with immense charm, with child-like openness, and said that Fenner's might be bearable after all, with the prospect of some reasonable conversation.

Except on special occasions, he still did mathematics in the morning, even in the cricket season, and did not arrive at Fenner's until after lunch. He used to walk round the cinderpath with a long, loping, heavy-footed stride (he was a slight, spare man, physically active), head down, hair, tie, sweaters, papers, all flowing, a figure that caught everyone's eye. ('There goes a Greek poet, I'll be bound,' once said some cheerful farmer as Hardy passed the scoreboard.) He made for his favourite place, at the Wollaston Road end, opposite the pavilion, where he could catch every ray of sunshine – for he was impatient when any moment of sunshine went by and he was prevented from basking in it. In order to deceive the sun into shining, he brought with him, even on a fine May afternoon, what he called his 'anti-God battery'. This consisted of three or four sweaters, an umbrella belonging to his sister, and a large envelope containing mathematical manuscripts, such as a Ph.D. dissertation, a paper which he was refereeing for the Royal Society, or some tripos answers. He would then explain, if possible to some clergyman, that God, believing that Hardy expected the weather would change and give him a chance to work, counter-suggestibly arranged that the sky should remain cloudless.

There he sat. To complete his pleasure in a long afternoon watching cricket, he liked the sun to be shining and a companion to join in the fun. But he was never bored by any cricket in any circumstances; he was fond of saying that no one of any vitality, intellectual or other, should know what it was like to be bored. As for being bored at cricket, that was manifestly impossible. He had watched the game since, as a child, he had gone to The Oval in the great days of Surrey cricket, with Tom Richardson, Lockwood, Abel in their prime: as a schoolboy at Winchester, an undergraduate at Trinity, with W. G. in his Indian summer and Ranjitsinjhi coming on the scene: through Edwardian afternoons, when Hardy was already recognized as one of the mathematicians of the age: in the Parks at Oxford after the first war, the serenest time of his whole life: and now in the 'thirties at Fenner's, his delight in the game as strong as ever.

His first interest was technical. He was secretly irritated when people assumed he knew every record in cricket history; in fact, his book-knowledge was considerable but in no way remarkable; it was greater than mine, but less than that of several acquaintances. He had been a creative person all his life, without the taste for that kind of recondite scholarship. He was far more occupied with the backswing of the man at that moment batting, or the way in which one could make a leg-break dip, or the difference between the hooking mechanism of Bradman and Sutcliffe. His interest was primarily a games player's, and not a scholar's. He himself had an unusually fine eye, and when well into the sixties could still offdrive or make an old-fashioned square leg sweep with astonishing certainty. Asked who lived the most enviable of lives, he' would have said, quite simply, a creative mathematician – for he knew that no one could have led a life more creatively satisfying than his own. His second choice would not have been a scientist (for science he had surprisingly little sympathy): I think he would have said instead a first-rate creative writer. And I am sure his third choice would have been a great batsman.

His second interest was in tactics, in that whole area of small decisions – about bowling changes, field-placings, batting orders, and the like – in which cricket is so rich. This was an interest which in exciting matches sometimes occupied him entirely. He used to say that P. G. H. Fender's famous passage about the last day of the fourth Test in the 1928-9 series was the finest expression of sheer intellectual agony in any language.

The point was this: there was nothing in the game, Australia needed about 100 to win with 5 wickets to fall, and J. C. White was the only effective bowler on the English side. White was bowling, of course, slow left arm, pitching on the leg and middle and going away a bit. Chapman had set a field with a fine leg to stop the glance for a single, but with no short leg to stop the push. The Australians kept making these safe singles. Fender's agony grew. Why could not the captain see that, if one cannot block both places, one should in all sanity block the safe push and leave the glance open, when it is the riskier of the two strokes against a bowler as accurate as White? Fender was, naturally, worried about the result as the singles kept creeping up: but chiefly he was dismayed by anyone missing such a pure intellectual point. At last lunchtime came. It is not stated in the book, but one imagines a desperate piece of lucid exposition from Fender. After lunch there was a short leg instead of a fine leg. Fender settled down in intellectual content; in the description, it comes almost as an anti-climax when England win by 11 runs.

With Hardy, it would have been just the same. I have sat by him, and seen him distressed for half-an-hour over some similar tactical blindness. How was it possible for a sentient human being to miss such a clear, simple, beautiful point?

Everything Hardy did was light with grace, order, a sense of style. To those competent to respond, I have been told, his mathematics gave extreme aesthetic delight; he wrote, in his own clear and unadorned fashion, some of the most perfect English of our time (of which samples can be read in *A Mathematician's Apology* or the preface to *Ramanujan*). Even his handwriting was beautiful; the Cambridge University Press had the inspiration to print a facsimile on the dust-jacket of the *Apology*. It was natural that he should find much formal beauty in cricket, which is itself a game of grace and order. But he found beauty after his own style, not anyone else's. He was deeply repelled by all the 'literary' treatment of the game; he did not want to hear about white flannels on the green turf, there was nothing he less wanted to hear; he felt that Mr Neville Cardus, despite gifts which Hardy was too fair-minded to deny, had been an overwhelmingly bad influence on the cricket writing of the last twenty years. Fender, analytical, informed, alive with intellectual vitality and a nagging intellectual integrity, was by a long way Hardy's favourite cricket writer. Fender has an involved and parenthetical style, which bears a faint family resemblance to Proust and Henry James. Hardy commented that all three were trying to say genuinely difficult things, but that Fender, like Proust and unlike Henry James, had within his chosen field an instinct for the essential.

Technique, tactics, formal beauty – those were the deepest attractions of cricket for Hardy. But there were two others, which to many who have sat within earshot must have seemed more obvious. Of these minor attractions, one was his relish for the human comedy. He would have been the first to disclaim that he possessed deep insight into any particular human being. That was a novelist's gift; he did not pretend to compete. But he was the most intelligent of men, he had lived with his eyes open and read much, and he had obtained a good generalized sense of human nature – robust, indulgent, satirical, and utterly free from moral vanity. He was spiritually candid as few men are, and he had a mocking horror of pretentiousness, self-righteous indignation, and the whole stately pantechnicon of the hypocritical virtues. Now cricket, the most beautiful of games, is also the most hypocritical: one ought to prefer to make 0 and see one's side win than make 100 and see it lose (J. B. Hobbs, like Hardy a man of innocent candour, remarks mildly that he never managed to feel so). Such statements were designed to inspire Hardy's sense of fun, and in reply he used to expound, with the utmost solemnity, a counter-balancing series of maxims.

'Cricket is the only game where you are playing against eleven of the other side and ten of your own.'

'If you are nervous when you go in first, nothing restores your confidence so much as seeing the other man get out.'

'After a pogrom, the Freshman's Match is the best place to see human nature in the raw.'

No match was perfect unless it produced its share of the human comedy. He liked to have his personal sympathies engaged; and, if he did not know anyone in whom to invest either sympathy or antipathy, he proceeded to invent them. In any match at Fenner's, he decided on his favourites and non-favourites: the favourites had to be the under-privileged, young men from obscure schools, Indians, the unlucky and diffident. He wished for their success and, alternatively, for the downfall of their opposites – the heartily confident, the overpraised heroes from the famous schools, the self-important, those designed by nature to boom their way to success and moral certitude ('the large-bottomed,' as he called them: the attribute, in this context, was psychological.).

So each match had its minor crises. 'The next epic event', Hardy would say, 'is for Iftikar Ali to get into double figures.' And the greatest of the minor joys of cricket for him was the infinite opportunity for intellectual play. It happens that unlike any kind of football or the racket games, cricket is a succession of discrete events: each ball is a separate mark in the scorebook: this peculiarity makes it much easier to describe, talk about, comment on, remember in detail. (Incidentally, it is this peculiarity which makes its great climaxes so intense.) It could not have been better suited to the play of Hardy's mind.

'Cricket is a game of numbers,' said Hardy cheerfully to those who wanted to compare an innings to a musical composition, and asked them what the maximum number of times the same integer could appear on the scoreboard at one instant in the innings. (The integer is 1; one batsman must have retired hurt: the score is 111 for 1, batsman 1 and 11 each 11, bowlers 1 and 11, last player 11, caught by 11.) As his professional life had been devoted to the theory of numbers, he could see something interesting in any scoreboard at any time.

Any newspaper in the cricket season had the same interest. Numbers, the structure of a score, the personal fate of clergymen, against whom he carried on an ironical private war: few things gave him more mischievous glee than to read that a clerical batsman had been run out. His great triumph in that direction, however, was a little different. It happened in a Gentlemen *v* Players match at Lord's. It was early in the morning's play, and the sun was shining over the pavilion. One of the batsmen, facing the Nursery end, complained that he was unsighted by a reflection from somewhere unknown. The umpires, puzzled, padded round by the sight-screen. Motor-cars? No. Windows? None on that side of the ground. At last, with justifiable triumph, an umpire traced the relection down – it came from a large pectoral cross resting on the middle of an enormous clergyman. Politely the umpire asked him to take it off. Close by, Hardy was doubled up in Mephistophelian delight. That lunch time, he had no time to eat; he was writing post-cards (such post-cards as came to many out of the blue) to each of his clerical friends.

But in his war against clergymen, victory was not all on one side. On a quiet and lovely May evening at Fenner's, the chimes of six o'clock fell across the ground. 'It's rather unfortunate,' said Hardy with his usual candour, 'that some of the happiest hours of my life should have been spent within sound of a Roman Catholic Church.'

Sometimes, not often, his ball-by-ball interest flagged. Then he promptly demanded that we should pick teams – teams whose names began with HA (first wicket pair Hadrian and Hayward (T.)), LU, MO – the combinations of any of our friends round us, the all-time teams of Trinity, Christ's (first wicket pair Milton and Darwin, which takes a lot of beating), teams of humbugs, club-men, bogus poets, bores. . . . Or he ordered: 'Mark that man,' and someone had to be marked out of 100 in the categories Hardy had long since invented and defined: STARK, BLEAK, 'a stark man is not necessarily bleak: but all bleak men without exception want to be considered stark', DIM, OLD BRANDY, and SPIN. There were other categories which cannot be printed; of the five above, STARK, BLEAK, and DIM are self-explanatory, SPIN meant a subtlety and delicacy of nature that Hardy loved ('X may not be a great man, but he does spin the ball just a little all the time,') and OLD BRANDY was derived from a mythical character who said that he never drank anything but very old brandy.

So, by elaboration, Old Brandy came to mean a taste that was eccentric, esoteric, but just within the confines of reason. To say that one would rather watch Woodfull than any other batsman would be a typical 'old brandy' remark. But one had to keep one's head in all these games with Hardy. Claiming Proust's novels as the best in the world's literature came within the permissible limits of old brandy: but a young man who did the same for *Finnegans Wake* was dismissed as an ass. 'Young men ought to be conceited, but they oughtn't to be imbecile,' Hardy grumbled afterwards.

Walking home after the close of play, he would maintain the same flow of spirits. At half-past six on a summer evening, Parker's Piece was crammed with boys' matches, square leg in one game dangerously near to cover in the next.

'I'll bet you sixpence that we see three wickets fall. Another sixpence that one chance is missed.' That bet meant that we had to keep a steady walking pace; as a rule, he wanted to stop and study any conceivable kind of game. He was too shy to offer to umpire, but if the boys invited him he settled down to an hour's entertainment.

Safely across the Piece, he would have some new concept, such as persuading me to stay in some dingy hotel. 'How much should I have to pay you to spend a night there? No, a pound is excessive.' Then the last excitement of the day's cricket, as he bought a local paper by the side of what was then the New Theatre. Stop press news and Surrey first: I can still hear his *cri de coeur*, some time in the middle 'thirties, when Lancashire were playing Surrey, and most of the present test team unknown. 'Washbrook 196 not out. Washbrook! Who the hell is *Washbrook?*'

The summer days passed. After one of the short Fenner's seasons, there was the University match; arranging to meet him in London was not always simple, for he had a profound suspicion of any mechanical contrivance such as a telephone. I do not think he ever used a fountain-pen: while in his rooms at Trinity or his flat in St George's Square, he used to say, in a disapproving and slightly sinister tone: 'If you *fancy yourself* at the telephone, there happens to be one in the next room.' His idea of communication was, if possible, to call in on foot: as a second line, to write a postcard.

Yet, punctually, he arrived at Lord's. There he was at his most sparkling, year after year. Surrounded by friends, men and women, he was quite released from shyness; he was the centre of all our attention, which he by no means disliked; and one could often hear the party's laughter from a quarter of the way round the ground. Having been a professor at both Oxford and Cambridge, he reserved the right to sympathize with either side; but in fact, except when his beloved friend John Lomas was batting for Oxford, his heart stayed more faithful to Cambridge than he liked to admit.

In those years, I used to go abroad soon after the University match, and to villages round the Mediterranean and Adriatic arrived post-cards in a beautiful hand, often mysteriously covered with figures. These postcards marked Hardy's August progress, Oxford, The Oval, Folkestone. Sometimes they contained nothing but a single sentence. 'How does N. F. Armstrong of your county hit the ball so hard without moving his feet, arms, or even apparently his bat?' 'Bradman is a whole class above any batsman who has ever lived: if Archimedes,

Newton, and Gauss remain in the Hobbs class, I have to admit the possibility of a class above them, which I find difficult to imagine.' 'The half-mile from St George's Square to The Oval is my old brandy nomination for the most distinguished walk in the world.'

In 1934 he sent me a large exercise book. On the left-hand pages he had written an over-by-over account of the fifth Test; on the right hand he had spread himself in disquisitions on the players, cricket in general, human nature, and life. Maddeningly, I lost the book in a move during the war, or it would give a better picture of him than any second-hand account. He promised that, when he had finished completely with creative mathematics, he would do something in the same form, but on a more ambitious scale, as his last non-mathematical testament. It was to be called *A Day at The Oval*. It would have been an eccentric minor classic; but it was never written.

Almost up to the end, I hoped that he would do it. His creative power left him, much later than with most mathematicians, but still too early: how harsh a deprivation it was for him, anyone can read in his *Apology*, which, for all its high spirits, is a book of intolerable sadness. His heart was failing: he took it stoically, but he had always been active, his enjoyments had been those of a young man until he was sixty, and he found it bitter to grow old. All this happened during the war: he hated war, not as we all do, but with a personal and desperate loathing. The world had gone dark for him, and because of the war, there was not much cricket for him to watch, which would have been an amelioration, which would, at least for occasional afternoons, have made him gay again.

So he never wrote *A Day at The Oval*. In his last illness, in the summer and autumn of 1947, he thought of it again, but he could not make the effort. Yet cricket, during those last months of his life, was his chief, almost his only, comfort and interest. His sister read to him every scrap of cricket news that she could find. Until the end of the English season, there was plenty of material, but after that she had to fill in with World Series Baseball before the Indians started their tour in Australia. That was his final interest. I had left Cambridge some years before, but during those months I went to talk cricket with him as often as I could get away; in each visit, he liked to spend a few minutes discussing death, and then hear everything I could tell him about the latest cricket gossip. Edrich was a particular favourite of his, and he showed all the old delight when I brought the news that Edrich had, right on the post, passed Tom Hayward's record. The last conversation I had with Hardy was four or five days before he died: it was about Vinoo Mankad: was he, or was he not, an all-rounder of the Rhodes or Faulkner class?

It was in that same week that he told his sister: 'If I knew I was going to die today, I think I should still want to hear the cricket scores.'

Each evening that week before she left him, she read a chapter from a history of Cambridge cricket. One such chapter was the last thing he heard, for he died suddenly, in the morning.

The End of an Era

ERIC MIDWINTER

W. G. Grace had one last duty to perform on behalf of cricket and that was help bring it to a shuddering halt. Like most of his generation, W. G. Grace viewed the 1914–18 War in simplistic and moral terms, an unreserved conflict of good against evil. It required total moral and emotional commitment, and, sorrowfully, that other overriding commitment, the one to cricket, had to be sacrificed. What the modern mind has difficulty perhaps in understanding is that it was the seriousness of cricket to its Victorian and Edwardian protagonists which made it a distraction, not its triviality. Rowland Bowen has astutely drawn the distinction between attitudes in the two World Wars in his *Cricket: A History of its Growth and Development throughout the World*. All major and competitive cricket, save for some northern league matches, was stopped in England during World War I, as cricketers turned their full attention to the foe. In World War II efforts were made to provide some good-class cricket by way of diversion for players and entertainment for war-weary spectators. The second war may have been, in the then current adjective, 'total' in its physical involvement, but the 1914–18 war was more 'total' in its psychological engagement.

Archie MacLaren, W.G.'s successor as England's captain, had called youth to the colours in sentiments – 'that crowned madman', 'that hog in armour', he called the Kaiser in *World of Cricket* – which sound shamefully jingoistic to modern ears. War had been declared on 4 August 1914 and the British Expeditonary Force, the true 'Old Contemptibles', was soon in action. Barely two weeks later Sir John French, after heavy fighting, was supervising its retreat from Mons. Grace was horror-stricken that cricket could meander on while such events were afoot, and he found it offensive that some cricketers might be dying in the trenches while others cavorted at the wicket. In one of the few direct attempts to publish his own thoughts he ever contemplated, he wrote a letter, not to *The Times* as many would have done, but, as he felt in terms of the readership he sought, more fittingly to the *Sportsman*. It is poignant indeed that his last public act was the tacit acknowledgement, by a man who had eschewed such ideas throughout his life, that politics and sport are inextricably mixed. The letter is dated 27 August 1914:

There are many cricketers who are already doing their duty but there are many more who do not seem to realize that in all probability they will have to serve either at home or abroad before the war is brought to a conclusion. The fighting on the Continent is very severe and is likely to be prolonged. I think the time has

W.G. Grace — massive authority
(G.W. Beldam)

arrived when the county cricket season should be closed, for it is not fitting at a time like this that able-bodied men should be playing day by day, and pleasure-seekers look on. There are so many who are young and able, and are still hanging back. I should like to see all first-class cricketers of suitable age set a good example, and come to the help of their country without delay in its hour of need.

How had cricket reached so far into the consciousness of society that it could be discussed and accepted in the solemn terms of Grace's letter to the *Sportsman?*

W. G. Grace said that cricket 'cultivates the manly attributes'. Church and school encouraged the ideal of cricket as the proving ground. Newbolt's 'There's a deathly hush in the close tonight', with its final stanzas of this remembered in the heat of battle, presaged the dreadful challenge for those who 'played their game in the fields of France'. And, as the Rev. Thomas Waugh wrote in 1894, after death 'The whole redeemed Church of God meets you with the words "Well Played, Sir"!' The games cult arguably altered Christianity. In death, as in life, 'he marks not that you won or lost but how you played the game.'

Cricket was a weighty alternative to, and not a relief from, the war effort: one could not mix business with business, and, for the Christian Englishman, there was no room for both a patriotic war and first-class cricket. It was during Grace's career that cricket had adopted this ritualistic dimension.

In an age of 'games-dominated Tory Imperialism' and when Thomas Carlyle fiercely espoused the notion of the heroic individual, W. G. Grace was the prophetic figure, the Ecce Homo, of Victorian cricket. Each game allowed the ritual Grace personified to unfold, its arcane rigmarole negotiating a slow, Talmudic processional from the pitching to the drawing of stumps, with the white-clad figures (how different, say, from the MCC in 1798 in sky-blue coats, nankeen breeches, hats and green beaver) adding to the trance-like, religious quality. There was even the necromantic rites of the Ashes.

Rowland Bowen wrote of this 'special new aura' with cricket becoming 'somehow a rather saintly game'. He records how W. G. Grace's cousin and Gloucestershire colleague, W. R. Gilbert, had been discovered stealing from his fellow players. 'The Colonel', as he was nicknamed, had scraped a precarious living mainly as a member of Grace's United South team. When this folded, he turned professional in 1886, but was found pilfering in the sacristy of the dressing-room. The matter was kept quiet by the Graces and the culprit, rather in the *Beau Geste* tradition, emigrated to Canada – and nearly ninety years on, Bowen was advised not to publish the story! The sin was too awful to contemplate.

The ceremonial of cricket was respected. Grace contemptuously dismissed 'barracking' as an Australian coinage, and the Grace brothers were all prepared to deal summarily with barrackers. It was like laughing in church. Even the humour could be church-like. When an MCC side, including Grace, was cheaply dismissed by a public school's opening bowlers, by the names Wood and Stone, the headmaster's scholarly choice of hymn in chapel that evening was 'The heathen in their blindness bow down to Wood and Stone'. The joke is in the dignified tradition of Anglican wit, like 'How should it stand before all resistless Graces?'

Grace also spoke of cricket as marked by 'the absence of occasion for passion', and, while he sometimes honoured this precept in the breach rather than the observance, there is no doubt that W.G. and his fellow Victorians played cricket, as Victorian armies fought such battles as that at Rourke's Drift in 1879, with a strange mixture of bravado and discipline. According to the old professional, when Grace blocked 'em, he blocked 'em for four. In a loop of film of the Champion at practice one notes that Grace adds a potent flourish of his giant's forearms at the moment of execution of every single stroke. It was this passionless enthusiasm, this controlled zeal, which helped Grace and the other maestros of the Golden Age to excel, and thousands of players and spectators approached the sport with the gravity of Phileas Fogg attempting his madcap circumnavigation of the world in eighty days. . . .

Cricket, therefore, was a discipline, as well as a ritual which became, in Grace's time, a metaphor for life. In his novel *The Go-Between*, set in 1900, L. P. Hartley perceptively uses a cricket match between the country Hall and the village to throw into relief the central plot of Ted Burgess, small-scale farmer and clandestine lover of Marian Maudsley, the local magnate's daughter. He is opposed to Lord Trimingham, stylish crack of the 'Hall' XI and Marian's fiancé. Young Leo Colston, the go-between of the two lovers, catches out Ted and wins the game, just as, unavoidably, he leads to the catching out of the secret affair. 'White clad figures sliding purposefully to and fro . . . as if a battle were in prospect . . . the ceremony of taking centre . . . its awful ritual solemnity . . . all our side were in white flannels . . . the village team . . . distressed me by their nondescript appearance . . . it was like trained soldiers fighting natives.' Leo's thoughts encapsulate the mood of the age exquisitely. It was not cricket for Ted Burgess to enjoy dalliance with Marian, and Ted Burgess shot himself, not for sinning against Victorian social standards, but, like W. R. Gilbert, for being discovered.

Then came the 1914–1918 War to close that era suddenly and tragically, and with it came the death of W. G. Grace. He died in October 1915 . . . as the lights were going out all over Europe; and, in his passing, he seemed to symbolize the closure of an era. One might be forgiven for the conjecture that it was. Perhaps it was more than a dismally neat coincidence. When old Martha Grace died, the game between Lancashire and Gloucestershire at Old Trafford was abandoned, and, when Edward Grace died, the flags at Northampton, where Gloucester were the visitors, were immediately flown at half-mast. When William Gilbert Grace died cricket had already been abandoned and the flags lowered. He died in the autumn following the first season in which no first-class cricket had been played in England since the very concept of such cricket had been specified. Grace, with his juvenile refusal to take politics seriously, was bewildered by the war; he hated, and rightly, the thought of cricketers and other young men being 'mown down', but, more than that, he was bewildered and, for all his full-hearted courage, frightened by it. But for Grace the immediate, searing wound was the total collapse and absence of cricket. Into that hollowness must have drained the remnants of the Champion's resolve to live. His obsession starved, his will was vanquished. . . .

Be that as it may, cricket itself came to a fulsome maturity under the Victorians with W. G. Grace, both at home and, under the British flag abroad. In the last decade of the last century and in the first decade of this, cricket ripened to its proudest flower, and is unlikely ever to bloom so again. It was a Victorian triumph, reaching its zenith late in that era and maintaining its glory throughout the Edwardian period, that apposite epilogue to Victorianism. Brilliant although the quality of play was in this period, it was also in its cultural and social aspects that cricket reached its highest point of development. The two – the expertise of the players and cricket's socio-cultural context – naturally interlocked. Part of, for instance, cricket's tremendous popularity at that time stemmed from the unparalleled zest and command of its exponents, while, in turn, they were doubtless inspired by being revered as the high priests of an almost sacred cult. Certainly all the lines of cricketing development peaked together to create a well-rounded and complete social phenomenon. If cricket had demonstrated that the English never grew up but indulged, in all classes, in child-like pastime, then 1914 was a national coming of age. W.G. himself sounded the clarion, and told young men to beat their cricket bats into rifles and turn their attention from Australia to Germany.

Arguably, cricket and Grace died together. Naturally, this does not mean that cricket, as a sport, was played no more. A clearer statement is that cricket atrophied then and has not, in any major way, evolved further since that time. The game had completed its development and was practised at its highest degree of competence. All-round fielding and field placing may now be more generally efficient and consistently so, but the actual skills of fielding, as well as those of batting, bowling and wicket-keeping, have not basically changed, and, although equalled, have not, in chief, been bettered. That imagined transferability of players, from age to age, so beloved of the buffs of any sport, is not as difficult in cricket as in other sports: compare, for instance, the Wimbledon tennis championships with those of a hundred years ago or even less.

An illuminating example is that cricket (like football in earlier times) had no fouls or sanctions: a typically Victorian stance on the cult of sportsmanship and acceptance of the law. A cricket match cannot progress far without the players' self-discipline and without their basic acceptance of the overall structure of the game. If players actively started to 'foul' one another, umpires would have little chance to arbitrate and no penalties to award. One should not whitewash cricket. There is and has been plenty of sharp practice of the Grace brand, ranging from appropriately prepared pitches to rank psychological warfare; but it has not yet had to accept the late twentieth-century stock-in-trade of the 'professional foul'.

The fact is that, for better or worse, cricket is a Victorian game, and represents the vices and virtues of that stimulating and arrogant epoch. What we have played, watched and read about since 1919 has been the celebration of that ritual, and, particularly in the inter-war years, it was blessed with writers worthy of that reverential treatment: the mellifluous prose of Neville Cardus helped enshrine cricket in this manner. It was he who made the point eloquently apropos W. G. Grace: 'easily the most spectacular man that ever played the game'.

One of Harry Furniss's
expressive cartoons of W.G. —
authority, again, over a tiny ball!

Cardus continued, 'He was the Dr Johnson of cricket – as full of his subject, as kindly and as irascible, and just as dogmatic in his dispensations of authority.'

This ability to watch cricket, backwards and from memory, means that its escapist quality is finely marked. It is a reverie, and, in one sense, it is anticlimactic. It has been a cultural effort to make time stand still and re-live, over and over, through the gifts of generations of cricketers, that Victorian experience. The continuous re-catching of that mood has implied a maintenance of the studied manners as well as the peculiar skills of the game, despite internal fiddling with the small points on the laws and alterations to the county competitions.

There are many who watch this processional of first-class cricket in a numbed state of ambivalence. On the other hand, they will wax sardonic about the snobbery and fuddy-duddyness of the MCC; on the other hand, they will be as shaken and offended as the blimpiest greybeard on his high chair in the Long Room at Lord's at the sight of a white sun hat, never mind a protective helmet. The impact of Kerry Packer was largely cultural and psychological. It was the threat to the context of the game rather than to the quality of the performance which most offended his opponents and led them into legal byways. The shock that players would prefer to earn more money in trumped-up exhibition matches in the strangest of conditions and with no hope of them being designated 'first-class' was acute. Many of the Packer fancies – coloured uniforms, white balls, night matches – are much less revolutionary than the changes cricket underwent in the nineteenth century. But by the Edwardian era the cricket authorities had more or less decided that all was well in the best of all possible worlds, and that a self-perpetuating oligarchy could nurse cricket, petrified at that point in time, for ever. It has meant that cricket's twentieth-century organizers have out-Heroded Herod. They have been considerably more conservationist and conservative than their predecessors, precisely because their referential frame was in the past – and that of their predecessors had been in the future.

That cricket since 1919 has been little more than a breath-taking and gripping exercise in mellow nostalgia and romantic anticlimax is a brave claim. But, even if it is an unfair hypothesis, it is undeniable that by those twenty or thirty years before 'the great game' of 1914, cricket had reached its highest and headiest point ever. It reigned in triumph as the premier game of England and her Empire in years when England and her Empire commanded the world's attention, if not always affection. And at the helm throughout this period was W. G. Grace. The then editor of *Wisden*, Sydney Pardon, said in the obituary in the 1916 edition: 'when he was in his prime no sun was too hot and no day too long for him', and, from a million incidents, he perceptively chose as the epitome of Grace his innings of 221 against Middlesex at Clifton in 1885, during which he stayed at the bedside of a patient the whole night.

Grace, in large part, created modern cricket and established it as a social and cultural reflection of his age. In at least two ways – the well-paid gentleman and the schoolboy in ogre's guise – he appears superficially paradoxical, but, in depth, this was all of a piece with his Victorian surrounds. An interesting final test of both his consummate greatness as a cricketer and the curious petrifaction of cricket in its Victorian-English stage of evolution is to wonder whether W. G. Grace would be an automatic choice for England's all-time cricket team.

The answer must be a resounding and unqualified 'Yes', and it is the essence of the point that, for any Victorian jockeys, boxers, footballers, athletes, swimmers and tennis-players, it would be difficult to make a similar case. If a benign providence could reincarnate the Champion, his eyes would glint at the sight of the bland, docile wickets and well-manicured outfields, and, given the news that boundaries were reduced to a shorter yardage, he might give vent to one of his high-pitched chuckles. His quick cricket intelligence – what *Punch* called his 'Ulysses-like astuteness of tactics' – would briskly assimilate the latest vagaries of the no-ball and LBW rules, and he would be pleased to learn that, at all levels, only eleven fielders would be mustered to foil his efforts. He would sniff appreciatively at the improvement in equipment, while probably declining the use of the helmet. He would be gratified to note that, in each term, more fielders reached the standard set by himself, in his prime, and by his brothers, by Gilbert Jessop, by Hirst, Braund, MacLaren and others, than in his own age. And his superb powers of sighting, hitting and placing deliveries would, to his enjoyment, be rather more challenged than of yore by more versatile field-setting. In short, he would probably soon feel acclimatized and prepared to take his place in any first-class side and, as supreme batsman and devastating all-rounder, perform with distinction in every present-day style of encounter from a forty-overs thrash to the solemnities of the five- or six-day Test. After all, it is, more or less, his game: in the words of E. V. Lucas, in Grace's obituary in *Punch*, 'There will never be another not only to play cricket as Grace did, but to be cricket as Grace was.'

D. L. A. Jephson's valedictory verse ended:

> Dead; and from death a myriad memories rise
> Deathless; we thank you, friend, that once you lived.

From *W. G. Grace* (1981)

Cricket on the green — at Brockham, Surrey

Envoi

Cricket's Itself Again and All's Well

J. M. KILBURN

The day at Old Trafford had been discouraging. Cricket of modest quality had ended shortly after lunch in a torrential downpour. Boycott, as Yorkshire's captain, had followed with public apology a conversational indiscretion in which he disparaged both his opponents and his companions of the match. Boycott had spoken wrongly and rashly and provocative journalism had mercilessly given quotation precedence over the social conventions. I left Old Trafford with fear for the future of first-class cricket. . . .

By the time I had reached the quiet hotel in which I was resident for the match the rainclouds had cleared to leave a lovely evening of early summer. The sky was new-washed blue, the sun, still high, gave sparkle to the innumerable greens of burgeoning foliage. I took my pessimism for a walk.

Unexpectedly I came upon a cricket field. It was clearly the home of a club of substance, the playing area extensive and well tended. Pavilion and scoreboard shone with fresh paint. The boundary line was neatly marked and accentuated with foot-high flags. The batting on soft turf was to slow bowling of a right-hander and a left-hander and though I could not read the scores from my distance, the concentration of the players suggested a critical stage in the match. An on-drive sent a fieldsman in pounding pursuit towards the boundary, the stroke assuring a comfortable two runs but a hazardous three. The third was attempted and was adjudged incomplete and the scampering batsman raised a hand of acknowledgment to the umpire's signal of dismissal and turned to walk briskly to the pavilion. He was passed on the field by his successor and the fielding side were in position, the bowler ready to run up as soon as guard had been taken. For all who were playing and watching there was nothing in mind beyond the next ball, the challenge of the moment, the absorption in good-natured contest.

Time stood still in a distillation of delight. People and place and circumstances gave visual representation of a meaning, a conception, an ideal. Cricket was itself again and all was well with my world.

From *Thanks to Cricket* (1972)

Sheer Joy of Cricket

JOHN PARKER

Troughton, although angry with himself over the mix-up that had led to Radnam's dismissal, was too good a cricketer to brood on the incident. He knew that a good steady innings was needed, to brace the side after a heady start had been rather thrown away, and he took guard firmly, deciding to apply himself to the task. He was a safe rather than a spectacular batsman, but he had made some good scores against Tillingfold in the past, and he was not inclined to underestimate the fielding side's ability. He knew only too well the unpredictability of cricket; and the fact that he was forty years old, while the bowler was a mere sixteen (or that he was a respected solicitor and Norman Smith a stable lad), would make not a jot of difference to what was written in the scorebook.

Smith, no matter how young he was, had also realized the significance of the moment, and he determined to do his best to follow his captain's instructions. 'Try to bowl at the off stump, Norman, first five balls inswingers. Then give him an out-swinger if you can.' Gauvinier had once seen the England fast bowler, Geoff 'Horse' Arnold, dismiss New Zealand's record-breaking opening batsman Glenn Turner this way at Lord's. He knew it was a tall order to ask a youngster to bowl as accurately as that, but he was also aware that some direction for a young man was better than no direction at all, so he made the suggestion and hoped.

Smith, running in to bowl, felt a surge of confidence. He lengthened his stride, leapt smoothly at the crease and hurled his arm over. It was an inswinger all right – a beauty. It swung from outside the off stump, pitched high on a length and nipped 'through the gate' between bat and pad amid a loud roar, clipping the top of Troughton's leg stump and sending the bails flying over Deacon's head. Smith, with the rest of the Tillingfold side, leapt in the air, arms uplifted in triumph, only to be deflated on seeing Troughton recover his balance, turn and begin to mend the wicket, instead of heading for the pavilion. He looked round at Fanshawe. The umpire was signalling towards the scorebox. 'No-ball,' he called, and Norman realized that the roar he'd heard as the ball hit the stumps was not his own shout of pleasure but the umpire's call. Fanshawe walked to the popping-crease and pointed his toe, indicating where Smith had gone over the line. Gauvinier called, 'Hard luck, Norm. Let's have another one there.'

It said a great deal for Smith that he did not allow the misfortune to throw him off balance. Bowling more carefully, he delivered the rest of the over to order. Five balls went down, each of them swinging in to the batsman. Three of them Troughton was able to leave alone, as

'Playing till too dark to see'.
Edmund Blunden's village green
picture is echoed at Accra Beach,
Barbados

they swung across his body and down the leg side, making Deacon
leap and stretch to stop them from going for byes. True, Troughton
played carefully, once going right up on his toes to bring the ball
down on to the pitch in front of him with the straightest of bats,
dropping his wrists and slackening the fingers round the bat handle.
The seventh, aimed straight at the middle stump, had Troughton
driving across the line trying to work it away to mid-wicket. It moved
off the pitch again, but this time in the other direction, touching the
outside edge of the bat as it went and winging its way chest high to
Gauvinier at first slip – a straightforward, finger-tingling slip catch.
He flung the ball high in delight – for himself, for Norman, for the
ball, for the catch, for the score and for the sheer joy of cricket.

From *The Village Cricket Match* (1977)

EDMUND BLUNDEN

On the green they watched their sons
    Playing till too dark to see,
As their fathers watched them once,
    As my father once watched me;
While the bat and beetle flew
On the warm air webbed with dew.

From *Forefathers* (1922)

Acknowledgements

Acknowledgements and thanks are due to the following author; publishers, and copyright holders:

Hugh de Selincourt, *The Cricket Match:* the Executors of the Hugh de Selincourt Estate and Jonathan Cape Ltd. A. A. Thomson, *Cricket My Pleasure,* and Ian Peebles, *Talking of Cricket:* Pitman Books Limited. Undine Giuseppe, *Sir Frank Worrell:* Thomas Nelson & Sons Ltd. Bruce Hamilton, *Pro:* estate of the author. Learie Constantine and Denzil Batchelor, *The Changing Face of Cricket;* A. E. Knight, *The Complete Cricketer;* Rowland Bowen, *Cricket: A History of its Growth and Development Throughout the World;* C. S. Marriott, *The Complete Legbreak Bowler;* Bernard Hollowood, *Cricket on the Brain;* Trevor Bailey, *The Greatest of My Time;* and John Arlott, *Fred: Portrait of a Fast Bowler;* Michael Meyer and Godfrey Smith, *Summer Days:* Associated Book Publishers Ltd. (Eyre Methuen Ltd.). Neville Cardus, *Autobiography* and *English Cricket;* Jack Fingleton, *Fingleton on Cricket;* Ray Robinson, *Between Wickets* and *The Glad Season;* and Basil d'Oliveira, *Autobiography:* William Collins Sons and Co. Ltd. Geoffrey Moorhouse, *The Best Loved Game,* published by Hodder & Stoughton, copyright © 1979 by the author. Siegried Sassoon, *Memoirs of a Foxhunting Man,* and P. G. H. Fender, *The Turn of the Wheel:* Faber and Faber Ltd. Roy Hattersley, 'The Free Seats': author and the *Guardian.* Bernard Darwin, *W. G. Grace:* Gerald Duckworth & Co. Ltd. K. S. Ranjitsinhji, *The Jubilee Book of Cricket:* William Blackwood & Sons Ltd. Ben Travers, *94 Declared* (published by Elm Tree Books): Fraser & Dunlop Scripts Ltd. John Arlott, *Jack Hobbs,* and Arthur Crimble, *A Pattern of Islands:* John Murray Ltd. Michael Parkinson, *Cricket Mad,* and J. M. Kilburn, *Thanks to Cricket:* Stanley Paul & Co. Ltd. Dudley Nourse, *Cricket in the Blood:* Hodder & Stoughton Ltd. Sir Neville Cardus, *English Cricket:* Margaret Hughes. Irving Rosenwater, *Sir Donald Bradman:* B. T. Batsford Ltd. C. L. R. James, *Beyond the Boundary,* and C. P. Snow, 'The Mathematician on Cricket' from *The Saturday Book:* Hutchinson Publishing Group Ltd. Ronald Mason, *Walter Hammond,* and Herbert Farjeon, *Cricket Bag:* David Higham Associates Ltd. John Arlott, *Hutton, the Immaculate Artist;* Paul Fitzpatrick, *Proctor,* and David Frith, *Miracle at Leeds: Wisden Cricket Monthly.* Neville Cardus, on 'Compton' in *Playfair Cricket Monthly* (June 1960): *Playfair Cricket Monthly.* Alec Bedser, *Cricket Choice;* John Cleese and Mike Brearley in *The Return of the Ashes* by Mike Brearley and Dudley Doust; Peter Walker, *Cricket Conversations;* Louis Duffus, *Cricket Stars of Today;* and Tony Lewis, *A Summer of Cricket:* Pelham Books Ltd. Norman Gale, *Cricket Songs:* Constable & Co. Ltd. Ian Peebles, *Patsy Hendren:* estate of the late Ian Peebles. Jack Braithwaite, *First Game of the Season:* Time & Tide. Ltd. A. G. Macdonell, *England, Their England:* Macmillan Publishers, Ltd. Graham White, *Cricket on Saturday:* J. Whitaker & Sons Ltd. Mihir Bose, *Keith Miller,* and Eric Midwinter, *W. G. Grace:* George Allen & Unwin Ltd. John Arlott, *Indian Summer* (published by Longmans), the author. G. M. Trevelyan, *English Social History:* Longman Group Ltd. Egbert Moore ('Lord Beginner') *Victory Calypso, Lord's 1950:* Melodisc Records Ltd. John Arlott, on 'Laker' from *John Arlott s Book of Cricket:* Lutterworth Press. E. W. Swanton, 'Barbadian Heroes' from *The Cricketer's Bedside Book,* and Ron Roberts, extract from *Playfair Cricket Monthly* (January 1961): John Farquharson Ltd. Alan Gibson, from *The Times* of 24 June 1971: Times Newspapers Ltd. Norman Harris, *Great Moments in Cricket:* Macdonald & Co. Ltd. Ted Dexter, *From Bradman to Boycott:* Ted Dexter and Macdonald & Co. Ltd. Viv Richards and David Foot, *Viv Richards,* text and illustration copyright © 1979 by Viv Richards and David Foot: World's Work Ltd. Arthur Mailey, *10 for 66 and All That,* and Alan Ross, on 'H. T. Bartlett' from *Cricket Heroes,* both published by Phoenix House: Chatto and Windus Ltd. John Masefield, 'Eighty-Five to Win': The Society of Authors as the literary representative of the Estate of John Masefield. Colin MacInnes, 'Second Test, 1963, Fifth Day', from *New Society* of 4 July 1963: Davis-Poynter Ltd. George McWilliam, 'Epitaph': the author. Frank Keating, *Bowled Over:* André Deutsch Ltd. Alan Ross, 'Test Match at Lord's': the author. C. L. R. James, 'Cricket in West Indian Culture': New Society Ltd. Henry Newbolt, 'Vitae Lampada': Peter Newbolt. John Parker, *The Village Cricket Match:* George Weidenfeld & Nicolson Limited. Edmund Blunden, one verse from 'Forefathers', first published in *The Shepherd and Other Poems of Peace and War,* reprinted in *Selected Poems of Edmund Blunden,* published in 1982 by Carcanet Press: Claire Blunden.